Intimate Partner Violence

Intimate Partner Violence

Enduring Abuse and Twenty-First-Century Issues, Challenges, and Opportunities

Laura Elizabeth

ROWMAN & LITTLEFIELD
Lanham • Boulder • New York • London

Published by Rowman & Littlefield
An imprint of The Rowman & Littlefield Publishing Group, Inc.
4501 Forbes Boulevard, Suite 200, Lanham, Maryland 20706
www.rowman.com

86-90 Paul Street, London EC2A 4NE

British Library Cataloguing in Publication Information Available

Library of Congress Cataloging-in-Publication Data Available

ISBN 978-1-5381-9895-7 (cloth)
ISBN 978-1-5381-9896-4 (paper)
ISBN 978-1-5381-9897-1 (electronic)

♾™ The paper used in this publication meets the minimum requirements of American National Standard for Information Sciences—Permanence of Paper for Printed Library Materials, ANSI/NISO Z39.48-1992.

This book is for the deep loves of my life who have been my shining stars and have been invaluable to this process in various ways. For Connor, for Michelle, for St. Betty in heaven, for Katja, for Kara, for Mommy, for Lisa, for Lori, for Lauren, for Kelli, for Catherine, for Marcia, and for Tanya—thank you for taking your wounds and helping to add to global wisdom. For Laurel, you are incredible! For Cate, thank you and Elizabeth for the inspiration.

BRIEF CONTENTS

Contents

ACKNOWLEDGMENTS

Thank you so much to Becca for your impeccable counsel and insight during this process and being patient with me as a first-time author! Thank you to all my students for inspiring me with your creativity and insight. Thank you to Drs. Edwards and Gordon for being such singularly fantastic professors to the point that you inspired me to go into academia.

INTRODUCTION

Trigger Warning: This introduction includes intense discussions of intimate partner violence.

Note: If you are affected by the issues presented and want additional support, information, and resources, please consider contacting the National Mental Health Hotline at 866-903-3787 or the National Domestic Violence Hotline at 800-799-7233.

CASE STUDY

It is the mid-2000s on a hot and hazy day in a southern college town. Most of the students are back in their home states for the summer. A recent graduate is struggling along the sidewalk outside the university gift shop, holding her newborn baby, a diaper bag, and several shopping bags. The baby's father had a shopping spree that day, purchasing the whole lot on her credit card, which wasn't unusual. For the duration of her relationship with this young man, she has paid for almost everything.

She trudges along on the sidewalk, her eyes cast down and her chest heavy. That college town was once her haven and happy place, but now she returns as a new, and very nervous, young mother. She is both physically and emotionally beaten down by the relationship that she desperately wants to escape. She realizes that the man with her (whom she no longer considers a boyfriend but someone she has been unable to fully get away from) is an abuser. Even in her early 20s gentle naïveté, that fact is crystal-clear. Over the past year, her head has been shoved into a car door; she has been thrown onto a bed; she is routinely called fat, ugly, and derivations of cruel epithets. She is told that she is sexually boring, lazy, and that she will end up working as a secretary despite graduating from a top 10 university and currently enrolled in a master's program. She would be honored to be a secretary because her beloved grandmother had been one for many years, but her abuser views that occupation, like many others, as completely beneath him and his vast talents.

The man hates her mother, resents her family's wealth, and routinely ridicules her maternal grandmother's recent death. He makes a series of increasingly unhinged allegations that two of her close family members have an intimate relationship. He has stopped help paying bills, routinely sleeps until 1 or 2 p.m., and makes a point of chain-smoking around her—the young woman is both severely allergic to cigarette smoke and fearful of it, as her other grandmother's death was the result of lung cancer. She is terrified of the man and at the same time repulsed by his behavior. She wishes he would just disappear. Occasionally, that seems like a possibility, given his openness to having relationships with other women, their superiority, and how he is too important to be living in her hometown.

The current situation frustrates this young woman because in hindsight, there were many warning signs, such as his hatred for his family. He thinks they are beneath him and believes they never acknowledged his outstanding abilities in multiple areas. This unsettles her; she is used to Southern modesty, even if it is only on the surface level. Another red flag is his strange social habits, like bringing a newspaper to a restaurant and then reading it during the duration of the meal rather than speaking to his dining companions. She believes that behavior is brazenly thoughtless and rude. Another thing that clued her in was that if he didn't like a comment she made, rather than respond accordingly, he would wait several minutes in silence and stare at her angrily as she tried to figure out what she did wrong. If it happened while they were talking on the phone he would pause, wait a few minutes before answering her, and then hang up because she "didn't deserve to hear from" him further.

Perhaps most ominously, the man (who gained significant weight after stopping participating in sports) hates how she no longer looks like she did pre-pregnancy: lithe, size zero, and blonde, attracting significant male attention. It's all her fault, he says. As a result, she now walks in public with her eyes cast downward. She now realizes that she normalized his early displays of ill temper because of her father's own moments of rage while she was growing up. However, the man's fury had escalated significantly. Even when they had minor spats, he would stare her down and not break eye contact, looking at her with absolute hatred, behavior disproportionate to the situation. Early in their relationship he had a road rage incident with her in the car. An elderly woman driving behind him in a parking lot pressed her horn (maybe even inadvertently!). His response? Let her pass him, chase her, pull up beside her, spit on her car, and flip her off. The young woman was horrified and could not stop shaking.

On this steamy day back in the college town, the young woman knows that the trauma she is repeatedly assaulted with is making her retreat into herself. Every morning, she and the baby have an established routine. After a night of intense study for her classes she gets the baby up, puts on cartoons, makes breakfast, takes a walk outside, does tummy time with the baby, and then puts the baby down for a first nap. When the baby sleeps, she's able to escape from reality to a place that is safe, even if it is imaginary. She is fully aware that she is daydreaming her days away, possibly even dissociating, but emotionally she goes to a place where she is held gently and respectfully, far away from her abuser. In her dreams she is safe.

She is certain that the man won't hurt the baby, but she thinks there's a good possibility that, one day, he severely hurts her (or worse). As she weighs this likelihood, she notes to herself that he is both image-obsessed and convinced of his brilliance. He once expressed to her, in all seriousness, his plan to be elected president of the United States, despite demonstrating no proclivity for politics. His only evident talent was in athletics (though he was a member of a team that went winless in two of his four collegiate seasons). In fact, she routinely is forced to do his graduate school coursework. He often sits her down and tells her she can't leave until it's done, which amuses her since he constantly calls her dumb and useless. She wonders why he would want such a worthless and unskilled person doing his work. Regardless of his motivations, a domestic violence conviction might undercut a presidential campaign, she notes to herself. That could keep her safe.

However, she circles back to the fact that his temper is unfathomable. The young woman comes from a household with a bitter and angry father, but even though she is familiar with male rage, she has never experienced anything like this man's fury. She estimates that this will work against her and her safety but is not yet sure to what extent. He is image obsessed, but he cannot control his anger. He is convinced that he is held in high esteem by the community, and she notes ruefully that he can be a skilled phony. However, she is unsettled by his lack of self-control, which is unusual for an image-obsessed person. If she had to lay odds on it, she surmises that he may well do something to her in a moment of extreme rage. She doesn't think he would plan it, though that is of cold comfort.

This young woman is resilient if nothing else. She receives no support or protection from her father, is severely emotionally, physically, and financially abused, and yet is still standing, which gives her confidence for the future, to do what she knows she needs to. In the past few months, she has tried to leave her abuser multiple times. After the most recent time, he informed her that the baby would never know her name, which she realized was a direct threat. Several times over the past couple of months he confined her against her will and didn't let her leave the house. He is much physically larger than her and a former athlete. When he blocks the door, she knows she has no recourse. Yet still, she dreams of freedom, safety, and prays for a rescuer.

Even on this sweltering summer day, when she is both physically and mentally weighed down by the abuse, she has not given up. Her concerns at this moment, however, are more immediate. She is worried that she might drop the baby. As the man wanders the university gift shop, hands free and unconstricted, she places a couple of his shopping bags down on the hot pavement to get a stronger grip on the baby. She decides to pop her head into the store and quietly asks him to carry a couple of the bags. As she opens the door, two clerks notice her bearing both an infant and all the bags as the man saunters through the air-conditioned store. They exchange nervous looks. The man sees them glance at one another.

That millisecond of judgment is enough to upset his fragile ego, and his volcanic rage is now predictably directed at the young woman. As soon as they get back to the car, he begins screaming at her in full view of the baby. She is told that she is an effing lazy princess, a loser, all manner of invectives because she could not successfully carry everything in the heat. She withdraws deeper into herself, as is her pattern, which only enrages him more. Something within him senses that she is biding her time and that when the time is right, she will escape from him. He now launches his most direct and ominous threat to date: "Bitches like you make me understand why Scott Peterson killed Laci."

In that moment, he has telegraphed that her time is running out, and she knows it. She is naturally a people-pleaser, easily intimidated, and conflict-avoidant, but as she experiences one of the scariest moments of her life, with nowhere to turn, she knows what must be done and silently prays to God for the strength to do it before it is too late.

That young woman was me. It feels like a lifetime ago. I made it out to the other side earning my master's degree as well as my doctorate as a single mother. My doctoral dissertation was on specialized domestic violence probation. My child ran the PowerPoint during my dissertation defense. I am now a victimologist, a college professor and researcher, the mother of a 20-year-old, and with this book, an author. I have been deeply in love multiple times since that abusive relationship ended, I have traveled the world, and I have experienced countless joys.

Yet the scars of abuse remain palpable in ways large and small, and I hope that the knowledge gleaned from this book will prevent similar trauma in others. Today, I tend to elaborately praise men for meeting baseline expectations in relationships and not being abusive; the two great loves of my life are men who both fall under the "protector" rubric, both decorated veterans of Special Forces. My obsession with feeling safe and protected can be debilitating. I am hypervigilant regarding arguments to the point where I don't speak up when they occur. I have struggled with intense depression and anxiety over the years, and sometimes overwhelming grief that the one pregnancy I was able to carry to term was with an abuser who treated me cruelly throughout, rather than with a gentle man who honored what should have been the most sacred time in my life. My self-esteem is fragile. I self-medicated with alcohol during my 20s. I often struggle to concentrate on tasks. When I was being abused in my 20s, daydreaming was an emotional defense mechanism. I still rely on it heavily all these years later. All too often, it keeps me from fully being present in the moment. Being severely abused in my 20s, and surviving, has indelibly forged and shaped me into the person that I am today in both empowering and painful ways.

As a victimologist, domestic violence researcher, presenter, and moderator, as well as a survivor, it is my hope that *Intimate Partner Violence* proves interesting and illuminating to both the academic community and society at large. It is my goal that the combination of objective and scholarly assessment of the current research on domestic violence, merged with the personal stories of survivors, will help readers understand all aspects of domestic violence fervently, and consider issues within intimate partner violence that are historically neglected.

TOPIC AREAS

To that end, *Intimate Partner Violence* is organized as follows:

The opening chapters of the book consist of a broad overview on the phenomenon of intimate partner violence (IPV). Chapters 1 and 2 offer a full background on the topic and provide a clear definition and explanation of the scope of that violence both globally and domestically. Next, the history of domestic violence laws and the development of serious policies against intimate partner violence are discussed. Subsequent chapters offer a detailed explanation of who the victims and the batterers are as well as a description and explanation of the various theories behind why batterers abuse and why some victims and survivors stay in these relationships.

The second half of the book is organized into chapters that focus on twenty-first-century questions and issues surrounding domestic violence, starting with a discussion of contemporary interventions against intimate partner violence. Subsequent chapters consist of a broader discussion of domestic violence internationally before attention shifts to a concentration on the impact of domestic violence on marginalized populations. Analyses on policing strategies, judicial treatment of IPV, and guns and domestic violence will also be discussed. The last section will discuss updated research on the enduring impact of domestic violence before the final chapter concludes with a discussion on the current societal challenges and opportunities in confronting this ongoing serious crime. Case studies will be interspersed throughout the book.

CHAPTER BY CHAPTER

Introduction

In the introduction I introduce myself, my personal story, and my academic and professional expertise to establish my credibility in guiding readers through a discussion of IPV. I explain how this book came about and how we as a society have a collective opportunity to reexamine IPV as a phenomenon and how it can most effectively be addressed.

Chapter 1: Introduction to Domestic Violence

This chapter consists of a full overview of what IPV is, the behaviors of the abuser and victim, and what a vexing societal issue it is both in the United States and worldwide. I take care to distinguish the difference between violence between intimate partners from that of overall family violence, as this text focuses on intimate partner violence and its singular issues. As part of the definition of IPV and the types of violence that fall under its rubric, physical, sexual, psychological, and financial violence will be discussed, and ensuing behaviors therein will be described.

Chapter 2: The Scope of the Violence

This chapter informs readers about the concerning depth of the problem of domestic violence, including victimization rates for heterosexual men, heterosexual women, and members of the LGBTQA+ community. Attention focuses on data points indicating the prevalence of this type of violence both nationally and globally, as well as a consideration of its economic, physical, psychological, and societal impact.

Chapter 3: Tracing the Development of Laws on Domestic Violence

Chapter 3 focuses on an analysis and discussion on how domestic violence laws have evolved in the United States over the centuries. Attention is paid to early US laws that enabled domestic violence, and the fact that the first explicit laws forbidding a man from beating his wife and children were not instituted until the approach of the nineteenth century. The fact that domestic violence shelters for the abused did not become widespread until the 1980s and federal funding was not made available until 1994 will also be highlighted. Readers will learn about the government's lack of acknowledgment toward this crime for much of its national history.

Chapter 4: The Batterers

This chapter focuses on a discussion and presentation of the scholarship on the identity of batterers and the general conclusions researchers draw about abusers' motivations, behaviors, and amenability to rehabilitative efforts. The clear weight of the scholarship, that battering behaviors transcend gender, race, ethnicity, socioeconomic status, professional acumen, and educational attainment, are highlighted to illustrate the pervasive nature of this behavior. Additional consideration is given to mass media portrayals of batterers and contextualizing these depictions with the body of scholarship on batterers.

Chapter 5: The Victims and Survivors

Chapter 5 focuses on a discussion and analysis of the research pertaining to victims and survivors of intimate partner violence. The main foci consists of traits, vulnerabilities, and behaviors that researchers suggest are widespread in survivors and victims of IPV. Popular misconceptions about IPV victims and survivors are addressed, and the disconnect between mass media portrayals of victims/survivors and empirical conclusions from the available research is assessed.

Chapter 6: Theories on Batterers and Victims

This chapter focuses on the main theories behind IPV, including psychological, social, cognitive behavioral, and family and systems theories. Theories explaining the behaviors of victims and survivors will also be assessed, including learned helplessness and battered women's syndrome. An additional emphasis of the chapter is the importance of theoretical understandings of domestic violence to address root causes and best practices for interventions, treatment of batterers, and assistance to victims and survivors.

Chapter 7: Contemporary Interventions against Intimate Partner Violence

Chapter 7 consists of an examination of both the current legal and community interventions against IPV and an analysis of the empirical evidence for their efficacies. Assessments of various contemporary batterer intervention programs is a focus of this chapter, as is a discussion on contemporary treatments and therapies for victims and survivors. The necessity for any intervention effort to prioritize the safety and well-being of the survivor is also comprehensively discussed.

Chapter 8: The Global Struggle against Intimate Partner Violence

This chapter focuses on IPV on a global scale: the pervasiveness of it in both peer nations to the United States and less privileged developing countries. The prevalence of lifetime estimates of IPV and disparities therein between the West (Europe and the United States, as examples) and countries in the Middle East and parts of Africa and Asia are described and assessed. Disparate global laws addressing intimate partner violence will also be considered, as well as global implications for intimate partner relationships for the duration of the twenty-first century.

Chapter 9: Domestic Violence and Marginalized Populations

In chapter 9, the focus on the disconnect between popular portrayals of domestic violence consisting of a heterosexual couple with a White male offender and a White female victim (i.e., *The Godfather*, *Sleeping with the Enemy*) with the empirical reality that men, minority females (especially Latina and Asian immigrants), and members of the LGBTQA+ community are at significant risk for IPV is discussed. A full consideration of the respective reasons for the high victimization rates within marginalized communities is discussed, including poverty, racism, social isolation, social stigma, and reduced access to community resources.

Chapter 10: Policing Strategies and Domestic Violence

This chapter will trace the evolution of US policing in its treatment of domestic violence from a laissez-faire and informal policy that characterized the policing response until the latter part of the twentieth century, when more formalized intervention strategies and mandatory arrest policies were instituted. The impact of this change on rates of IPV is assessed, as well as the relationship between police and marginalized communities that have often hindered survivors' efforts to get help.

Chapter 11: Domestic Violence and the Courts

Chapter 11 describes and assesses the trajectory of IPV cases in the courts. It is emphasized that wife battering was deemed illegal in 1920, as well as the difficulty in prosecuting and obtaining convictions in IPV cases. IPV as a hidden crime with reluctant complainants is explained, and the efficacy of current civil court measures, like protective orders, is evaluated.

Chapter 12: Guns and Domestic Violence

This chapter focuses on the theme of singular relationships with firearms (as compared to peer nations globally), and how it can significantly intensify the risk of domestic violence fatalities in the United States. In fact, research indicates that intimate partners kill women (two-thirds) with a gun. A thorough discussion of the full research on gun ownership and domestic violence is conducted, and the significance of recent Supreme Court cases like *U.S. v. Rahimi* (a June 2024 case that focused on whether the government can bar gun possession for those who have domestic violence restraining orders) is analyzed.

Chapter 13: The Enduring Impact of Intimate Partner Violence

In chapter 13, the sometimes-lifelong consequences of domestic violence, from physical injury and disability to heightened rates of post-traumatic stress disorder, depression, anxiety, substance use disorder, and sexually transmitted infections is discussed. Careful attention is paid to the enduring impact of trauma on the body, including heightened risks for survivors to suffer cardiac issues, digestive problems, chronic pain, sexual dysfunction and pain, musculoskeletal injuries, and potential traumatic brain injuries. A key emphasis of the chapter is that trauma has a lifelong impact, and one of the many challenges in combating IPV is that the legacy of trauma and suffering can persist long after the abuse has stopped, and the relationship has ended.

Chapter 14: Domestic Violence in the Twenty-First Century: Lessons Going Forward

The final chapter consists of an examination of where the United States finds itself in the fight against IPV 25 years into the twenty-first century, as well as lessons and thoughts for individual readers to carry forward. A thorough analysis of the impact of the COVID-19 pandemic on IPV is conducted, and trends/evolutions in our collective understanding of this phenomenon are discussed and fully contextualized.

GOALS OF THE BOOK

In short, this book represents my act of love to my younger self and to all of those who have been impacted by relationship violence. While no act of scholarship can undo the abuse that other survivors and that I have endured, there is tremendous healing in confronting the reasons why domestic violence is such a pressing social issue. I am hopeful that an engrossing journey through all aspects of domestic violence will aid in giving a new generation, born many years after the most significant domestic violence-related murders in US history, that of Nicole Brown Simpson and Ron Goldman, a comprehensive understanding of this phenomenon. The 30th anniversary of the murders was in June 2024 and represented a time for quiet reflection on relationship violence in the United States and societal progress in the three decades since the crime took place. It is my goal that this book helps readers to objectively assess how far we have come, and how far we have yet to go.

Intimate Partner Violence is designed to be equally accessible for both scholars and laymen, and accordingly, discussions of the research into all facets of IPV are balanced with case studies and examples of domestic violence in both society and popular culture. It is my hope that readers will reexamine their own knowledge of domestic violence considering this book's treatment of domestic violence and marginalized populations. A key theme throughout the book is the disconnect between popular portrayals of IPV and the more complex reality of relationship violence. As clear as it is that IPV is morally and legally unacceptable, the answers on how to best address it are much more complicated.

1

Introduction to Domestic Violence

CASE STUDY

Kristie, a 19-year-old college student and her boyfriend Jack, also a college student, have been dating for four months. They met in a business class and connected over their shared participation in college sports—Kristie played volleyball and Jack football. Initially, they spent all their spare time together: working out, studying, going to events, and partying. They each envisioned a future together, but serious cracks emerged.

Unfortunately, Jack has a serious drinking problem. When he drinks, he becomes violent toward those around him: teammates, roommates, and Kristie. He has punched multiple male friends and was arrested his freshman year for disorderly conduct. The first two times he had hit Kristie, Jack had drunk to the point of blacking out and slammed her against furniture when she tried to stop him. Another time, Kristie started screaming and clawed his face. A few days later, they discussed what had happened. Jack told Kristie that he thought they had an issue with physical violence. He believed that they both were guilty of it and that they needed to work on anger management.

Kristie is confused and distraught. She has never been violent with anyone in her life, and she doesn't know much about the topic of intimate partner violence (IPV). In high school, she was taught a little bit about it and remembers learning that violence tends to escalate over time. She is not sure if her relationship is truly violent or is experiencing "isolated incidents," as she refers to them. Her best friend is deeply concerned and reminds Kristie that in less than six months of dating Jack there have already been three "isolated incidents." Kristie tells her friend that she is just as guilty as Jack and that the abuse is mutual. Her

---

best friend, who is studying psychology, explains that she has learned about IPV in several classes and that mutually abusive relationships are quite unusual. Instead, her friend posits that Kristie is exhibiting reactive abuse, which is lashing out against an abuser rather than initiating abuse. Kristie's friend urges her to visit the counseling center to discuss what has been happening. After another violent Saturday night (this time one that keeps her from volleyball practice for two days with severe back pain) Kristie decides to go.

Kristie's painful relationship is a disturbing example of the persistent societal issue of IPV. This chapter consists of a full overview of what IPV is, the behaviors of the abuser and the abused, and its impact on society both in the United States and worldwide. It is important to note that a distinction must be made between IPV and overall family violence, which is a pressing issue worthy of study and analysis. There are texts that explore the multiple aspects surrounding family violence, but the discussion in *Intimate Partner Violence* is narrower in scope. Throughout this book, the focus of our attention will be on IPV and particular issues pertaining to it. IPV in and of itself will be defined and the description of the types of violence that fall under its rubric—physical, sexual, psychological/emotional, and financial violence—will be discussed, as well as stalking and their behaviors.

THE DEFINITION OF INTIMATE PARTNER VIOLENCE AND ITS DISTINCTION FROM FAMILY VIOLENCE

Before we define the terms that will be so important for understanding the main ideas in this book, it is important to differentiate its goals, that is, to explain all aspects of IPV from the overall discussion of family violence. Family violence is often defined as abuse perpetrated within both traditional and nontraditional family units that include intimate partner violence and/or child abuse and/or elder abuse and/or animal abuse (Tiyyagura et al., 2020). This abuse need not only be physical; in fact, violence within the family unit also often manifests as emotional, sexual, financial, and economic, or some combination, as well as neglect (Paavilainen et al., 2014). All aspects of family violence are worthy of meticulous study and examination, and the results have obvious relevance to society overall.

Our focus is narrower in scope, as we examine IPV, commonly referred to as domestic violence, specifically. Other experiences of abuse will come up throughout the book, but the focus is on violence between **intimate partners**. Accordingly, we must settle on a working definition for IPV for ease of readability. Researchers have offered multiple definitions, and a concise and workable one is that IPV describes sexual abuse, physical abuse, stalking, and psychological/emotional abuse by a former or current intimate partner, which includes spouses, boyfriends/girlfriends, dating partners, or a current sexual partner (Breiding et al., 2015). Readers may notice that financial/economic abuse is not included within the rubric of this definition. We will address this omission in the formal definition by also including financial abuse in our working definition. This type of abuse will be addressed in this chapter and throughout the course of the book. We also note that we will also refer to IPV as **domestic violence** throughout the text because people often use that term within the public lexicon to describe abuse between intimate partners.

It is also important to describe more fully what an intimate partner relationship looks like. Experts in criminology characterize it by "emotional connectedness, regular contact, physical/sexual behaviors, and knowledge about each other's lives" (Breiding et al., 2015). Additionally, it is important to note that intimate partners do not have to reside with one another, can be of the same sex, and may or may not share a child together (Breiding et al., 2015). The importance of the overall term "intimate partner" is that it refers to a relationship of physical, sexual, and/or emotional closeness that distinguishes it from other, more casual, relationships in one's life. The elements themselves denote a particular importance, and accordingly, throughout this book, we will focus on close relationships that have turned abusive.

THE CONSTELLATION OF ABUSIVE BEHAVIORS IN INTIMATE PARTNER VIOLENCE

Physical Abuse

When people are tasked with describing IPV many might logically describe a host of toxic behaviors that center around physical abuses. In fact, most of the literature focuses on physical abuse (Postmus et al., 2020). This can certainly be an important aspect of domestic violence, but IPV can also include numerous other types of violence. However, the most well-known and most discussed is physical abuse. Again, it is helpful to have a working definition of physical abuse because some people may have a broad or narrow definition than others. For the sake of clarity, we will define physical abuse as a nonaccidental use of force, one that carries with it the potential of injury, death, physical disability, or pain (Breiding et al., 2015).

In terms of physical actions that fall under the rubric of abuse, we include scratching, shoving, pushing, grabbing, punching, slapping, biting, shaking, using any form of weapon on another (gun, knife, fists, and others), restraining, burning, or using one's size to compel a smaller or less strong person to do something against their will (Breiding et al., 2015). We also note that physical abuse can also include *attempted* forms of each of the above acts. For example, a girlfriend can attempt to slap her partner and miss, but the missed strike does *not* mean that an act of physical abuse did not occur. It did, though the abusive partner was not successful in completing the act. The attempt to physically hurt a partner is sufficient to qualify as abuse within this definition.

Until recently, researchers have overwhelmingly focused their attention on physical violence within the literature. In fact, much of that research simply divided IPV into physical violence and nonphysical violence, the latter of which encapsulated multiple aspects of emotional and sexual violence (Outlaw, 2009). This disparity and hyperfocus on physical violence is concerning because studies often suggest that physical violence is less common than other types of violence within intimate relationships (Outlaw, 2009). Yet historically, physical violence has been emphasized to such an extent that it is understandable that both experts and the public would think that physical violence is more common.

Sexual Abuse

A similarly devastating type of behavior within the rubric of IPV is sexual abuse. For purposes of our exploration of IPV, we will use a methodical definition of sexual violence: the commission or attempted commission of a sexual act or acts without the free and voluntary consent of the victim, or perpetrated against a victim who is unable to consent or refuse because of various circumstances (Breiding et al., 2015). As is true with physical abuse, it is important to note that an act does not need to be completed to qualify as sexual violence; the attempted commission of the act is sufficient to qualify as abuse within our definition. Methods of commission, or attempted commission, of sexual violence within a relationship can include (but are not limited to) use of force against the victim to compel their participation in a sexual act or acts; drugging the victim to make it easier to get the victim to comply; taking advantage of an intoxicated victim; sexual exploitation of a vulnerable or compromised person; intimidation; financial coercion; insulting or humiliating the victim; constant verbal pressure for sexual acts; false promises of marriage or staying in the relationship if the victim will do something sexual; nonphysical threats; and grooming behaviors (Breiding et al., 2015).

It is important to note that while there is considerable focus on the physical violence aspect of IPV, research indicates that intimate partners commit a staggering one-third of sexual assaults, yet this area of research within IPV is often overlooked (Bagwell-Gray et al., 2015). In terms of the prevalence of sexual violence within intimate relationships, recent research indicates that roughly one-tenth of women experience sexual violence within their intimate relationships (Black et al., 2011). It is essential that this area of IPV continues to receive the necessary research, because studies thus far suggest that individuals who experience sexual violence in their intimate relationships often experience substantially worse outcomes than those individuals who are abused in other ways. In fact, victimization from sexual violence in intimate relationships is associated with higher rates of post-traumatic stress disorder (PTSD), suicide, substance abuse, physical and sexual health problems, and death by homicide (Barker et al., 2019). The impact of sexual violence within IPV also appears to have strong implications for family members of victims, as children of those victimized demonstrate higher rates of depression, anxiety, and somatic symptoms (Barker et al., 2019). Overall, some criminology experts believe that sexual violence is a "marker" for more extreme overall violence in a relationship and is an important predictive factor for the escalation of violence within the relationship (Coker et al., 2000).

Psychological/Emotional Abuse

For purposes of definitional ease, psychological abuse describes nonphysical behaviors that are intended to exert control over the victim, harm them emotionally, or both (Breiding et al., 2015). These behaviors can include, but are not limited to, name-calling; humiliation; expressing excessive anger; gaslighting (playing intentional mind games with the victim); exerting coercive power over them and limiting access to family, friends, and/or money; monitoring the victim's private communications without permission; making manipulative threats to harm oneself if the victim ends the relationship; threats of committing physical or sexual harm to the victim; attempts at exerting control over the victim's reproductive freedom (e.g., a forced abortion or withheld birth control); exploitation of an area of vulnerability for the victim (e.g., immigration status); and/or threatening the victim's loved ones (Breiding et al., 2015). This constellation of behaviors can be conceptualized as the abusive partner's overall effort to diminish the victim psychologically, to take their power away, and to gradually crush their self-esteem and sense of agency.

The adage about "sticks and stones" has been corrosive in terms of understanding how serious psychological abuse is within intimate relationships because words *do* have an impact, and psychological violence has an intensely negative affect on many victims. In fact, some researchers have found that psychological violence was the strongest predictive factor for the development of PTSD in victims of IPV, even more so than physical and sexual abuse (Pico-Alfonso, 2005). While there is no clear research consensus about the most "serious" form of IPV, and all forms are highly alarming and potentially damaging to every aspect of a victim's person-hood, researchers have found multiple indicators that nonphysical modes of abuse are damaging. Among them, especially for women who have had childhood exposure to violence (Pico-Alfonso, 2005), psychological abuse may trump all other forms in the damage it inflicts on a victim's psyche.

Financial Abuse

Financial abuse is often used interchangeably with economic abuse, and for purposes of this book, we define it as an "intentional pattern of control" in which the abusive partner coerces their partner in terms of finances and/or interferes with their partner's ability to use their funds, earn money, or keep it (Postmus et al., 2020). This type of abuse is consid-ered "hidden" because it was not until recently that researchers focused on financial abuse as a major form of IPV; economic abuse has certainly been historically underconsidered as compared to physical abuse and psychological violence (Postmus et al., 2020). An additional key aspect of financial abuse is that it is often intended to isolate the victim and make them economically dependent on the abusive partner (Braaf and Barrett-Meyering, 2010). Also significant is the fact that restricting someone's resources or access to resources can result in the victim's isolation and difficulty participating fully in society. It is evident that different types of IPV overlap, as behaviors common within financial abuse serve to help isolate a victim, which is a key behavior in psychological abuse.

Researchers have found that financial abuse can cause sustained pov-erty for victims, and at minimum, damage their financial status (Eriksson and Ulmestig, 2021). The financial limitations also caused by this kind of abuse can isolate women from full participation in their social lives; for example, they become financially limited because their partners had controlled access to their funds and/or misappropriated it. As a result, victims often experience isolation, extreme financial stress, damage to their physical health because of intense stress, and serious damage to their self-esteem (Eriksson and Ulmestig, 2021). As experts in domestic violence note, financial abuse is "not just about the money" (Eriksson and Ulmestig, 2021), and money is not just "money." Money represents freedom to so many abused partners, and the limitation of this valued resource can often limit their abilities to leave violent relationships (Con-ner, 2013). Researchers have concluded, "Economic instability is a tie that binds [individuals] to their abusers" (Conner, 2013). Thus, financial abuse is often a key tool within the arsenal of abusive partners, one that prevents victims from leaving. It deserves further attention within the body of literature on domestic violence so that both policymakers and practitioners can confront this type of violence.

Stalking

It is important that stalking behaviors be fully defined and understood because studies have shown a clear link between stalking and an increased chance of lethality within IPV (Brady et al., 2020). For purposes of this book, we define stalking within IPV as a series of behaviors perpetrated by a fixated individual on another partner, often after the relationship has ended (Bendlin and Sheridan, 2021). These behaviors can include periodic actions that may seem charming between *willing* partners, like unsolicited love letters, repeated phone calls, unwanted gifts, and constant messages (Bendlin and Sheridan, 2021). The key factors that separate stalking from wooing a lover are sometimes misunderstood. Stalking differs from courting or romancing because it encapsulates harassing behavior from obsessed individuals who abuse the victim's agency and boundaries by refusing to go away.

Also central to understanding the worrisome nature of stalking within IPV is the fact that it is an escalating and dangerous behavior. In other words, stalkers are not harmless pests. Stalking situations within IPV are generally not solved by victims simply telling the perpetrator to go away. Once a stalker has started their harassing behaviors, the risk for future violence inflicted on the victim is staggering. In fact, one study indicates that almost 40% of stalkers within IPV ultimately physically assault their victims (Mullen et al., 1999). Perhaps most alarmingly, researchers have found that over three-quarters of US homicides against females had been preceded by prior stalking (McFarlane et al., 1999). Accordingly, it is essential that stalking is not minimized or dismissed when it occurs in any setting, including within IPV. There is no aspect of this behavior that is charming, loving, or caring because stalking involves harassing victims with actions that are often associated with love affairs. There can be a societal tendency to not understand how concerning stalking is and the degree to which it increases the risk of violent and possibly lethal outcomes.

It is also important to note that the internet and social media platforms can facilitate the efficacy of the stalkers' efforts. The anonymity of some spheres of the online space, as well as the instantaneous global reach of the internet, can assist stalkers to torment victims with a fraction of the effort required for in-person actions (Shimizu, 2013). In other words, the digital emphasis of current society can both aid stalkers because of the ease of online communications, as well as potentially lure other future stalkers to engage in harmful and harassing activities (Shimizu, 2013). It is essential that strategic cyberstalking laws address this alarming type of IPV when it manifests online.

THE TOLL OF DOMESTIC VIOLENCE

Domestic Violence in the United States

Recent analysis within the United States indicates that IPV is a destructive social phenomenon, one that represents a serious challenge to law enforcement and the criminal justice system. In fact, researchers have found that from 2003–2012, IPV cases in the United States made up over 20% of all violent victimizations (Truman and Morgan, 2014). Most of the violence was perpetrated by male offenders against females (76%), and most of the intimate partner relationships in which there was violence were characterized as boyfriend-girlfriend (Truman and Morgan, 2014).

While these numbers are concerning, there is also heartening information in the official statistics. Foremost, data indicates that rates of IPV declined in the United States an impressive 63% between 1994 and 2012 (Truman and Morgan, 2014). This decline in IPV rates parallels the overall decline in violent crime in the United States during that time period. However, we also note that the most significant portion of the decline occurred between 1994 and 2002, with rates of IPV remaining mostly stable and not declining significantly between 2010 and 2012 (Truman and Morgan, 2014).

We will discuss the spike in domestic violence during the COVID-19 pandemic in both the United States and globally in the final chapter of this book. It is not addressed here because we are looking at long-term trends within IPV rates in the United States, not temporary data points within a global health crisis. From these recent statistics, we can gain the fullest understanding of the toll that IPV takes on the criminal justice system and wider American society. We can conclude that IPV numbers have dropped significantly in the past 30 years in the United States, but it *still remains an* issue. There are multiple metrics that we will discuss in chapter 2 that illustrate its serious impact on society, and we urge readers to not dismiss IPV as an unfortunate behavior that occurred in this country during a less enlightened time. This crime is still occurring regardless of gender, sexuality, race and ethnicity, religion, economic status, and age, which is a theme that we will continue to discuss throughout this book.

Domestic Violence Worldwide

We note similar global issues in domestic violence and will discuss rates and trends in IPV in various nations and regions throughout the world in chapter 8. However, there are initial important facts to share about the impact of global IPV. Global data from 161 countries participating in the

WHO's Global Database on Violence against Women is concerning in multiple respects and illustrates the impact that IPV has had on women around the world. In fact, research has shown that women ages 15–49 who had ever had an intimate partner indicates that a staggering 1 in 3 had experienced IPV over the course of their relationships (Sardinha et al., 2022). Global IPV also appears to start at a young age in many cases, with 24% of teenage girls aged 15 to 19 already having experienced at least one incident (Sardinha et al., 2022).

IPV appears to occur more often in low-income countries globally, but this does not mean that it does not have a pronounced impact on numerous high-income countries, as we will learn in chapter 8. It is also important not to view IPV as an "us versus them" situation domestically and globally. While we will fully discuss the religious, social, cultural, and economic conditions in countries and regions of the world that experience disproportionately high rates of IPV, it should be examined in an objective manner, one that is grounded in research and data, not by stereotypes or preconceived cultural notions. IPV poses a significant challenge both domestically and globally that transcends national, economic, and cultural differences. Data indicates that a stunning 1 out of every 3 female homicide victims globally are killed by intimate partners (Mercy et al., 2017), and it is crucial that we understand the roots of this staggering figure.

CONCLUSION

In this chapter, we have focused on the necessary definitional explanations within IPV and have discussed the different types of abuse that it encapsulates under its wide umbrella, including physical violence, sexual violence, psychological violence, financial abuse, and stalking. We have briefly discussed how IPV can be found domestically and globally. In the next chapter we will devote our attention to the full scope of the violence, victimization rates, prevalence rates, and the impact that IPV has on multiple sectors throughout society.

SAMPLE QUESTIONS FOR CRITICAL THINKING

1. What is the definition of IPV?
2. What is financial abuse within IPV and how does it intersect with other types of abuse?
3. What are psychologically abusive behaviors within an intimate partner relationship and how do they impact victims?
4. What are sexually abusive behaviors within intimate partner relationships?

CONTEMPORARY APPLICATION

The Asheville Police Department in North Carolina posted a meme on their website that appears to poke fun at/mock the seriousness of stalking and other IPV behaviors that would necessitate a restraining order. This meme illustrates how different behaviors within the constellation of IPV can be minimized and not treated with appropriate sobriety (DeGrave, 2018).

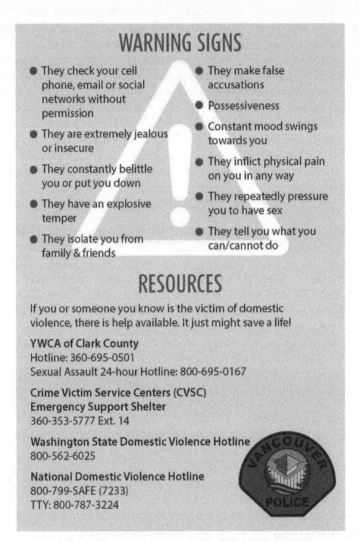

Figure 1.1. Domestic Violence Awareness Month sign from the Vancouver Police Department, posted on X. https://x.com/VancouverPDUSA/status/1446517150034845699.

2

The Scope of the Violence

CASE STUDY

Amani is a 28-year-old employee of a nonprofit organization. In the evening, she attends graduate school, working toward a degree in social work. She is bubbly, excited for the future, and fully embraces her trans identity. She is grateful for the support from family and friends, as she has heard horror stories from some of her friends about their own experiences as trans women. In fact, helping those who have been impacted by ignorance and prejudice is a motivating factor in both her professional and academic work. Her romantic life has been blossoming, as she recently met Justin, a 23-year-old law student. He is very charismatic, a fantastic storyteller, and a gifted mimic. Amani is smitten with that side of him. They immediately clicked, and their relationship has turned intimate. However, Justin does not have the same family support that she does, and he insists that their relationship must remain a secret because of her trans identity.

Amani is torn because she knows that she is too special to be a secret. At the same time, she understands the reality of ongoing bias against her community. She also knows that Justin's family is conservative. Another complicating factor is that Justin's family is financially supporting him while he goes through law school. She understands that it is early in their relationship, but Justin's secrecy causes her pain. They spend most of their weekends at her apartment, ordering in from restaurants as they binge-watch Netflix.

Unfortunately, there is a side to Justin that is troubling. He is a terrible financial manager and has managed to accumulate substantial debt. Amani has spent years saving up to attend graduate school and planned carefully so that she has enough money for her expenses. In her early 20s, she worked a weekend job, but that it is no longer possible due to all her other obligations, so she is very careful with her finances.

Two months into their relationship, Justin asks Amani for $300 so that he can pay his rent and utility bills. When they order out, she is the one who usually pays, but she attributes it to his age and lack of employment. She is by nature a generous person and given that Justin has promised to pay her back within the month, she sends him Apple Cash.

After the expected payment date comes and goes, Amani casually asks Justin if he plans to pay her back soon. She kindly tells him that it's fine if he needs more time, but she would just like a timeline of payment so that she can budget accordingly. Justin smiles his megawatt grin and assures her that he will be paying her back over the next few days. Amani is reassured and enjoys the rest of the weekend with her new boyfriend.

A few days later, Amani opens her credit card statement and is stunned to see several charges that she never authorized. The only person who could have had access to the card was Justin because she always kept her purse open in the apartment during their weekends together. She can't imagine he would ever do this to her, but she must figure out if some sort of mistake has been made. She immediately calls him and asks if he knows anything about the charges. He becomes nervous and stammers. He explains that he was shopping online using her laptop and he guesses that her card details were saved automatically as the default payment method, and that the "mistake" occurred there. He assures her that he will itemize all charges that are his and will pay her back as soon as he can, along with the $300.

Amani continues to worry throughout the course of the day. She knows that his explanation makes little sense, so she texts him some follow-up questions. She becomes startled when she realizes that her texts aren't going through. They are not friends on social media, and she has a sinking feeling that he blocked her. She can barely sleep that night. When she gets to work in the morning, she calls Justin from her work phone. He picks up and answers in his typical cheerful voice, but as soon as he hears her voice he hangs up.

Utterly distraught, Amani makes an appointment with her Employee Assistance Program counselor. She feels completely used and betrayed and isn't even sure how to proceed. Justin owes her well over $1,500, but she is fearful about the implications of taking him to court. She is attempting to dispute the credit card charges but is having little luck. As she and her counselor discuss the pros and cons of filing a court case or even going to the authorities on the grounds of credit card fraud, her counselor gently brings up another point to consider. Has Amani considered that she was a victim of emotional and financial abuse during this relationship and is now dealing with the trauma of surviving intimate partner violence (IPV)?

Amani is confused and tells her counselor that Justin never hit her, never raised his voice to her, and had always respected her sexual boundaries. Her counselor points out that Justin may not have abused her physically or verbally, but he clearly did not respect her financial boundaries. Further, ghosting someone after keeping their relationship a secret and borrowing/stealing a substantial amount of money from them is emotional abuse. The counselor further explains to her that IPV describes multiple behaviors and types of abuse and is certainly not limited to physical violence. In the ensuing weeks, Amani battles deep depression and sadness, and struggles to decide what to do about the stolen money.

Amani's harrowing plight is one example of the pervasive scope of IPV, as well as the toll it takes on its victims, both of which are the focus of this chapter. The concerning depth of the problem of domestic violence, including victimization rates for heterosexual men, heterosexual women, and members of the LGBTQA+ community will be discussed. Attention will focus on the data points that indicate the prevalence of this type of violence in the United States, as well as the implications of economic, physical, psychological, and societal violence, which are disturbing both individually and collectively.

THE PREVALENCE OF DOMESTIC VIOLENCE FOR HETEROSEXUAL MEN

While we examine marginalized and/or historically ignored victims of IPV in chapter 9, male victims of heterosexual IPV can be categorized as misunderstood and sometimes ignored. There are some initial themes of IPV regarding heterosexual males that should be discussed in order to understand the prevalence of this type of abuse. While statistics on intimate violence perpetrated against heterosexual males varies, estimates indicate that at least 12% of men in the United States are physically abused at some point by their female partners and that at least 4% (roughly 2.5 million men annually) are abused in a manner that would be categorized as severe (Straus, 1995). It is also important to note that unlike the decline in domestic violence rates in the United States since 1994, nonlethal IPV rates against males have remained steady and have not generally declined (Straus, 1995).

The National Violence Against Women Survey (NVAWS) indicates a concerning amount of violence perpetrated against men (Tjaden and Thoennes, 1998), the roots and implications of which we discuss in chapter 9. Essentially, NVAWS indicates that female-perpetrated violence against males constitutes 40% of injuries caused by intimate partner violence over a one-year period (Hines and Douglas, 2014). It is additionally important to note that women appear less likely than men to report their abuse from intimate partners on surveys, particularly when IPV is described as a crime. Estimates indicate that women underreport their use of IPV by approximately 75% (Mihalic and Elliott, 1997). What the body of research indicates is that IPV is perpetrated against heterosexual men as well, though as we will learn in the next section, statistics show that in heterosexual relationships, the majority of the violence is male perpetrated against women.

THE PREVALENCE OF DOMESTIC VIOLENCE FOR HETEROSEXUAL WOMEN

Researchers conclude that within cisgender/heterosexual relationships, female partners sustain the brunt of IPV. In fact, data indicates that women in the United States suffer IPV to a surprising extent. The National Domestic Violence Research Center estimates that between 600,000 and 6 million women were victimized by IPV in 2003 (Alejo, 2014). Additionally, NVAWS estimates that 25% of women had been abused within their intimate relationships, as well as around 7% of men (Tjaden and Thoennes, 2000). Disparities in IPV rates in heterosexual women by ethnicity, age, and other variables will be explored throughout this book, but for purposes of this chapter we contextualize IPV perpetrated by men against their female partners as statistically more common than perpetrated by women against their male partners. We also note that this research finding is consistent over time when assessing national rates and trends for IPV. Additionally, it is important to note that research findings are consistent in that female IPV victims are more likely to be killed by their abusers than male IPV victims. This finding holds true regardless of the victim's race, age, or socioeconomic status (Johnson, 2008). At the same time, a central point of this book is that all aspects of IPV are important to learn from and understand fully. Its aim is to address IPV in heterosexual relationships as comprehensively as possible, focusing on both female and male victims as well as perpetrator dynamics.

THE PREVALENCE OF DOMESTIC VIOLENCE FOR
THE LGBTQA+ COMMUNITY

Chapter 9 examines all features of IPV perpetrated within the LBGTQA+ community, but there is important data to consider here that illustrate how pervasive IPV is within the sexual minority community. It is essential to understand that the data indicates that IPV is *not* limited to heterosexual relationships and in fact, there are multiple studies that suggest that some aspects of IPV are *more* prevalent within the LGBTQA+ community. Sexual minorities include those who identify as lesbian, gay, bisexual, transgender, asexual/agender, as well as those who question features of their sexuality. Nonbinary individuals are also included in our categorization of the sexual minority community, even though they are not specifically named within LGBTQA+ per se.

While the exploration of sexuality is complicated and the LBGTQA+ abbreviation is not exhaustive, what is clear is that sexual minority individuals are statistically victimized by IPV at stunningly high rates. In fact, research indicates that almost 44% of lesbian women experience IPV over the course of their lifetimes, 61% of bisexual women experience IPV over the course of their lives, 26% of gay men experience IPV during their lives, and 37% of bisexual males experience IPV over the course of their lives (Walters et al., 2013). Research also indicates that bisexual women are at a uniquely high risk for physical and sexual victimization from intimate partners, and that lesbian women also experience significant relationship violence (Walters et al., 2013). Paradoxically, given these numbers, IPV researchers have focused most heavily on heterosexual relationships (Chen et al., 2020).

THE ECONOMIC TOLL OF DOMESTIC VIOLENCE

It is important to understand the toll of economic violence on its victims in order to grasp the depth of the problem. We do not imply that financial implications trump the personal toll that this crime takes on its victims, but it is important to note the economic consequences for both victims and society in order to address all aspects of IPV. The statistics are staggering, with costs defined as decreased health, lost professional productivity, and the financial toll on the justice system (Peterson et al., 2018). Estimates of the lifetime economic costs of IPV were $100,000 per female victim and over $23,000 per male victim (Peterson et al., 2018). The estimated economic toll of IPV for society as a whole is astounding: $3.6 trillion over victims' lifetimes when the 43 million US adults with IPV victimization histories are measured (Peterson et al., 2018).

This figure is so high that it could be construed as outlandish or exaggerated, but when experts break it down, the reality of it becomes apparent. This figure reflects collective costs of $2.1 trillion in medical costs (59% of the national economic toll), $1.3 trillion in lost productivity for *both* victims and perpetrators (37% of the overall national economic toll), $73 billion lost in criminal justice system costs (2% of the overall total), and another $62 billion allotted for other costs, including lost and damaged victim-owned property (Peterson et al., 2018). Obviously, these figures speak for themselves and illustrate the intense economic damage that IPV inflicts on the United States. They further emphasize that IPV cannot be dismissed or minimized as a private problem within relationships; rather, it is a societal challenge born out of violent crime that affects us all and thus requires thoughtful and collective action.

THE PHYSICAL TOLL OF DOMESTIC VIOLENCE

IPV takes a significant toll on the physical health of its victims. Chapter 13 explores the potential lifelong toll for physical and sexual health consequences more in-depth. This section is more general in nature. Sadly, one study found that women who suffer from IPV have chronic headaches, significantly heightened gastrointestinal symptoms, cardiac issues like hypertension and chest pain, and have three times the rate of gynecological problems (e.g., STIs and UTIs) and sexual pain as compared to nonabused partners (Campbell, 2002). Additionally, data indicates that abused women accrue 92% more health-care costs annually than nonabused women, though we note that these studies include both physical health care and mental health care (Campbell, 2002). In other words, these heightened costs are not due solely to the damage to physical health from IPV.

Additional research indicates that the overall physical health of abused women is significantly worse than nonabused women. In fact, researchers have found that severely battered women annually spend twice the number of days in bed than nonabused women and are much more likely to describe their health as fair to poor as compared to nonabused women (Gelles and Straus, 2017). Experts have concluded that IPV is associated with injuries like broken bones, pain, facial trauma, and ligament injuries, and that victims commonly present to outpatient clinics with these symptoms (Goldberg and Tomlanovich, 1984). Finally, it is important to note that many of these physical health consequences may not be properly treated at the time the initial IPV injury was inflicted, especially for abused partners who were intimidated/coerced to not seek medical treatment. Disturbingly, some research suggests a correlation between IPV and undiagnosed hearing, vision, and concentration problems in abused women (Eby et al., 1995). Some experts conclude that one common physical health consequence of IPV is undiagnosed neurological injuries, which can have lifelong implications on their daily functioning.

IPV is a significantly underreported phenomenon. Researchers estimate that between 1994 and 2005 only 58% of women and 52% of men reported their victimization to the authorities (Tjaden and Thoennes, 2000). Reasons for this silence range from fear of retaliation to embarrassment to multiple other factors, but what is most salient is that there is a substantial amount of physical suffering from IPV every year that is not captured in the physical data. In fact, estimates from emergency rooms suggest that rates of IPV are four times higher than the "official" numbers (Hafemeister, 2010). The import of reconciling the official data with unofficial research estimates is that while we know that IPV significantly damages the physical health of victims, it can also postulate that, chillingly, many victims are likely walking around with untreated and significant physical injuries each year.

THE PSYCHOLOGICAL TOLL OF DOMESTIC VIOLENCE

The destructive toll that IPV takes on victims' mental health cannot be overstated. Various psychological considerations of IPV are explored over the course of this book, and the emotional states of both victims and offenders are discussed. For purposes of this chapter, however, attention to the damaging effects of IPV on overall mental health is covered. Sadly, researchers have consistently correlated IPV to a range of alarming mental health disorders and challenges.

Numerous studies indicate that depression is an overwhelming consequence of women in abusive intimate relationships (Hamberger et al., 1992). This is deeply concerning when one considers the risks of clinical depression, including the lack of ability to function, loss of sleep, loss of once-pleasurable activities, and suicidal ideation (Karakurt et al., 2014). Tragically, researchers have found that severely battered women by males are four times more likely to attempt suicide than nonabused women (Straus et al., 1990). Depression is a complex illness that commonly requires intense treatment and diligent collaboration between individuals experiencing the illness and their clinical team. Sadly, psychological experts conclude that less than half of patients with depression achieve remission (Zajecka, 2003). The strong link between IPV and depression is one of multiple indications that the mental health impact of IPV is serious and sustained, and when abused partners exhibit clinical depression, the odds are against their full recovery.

Additionally, battered women in shelters demonstrate disproportionately high rates of post-traumatic stress disorder (PTSD) as compared to women overall (Astin et al., 1993). Research indicates that between 40% to 60% of female IPV victims exhibit PTSD symptoms (Mertin and Mohr, 2001). PTSD has a strong impact on the lives of those afflicted. It can include interfering thoughts, flashbacks, hypervigilance, difficulty sleeping, and a host of other alarming symptoms (Mertin and Mohr, 2001). There are other important mental health symptoms that are commonly identified in battered partners, including heightened rates of anxiety, diminished self-esteem, and substance abuse (Afifi et al., 2009). Emotional disorders commonly associated with IPV pose significant challenges to one's functioning and overall enjoyment of life. Mental health experts note that there is significant room for improvement in psychological treatment both domestically and globally, and that only one-third of mentally ill Americans receive proper treatment appropriate to their diagnosis (Wang et al., 2002). The fact that a significant proportion of IPV survivors appear to experience mental health challenges related directly to their victimization experiences is concerning given the relatively low odds that they will receive fundamentally helpful treatment.

CONCLUSION

The societal toll of IPV in the United States is considerable when we examine its physical, emotional, and economic impact. We have discussed concerning rates of IPV throughout all typologies of relationships and the significant injuries inflicted by it on all sectors of society. Given these overwhelming facts, it is fair to say that IPV is a public health crisis, as some global experts assert (Ellsberg, 2006). While this observation seems intuitive, it is worth noting that it is unlikely that any society in which there is extensive violence between intimate partners can ultimately succeed. A nation in which a notable proportion of its population that's physically battered, psychologically struggling, traumatized, and unable to fully participate in the workforce faces considerable challenges competing on the global stage. Accordingly, for both individual citizens and nations, it is crucial that proper resources be dedicated to combating IPV.

The subsequent chapter examines the development of IPV laws in the United States. It will be shown that domestically, laws have not been aggressive enough in dealing with this public health crisis. In fact, the historic trajectory of laws to combat IPV tells a story of centuries of nonintervention and a lack of proactivity, which remains a controversial topic today.

SAMPLE QUESTIONS FOR CRITICAL THINKING

1. How has the rates in IPV victimization for both heterosexual women and men as well as members of the LGBTQA+ community affected both victimized people and society overall?
2. What are the economic tolls of IPV on the United States over the course of a victim's lifetime?
3. What is the impact of IPV on overall mental health?
4. Do you think IPV constitutes a "public health crisis"? Thoroughly explain your answer.

CONTEMPORARY APPLICATION

Bhaya, 2017. *New study highlights impact of domestic violence on workplace, productivity.* CGTN. https://news.cgtn.com/news/3051444f7a6 37a6 333566d54/share_p.html

Tracing the Development of Laws on Domestic Violence

CASE STUDY

Christina is a 19-year-old Black woman living with her sister in public housing. She has one toddler daughter and is expecting a baby
in several months. She shares the children with her longtime boyfriend, Jordan. Christina is unemployed, has no vehicle, and relies
on public assistance. Jordan works a variety of cash-only construc-
tion jobs and never seems to struggle for money. He is a full decade
older than Christina and helps her out financially when he feels like
it. Christina desperately wants to get a job and further her education, but she is hampered by her lack of a car, the dearth of reli-
able public transportation, and her responsibilities to her family.
Not only does she care exclusively for her daughter, but she also
watches her sister's two young children during the day while her
sister is at work.

Christina's career interests are in psychology and counseling, particularly understanding the post-traumatic stress experience of children who grow up in high-crime areas. She grew up in public housing.
Some of the things she witnessed have left an indelible impact on her.
She fervently hopes and prays that she can get a studio apartment away
from the chaos of the housing community but knows that Jordan is her
biggest obstacle. They started dating when she was 15 years old. Since
then, he has become progressively more controlling and violent.

One evening, Christina's sister returns early from work unexpectedly
to discover her sister and Jordan arguing. Christina has a swollen eye
and marks on her neck, and her sister, furious, immediately phones the

police. Christina begs responding officers to just warn Jordan or make him leave for the night and says that his behavior is an aberration. She insists that their argument is a private matter and that she wants to resolve the situation between the two of them. The officers listen attentively before handcuffing Jordan; they explain to Christina that domestic violence is a serious crime and a high priority for their department. One officer tells Christina that domestic violence may have been considered a private family matter 60 years ago, but in 2024 society will not tolerate abusive behavior.

Christina's experience is emblematic of the sea change that has occurred within domestic violence laws in the United States, especially during the twenty-first century. Accordingly, this chapter focuses on analysis and discussion of the evolution in domestic violence laws in the United States. Close attention will be paid to early laws that actually enabled domestic violence. For example, the first laws forbidding a man from beating his wife and children were not instituted until close to the nineteenth century. Domestic violence shelters did not become widespread until the 1980s, and widespread federal funding was not provided for domestic violence until 1994. History shows the lack of US governmental attention toward this crime for much of its history. As much as contemporary domestic violence laws can largely be contextualized throughout the United States as conveying zero tolerance toward this crime, laws regarding intimate partner violence (IPV) during much of our national history can be termed as enabling and archaic.

EARLY DOMESTIC VIOLENCE LAWS

Husbands' Power of Correction

IPV laws did not exist in the United States in its early years. In fact, husbands were given the power to correct their wives if the "correction" was suitably mild. Essentially, IPV was sanctioned by the state, within limitations that were meant to prevent wanton violence. Husbands were allowed to use a stick or a rope that was no broader than their thumb to inflict abuse (Randolph, 2014). The encouraged weapon of correction was a switch, yet the historical records indicate that, not surprisingly, much more dangerous and extreme weaponry characterized IPV in the eighteenth and nineteenth centuries (Randolph, 2014). The records suggest that common household implements were often used in IPV, including clubs, fists, pots, pans, and feet (Randolph, 2014), which indicate that private corrections significantly diverged from the legal allowance.

It is important to note that the prevailing societal paradigm of the era was that a husband was responsible for his wife's behavior and reserved the right to control it through "chastisement," a gentler term for physical abuse, which was supposed to not result in injury (Hafemeister, 2010). The husbandly control of the family was supposed to encourage stability in domestic relations and society overall, though it appears that the lack of laws forbidding IPV were correlated with rampant familial violence.

Unsurprisingly, given the patriarchal laws and mores that characterized early American society, records indicate that IPV was common in the early years after the nation's founding. Wives were forbidden from using corporal punishment or "correcting" their husbands, yet the records indicate early America was a violent society in which wives also targeted husbands with violence (Randolph, 2014). Spousal homicides were quite unusual, but nonlethal IPV was alarmingly common. Historical records indicate that the impetus for violent arguments typically centered around work, money, children, and drinking (Randolph, 2014).

Despite clear manifestations of societal chaos in intimate relationships, the underlying patriarchal norms generally went unchallenged for decades in the country's early years. Tellingly, in the beginning of the nineteenth century, feminists did not challenge the legitimacy of husbands to physically correct their wives; rather, they raised substantive concerns over the prevalence and severity of wife-battering (Hafemeister, 2010). Accordingly, social reform measures for which early feminists advocated often centered around mitigating the damage of IPV, so to speak. As a prime example, the burgeoning feminist movement urged that temperance be adopted as a remedy for the alcohol abuse that was thought to trigger severe episodes of IPV (Hafemeister, 2010). This was symbolic of the theme that most elements of society did not challenge IPV until the twentieth century, and that the prevailing legal framework until then was

Figure 3.1. *Temperance Movement,* #2 Painting by George Cruikshank, 1847. https://fineartamerica.com/featured/4-temperance-movement-1847-granger.html.

simply to attempt to limit the severity of IPV (Hafemeister, 2010). The underlying abusive behavior remained essentially unchallenged for more than a century.

Massachusetts as a Case Study

In Massachusetts, laws addressing IPV during colonial times represent an interesting example of various treatments of abusive/neglectful spouses. The nature of colonial society made it very difficult to conceal abusive behaviors, and laws that the colony put in place made it clear that IPV was widespread. However, there were certain official remedies implemented to prevent abusive behavior from spiraling out of control in a way that would destabilize wider society: legal sanctions for "neglectful" husbands mandated them to provide support to their wives, possibly be whipped, produce a bond for good behavior (which essentially meant that problematic husbands made a formal legal promise to change their ways under penalty of more stringent legal sentencing should further issues occur), or even be sent to the workhouse (McDonald, 1986).

In Massachusetts an additional measure that limited the scope of violence while not criminalizing IPV itself was founded in 1641 in the Body of Liberties, which allowed husbands to strike their wives only in self-defense (McDonald, 1986). Surprisingly for the period, verbal abuse was criminalized within the codes of the colony, with penalties ranging from placement in the stocks to whipping (McDonald, 1986). These examples emphasize widespread IPV in colonial Massachusetts and how the colony attempted to mitigate it with various provisions while still not fully criminalizing the perpetrators.

Post–Civil War Reforms in Intimate Partner Violence Laws

Social changes in the wake of the end of the Civil War, coupled with women's strong participation in industrialization, prompted reform efforts within IPV laws and policies (Baggett, 2014). The legal environment of IPV cases in the pre–Civil War period is illustrated by the 1851 case of William Hussey in North Carolina who kicked his wife, Beulah, in the leg and punched her in the head, crimes for which he was convicted. Hussey appealed and the North Carolina Supreme Court reversed the decision and upheld principles of the male's right to "chastise" his wife, as well as matters of the family home to remain private (Baggett, 2014).

However, just over 30 years later, Joseph Huntley whipped his wife, Rachel, more than 20 times, not surprisingly leading to cuts all over her body. The lower court found him not guilty on the grounds that Rachel was not so severely injured that she could not "go about as usual"

(Baggett, 2014). In contrast to its decision with Hussey, the North Carolina Supreme Court stepped in, reversed the lower court's decision, and found Huntley guilty of assault and battery in a decision that accused him of damaging the "peace, decencies, and proprieties of the public" (Baggett, 2014). This shift signaled a wider trend in American law and jurisprudence, one in which IPV was not fully dismissed as a private matter, especially when the violence was severe. The Supreme Court did not find Huntley guilty of IPV because he assaulted his wife once and that itself constituted IPV; rather, he repeatedly and brutally whipped her causing visible injuries, which offended the sensibilities of the court.

Disturbingly, however, public perceptions of IPV shifted over the course of Reconstruction to a point where, especially in the South, society widely and wrongly ascribed it to a practice solely existing within the Black community (Baggett, 2017). In this way, the increased prosecutions for IPV disproportionately targeted Black husbands who abused their wives, all but ignoring abusive White husbands who treated their wives markedly like Black men who were convicted and jailed (Baggett, 2017). Accordingly, experts in the field have posited that the increasing criminalization of IPV in the post-war years reflected *both* the success of female advocates who urged for IPV to be treated as a crime, as well as a mechanism of racist Jim Crow governments to gain additional controls over Black former slaves with convictions and jail time for behaviors for which White men largely escaped sanctions. Legal observers conclude that the judiciary punished IPV cases in the Reconstruction era in a manner more consistent with exerting control over segments of society, rather than protecting victims, which can be understood as "selective prosecution" of batterers (Siegel, 1995).

THE MOVE TOWARD MORE FORMAL INTERVENTIONS AND CRIMINALIZATION LAWS

As the nation moved through the late nineteenth and early twentieth century, it was clear that societal views toward IPV were evolving, and that state and federal laws would need to be updated to reflect this growth. In 1871, Alabama took the first tentative steps toward adapting their laws by rescinding the right of husbands to beat their wives, though the state did not flat-out criminalize the conduct (Barr, 2012). The tentativeness of the Alabama Supreme Court's decision is reflected in the language therein, in which judges specifically named a variety of severely abusive behaviors including "beat[ing] a wife with a stick, pulling her hair, choking her, spitting in her face or kicking about the floor" (Hafemeister, 2010). Rather than expressly condemn or criminalize these dehumanizing and battering actions, judges simply said they were "not now acknowledged in our law" (Hafemeister, 2010). It is a powerful statement of the mentality toward IPV in the latter nineteenth century that judges did not condemn abusive behaviors perpetrated against wives; rather, they refused to "acknowledge them" in state law. This crucial distinction meant that IPV was not explicitly illegal in the state. In fact, the prevailing societal paradigm was that husbands had authority in their households, but with that authority came the obligation to exercise that power in a responsible way; when the power spiraled into serious abuse, this threatened societal good order and necessitated a more formal intervention (Edwards, 2023).

Maryland, Delaware, and Oregon criminalized domestic violence during the latter part of the nineteenth century and early twentieth century, authorizing punishments against abusive husbands (Gregory, 2002). IPV became such a serious matter that then-president Theodore Roosevelt lamented in his 1904 address to Congress that IPV was "inadequately" punished (Gregory, 2002). Unfortunately, the legal deck was still stacked against abused women for the first half of the twentieth century, as IPV perpetrated against women from lower socioeconomic statuses was not pursued aggressively, and legal, economic, and psychological barriers prevented many abused women from seeking divorces (Hafemeister, 2010).

It would take the growth of the civil rights and feminist movements in the 1960s for US criminal law to substantively change its posture toward domestic violence. The genesis of formalized legal interventions with IPV will be discussed in chapter 8, but for purposes of this chapter, we note briefly that feminist leaders partnered with battered women's advocates and conservative lawmakers throughout the 1970s to promote a "get tough" approach to IPV (Fagan, 1996). This collaboration proved to be resoundingly successful, as by 1980, 47 states had passed laws that allowed police to make warrantless arrests for IPV and to enforce civil protection orders for victims (Fagan, 1996). If we were to trace the trajectory of IPV laws in the United States, it would be fair to say that the nation has evolved from a noninterventionist stance in which IPV was seen as a private matter and the state should only intervene legally to *limit the severity of the violence*, to a country with a legal paradigm that is currently best classified as zero tolerance toward IPV.

CONTEMPORARY DOMESTIC VIOLENCE LAWS

Many of the IPV laws and policies of the last 30 years are directly correlated with the passage of the 1994 Violence Against Women Act (VAWA), which gave federal funding to states that passed robust anti-IPV laws encouraging mandatory arrest and prosecution (Messing et al., 2015). In the years since, VAWA has been used to enforce the civil rights of gender-based victims of IPV (Messing et al., 2015). However, this changed in 2013 when Republican lawmakers objected to the designation of formalized protection within VAWA for LGBTQA+ survivors of IPV (Messing et al., 2015). This politicization of victim-survivor protection is concerning given the weight of the data that indicates disproportionate IPV victimization within the sexual minority community, a theme that is highlighted throughout this book.

When experts assess the helpfulness of VAWA, one point of hesitation is raised: in 1994, VAWA disproportionately allotted resources to a criminal justice system response for IPV with 62% of funds devoted to that system and only 38% to social services (Messing et al., 2015). Some worry that the heavy emphasis on legal prosecution of IPV exhibits a lack of understanding to the point of actual harm for the care of marginalized victims who may not trust the criminal justice system (Arnold and Ake, 2013). Other critics of the VAWA have raised concerns that the women who conform to "patriarchal norms" (i.e., married and heterosexual) are the most likely to be helped by it (Goodmark, 2012), as well as that mandatory arrests and prosecutions subordinate the agency of victims to what continues to be a male-dominated criminal justice system. Finally, male rights activists have criticized VAWA on the basis that it supports feminism and believes women' s claims indiscriminately and at the expense of men (Dragiewicz, 2008). Objections of this type are often termed "antifeminist" (Messing et al., 2015).

When considering the quantitative impact of VAWA, we must consider that since its passage, all states have strengthened their anti-IPV laws (Messing et al., 2015). While federal funding is tied to the robustness of states' anti-intimate partner violence laws and policies, it is important to note that states have the final say (National Task Force to End Sexual and Domestic Violence Against Women, 2012). This means that there is not a federal standard throughout the country for laws combating IPV, and while the federal government can use funding as an incentive for states to show a strong response against IPV, individual states ultimately control their own laws.

Gender-Based Intimate Partner Violence as a Civil Rights Violation

A question debated by contemporary legal scholars concerns the categorization of gender-based IPV as a civil rights violation (Goldscheid, 2013). Historically, federal civil rights investigations were based on addressing gaps in state protection of individuals' constitutional rights, particularly during the civil rights movement, during which southern states often responded to racial violence and domestic terrorism perpetrated by hate groups with nonprosecution (Goldscheid, 2013). For example, the Emmett Till Unsolved Civil Rights Crime Act was inspired by the horrifying abduction, torture, and lynching of 14-year-old Emmett Till in Mississippi in 1955, a crime for which members of a family of avowed White supremacists were acquitted in what was essentially a show trial in state court (Schwabauer, 2010). The act itself provided funding to federal investigators who were reexamining notorious cases from the civil rights era (like the Till lynching) to see if charges could be brought for violations of constitutional rights (Schwabauer, 2010).

Proponents of classifying gender-based IPV as a civil rights violation appear to be moving on a parallel path with advocates for civil rights–era victims who had not received justice at the state level. The idea of categorizing gender-based crimes as a civil rights violation is that it allows federal authorities to have a means for redress for cases of gender violence where there was not sufficient protection for the victim within the individual state's justice system.

The Impact of the O. J. Simpson, Nicole Brown Simpson, Ron Goldman Case on Intimate Partner Violence Laws

The June 1994 murders of Nicole Brown Simpson and Ronald Goldman in Los Angeles, California, garnered international attention on IPV and renewed fears that state laws were not sufficient in combating the crime (Hafemeister, 2010). Nicole's ex-husband, famed football star and movie actor O. J. Simpson, who had previously been arrested for beating her, was arrested for the murders, and ultimately acquitted after a trial that was televised worldwide and reintroduced the concept of IPV to a global audience (Hafemeister, 2010). In the wake of the case, and the public perception that IPV had not previously been treated with appropriate severity, state legislation that combated IPV more strongly was passed. As a result, fatality review boards were established to investigate domestic violence fatalities (Hafemeister, 2010). The idea behind these boards was that fatal IPV cases must be investigated by a variety of stakeholders in the criminal justice system and community to assess the previous response, determine how the response could have been more effective, specify lessons that could be learned, as well as promoting enhanced community understanding of IPV (Hafemeister, 2010).

Evolution in Laws on Marital Rape

As discussed in chapter 1, IPV can and often does include sexually abusive behaviors perpetrated by one intimate partner against the other.

Unfortunately, for much of the nation's history, laws on marital rape indicated no understanding of sexual violence within IPV. The data indicates that up to 14% of married women and 50% of battered women experience sexual violence within their relationships (Martin et al., 2007). Yet it was only since 1993 that all 50 states finally criminalized marital rape, historical nonaction that is even more staggering when one examines the lifelong impact of this crime, including PTSD, depression, gynecological issues, and assorted health problems (Martin et al., 2007).

The Hale doctrine governed sexual mores between husband and wives in the seventeenth and eighteenth centuries and essentially posited that husbands could not legally rape wives because upon marriage, a wife "gives herself" to her husband and cannot retract this consent (Martin et al., 2007). Shockingly, this doctrine remained legally unchallenged until the 1970s, when the growing feminist movement strongly advocated for fundamental reform within this area of IPV (Gelles, 1977). These advocates accumulated dramatic wins that forever changed the legal environment for marital rape laws. In 1979, the *Commonwealth v. Chretien* case represented the first conviction of a man for raping his wife (Pagelow, 1988). All US states ultimately followed suit by July 1993 and criminalized marital rape (Martin et al., 2007), as did the federal government with measures like the Federal Sexual Abuse Act, which made marital rape illegal within federal properties (Martin et al., 2007).

However, there is an important caveat: as of 2024, multiple states still have what can be considered as "loopholes" in marital rape laws. The other remaining states had some type of "allowances" for sexual misconduct within intimate relationships that depended on things like the degree of force used and the inability of the wife to give consent (Martin et al., 2007). These allowances are quite disturbing because they (intentionally or not) send the message that sexual assault within intimate relationships is somehow less serious; that if ever there was a sexual relationship between partners, one cannot rape or sexually assault the other in the future. This is simply untrue, as sexual ethics experts have clearly asserted that consent is an ongoing process. In other words, a partner giving consent one time does not mean that consent is "good" for every encounter in the future; instead, voluntary consent is a necessary part of every sexual encounter, and past sexual relations do not imply future consent (Muehlenhard et al., 2016).

It is concerning that aspects of US marital rape laws still do not fully reflect this understanding of the importance of complete consent within intimate relationships. While the laws on IPV in the United States have fundamentally shifted since the early days of the nation and are now characterized by their assertive criminalization of IPV, there are still multiple areas of growth that are necessary. Most notably, gaps exist within the rubric of approaches to marital rape, as there are still allowances in some states that indicate this crime is not treated as such in every single case. As discussed in chapter 1, sexual violence is common within violent intimate partner relationships and national laws must reflect the absolute importance of consent, not a fixation on the past sexual relations of the parties involved.

CONCLUSION

This chapter has explored the development of laws in the United States that address IPV. The achievements of advocates for criminalization, as well as areas where additional efforts may be necessary have been noted as well. The underlying theme of this chapter is that, over time, society evolved and no longer saw IPV as a private family matter that only merited intervention when it became too severe. Rather, there was a growing consensus over the years that IPV was a concerning crime that needed to be properly addressed by the legal system. While the criminality of abusers' behaviors was the focus of this chapter, our attention shifts in the next chapter to examining all aspects of abusive partners as people. The criminality of their conduct is no longer in dispute, but other aspects of batterers' lives, motivations, and amenability to treatment are less clear. These questions will form the basis of our exploration in chapter 4.

SAMPLE CRITICAL THINKING QUESTIONS

1. What are the noninterventionist philosophies and legal trends of IPV in the early years of the United States?
2. What is the importance of the Violence Against Women Act in combating IPV?
3. How have marital rape laws in the United States told us about larger public understanding about IPV and consent?
4. What is the significance of the O. J. Simpson case in regard to IPV laws of the 1990s?

CONTEMPORARY APPLICATION

National Library of Medicine (2015). Domestic Violence in the 1970s. https://circulatingnow.nlm.nih.gov/2015/10/15/domestic-violence-in-the-1970s/.

4

The Batterers

CASE STUDY

Brent is a 50-year-old surgeon who is twice divorced and now engaged to his fiancée, Carolyn. Carolyn is 13 years younger than Brent. They met when their children were teammates in a youth league. Initially, everything was great—Brent could not have been more excited about his new relationship. Over time, however, problems began to surface. Brent began to exhibit behaviors that were issues in past relationships. Carolyn is a former model, and Brent now finds himself constantly fixating on the possibility that she will leave him for someone else.

Brent works long hours and sometimes, when doing paperwork, becomes distracted with thoughts of Carolyn with other men, even though she herself has a busy career as a realtor. She is extroverted, which is something he tries discouraging. He believes that her friendliness may give the wrong impression, so he asks her to be more "subdued" and consider wearing less makeup. Additionally, he tells her that her platinum-blond hair is attractive to older men having a mid-life crisis seeking out a younger woman. Carolyn is hurt and tells Brent that he's being controlling and trying to change all the qualities that make her "her." She feels that he is attacking fundamental tenets of her personality and tries to set a boundary in terms of changes that she is unwilling to make.

Brent's jealousy fuels many conflicts, which lead to a deterioration in their relationship. His behavior makes Carolyn very nervous, so she turns to wine to relax when they're both at home. Brent's anger continues to build as he becomes hyperfocused on the false claim that Carolyn is secretly dating a successful male colleague and is only using Brent for his money. After multiple verbal arguments, Carolyn heads into the bedroom one evening to pack an overnight bag and head to a hotel. She is not planning on ending the relationship but realizes that she can't accept things as they currently stand.

As she is packing, Brent storms into the bedroom and tells Carolyn that she is not leaving him. She must stay and they will figure things out. Carolyn calmly tells him that she is leaving. Brent's rage boils over. He grabs Carolyn, violently shakes her, and shoves her into a wall. Carolyn breaks free and immediately calls 911. She recognizes the signs because she was in an abusive relationship when she was in her 20s. She knew that his jealousy was a huge issue, but she never thought that he would physically abuse her. That's crossing a line. Brent realizes his mistake, but rather than apologize, he immediately begs her to hang up and consider the professional repercussions he will face if the police come. He is fully aware that they will make an arrest for intimate partner violence when they can determine the primary aggressor. Carolyn's torn blouse is confirmation of what took place between them.

The police arrive and, to Brent's horror, they arrest him on two charges of domestic violence. Additional charges for false imprisonment are considered. The media learns of the celebrated surgeon's arrest for domestic abuse and as a result he is immediately suspended from his job at the hospital. He retains an attorney who gets him a plea deal with the district attorney. Brent, as a first-time offender, is allowed to plead guilty to two misdemeanor offenses and as part of his sentence is mandated to attend a year's worth of batterer intervention classes. Initially, Brent keeps his guard up around his classmates because he feels that he, as a surgeon, has little in common with them. Over time, however, their stories resonate with him, and he feels more connected to them. When his classmates speak about their issues with jealousy and control, he has a stinging and painful awareness of this same problem in all of his relationships. He used to tell himself that the women he dated and married didn't try hard enough to him to prove themselves to him, but as the months pass and he attends more classes, he starts to accept that it was his own violent behavior that brought him to this class. He understands that his issues with jealousy, insecurity, and control fueled a moment of violence that he would have once thought unfathomable. While his relationship with Carolyn is over, Brent resolves to continue weekly therapy long after his completion of the class.

Brent's story illustrates the need to deeply explore the experiences and psychology of abusive partners so that society at large can best understand how to confront the persistent societal issue of domestic violence. This chapter focuses on the identity of batterers and the general conclusions researchers can draw from abusers' motivations, behaviors, and amenability to rehabilitation. In this chapter, research will reveal that battering behaviors transcend gender, race, ethnicity, socioeconomic status, professional acumen, and educational attainment. Additional consideration will be given to mass media portrayals of batterers and contextualizing these depictions with the body of scholarship on batterers. If we are to make sustained progress in the fight against intimate partner violence (IPV), understanding abusive partners is an essential ingredient.

WHO ARE THE BATTERERS?

Before we delve any deeper into our examination of IPV perpetrators, it is important to note that there is no prototypical batterer. The behavior transcends age, race, religion, professional status, and sexuality, but exhaustive research has helped us to identify certain risk factors for battering. One consistently high-risk factor is low socioeconomic status (Caetano et al., 2008), but we must note that this certainly does not exclude the wealthy from the population of IPV perpetrators. While the wealthy can be victims/perpetrators of IPV, it is important to note that there are situational factors associated with households experiencing poverty/an overall lack of economic resources that are empirically linked to higher rates of IPV. We will examine all demographic factors related to battering behaviors in the next section.

Demographics/Socioeconomic Characteristics

Research that focuses on the role of ethnicity in IPV indicates that rates among different ethnicities are roughly similar when other factors like alcohol use and socioeconomic status are taken into consideration. However, Black couples appear to be at a unique risk for violent relationships even after these factors are accounted for, as compared to White couples and Hispanic couples (Cunradi et al., 2002). There is research that also indicates that Black male abusive partners use more severe violence against their partners than White male batterers (Smith, 2008). While a lower socioeconomic status and a greater use of alcohol were also factors correlated with batterers, there was a clear ethnic disparity in the identity of IPV perpetrators (Cunradi et al., 2002) and the severity of the violence (Smith, 2008). This has prompted researchers to question why this disparity exists.

Research that has focused on understanding the lived experiences of Black male batterers suggests that there are several factors unique to their experiences in the United States that are critical to understanding disparities in rates of domestic violence. An in-depth study of Black male batterers indicates that several factors were helpful to understanding the previously mentioned disparity in IPV rates. Essentially, there are structural factors behind the violence, including the expectation of Black men to serve as breadwinners in their relationships, but there is a considerable dichotomy between that expectation and the reality of mass incarceration disproportionately affecting Black males, as well as racism in the labor market (Smith, 2008). Almost 33% of Black men will be incarcerated in the United States over their lifespan (Hattery and Smith, 2007). This statistic is simply shocking and provides a vivid illustration of the degree in which Black men still experience discrimination in this country, especially when one examines the postprison societal punishments against those with a felony conviction and how those punishments eliminate a candidate from much of the job market (Hattery and Smith, 2007).

Additionally, researchers found that the internalization of harmful norms of masculinity was also key to understanding these heightened rates of domestic violence. Essentially, in the United States there is a notion of masculinity that is inculcated into boys at a young age, which has ramifications as they age and face obstacles in adulthood. For Black men, these obstacles are structural and institutional. Essentially, some Black men have internalized the belief that they need to provide for their families, but when institutional racism prevents this via incarceration, unemployment, and underemployment, their masculinity becomes threatened and violence against a partner is more likely (Smith, 2008). Finally, some Black men experience unique exposure to violence during childhood as compared to their counterparts of other ethnicities, which is crucial to understanding IPV perpetration. Researchers have found that a little boy who witnesses his father beat his mother has a three times greater risk of being a batterer in adulthood (Smith, 2008). Early childhood experiences are helpful to understanding ethnic disparities in IPV perpetuation and increased rates of Black batterers as compared to their proportion within the general population.

Research also suggests that Hispanic couples experience IPV at higher rates than do White couples and that there are unique factors behind this disparity (Caetano et al., 2005). According to a review of the literature, young Hispanic men are at a higher risk of perpetration of IPV (Lown and Vega, 2001), but there are additional factors unique to the Hispanic experience in the United States that are also explanatory of observed ethnic disparities in IPV. First, it is important to note that some Hispanic men experience the tension between cultural expectations and assimilation to majority culture and traditional Hispanic patriarchal notions of the supremacy of the father/husband in the household. Research indicates that there are higher rates of battering observed for Hispanic males who feel their authority in their households slipping away (Davila et al., 2007). Similarly, higher rates of IPV were observed in Hispanic males whose partners had more education than them (Perilla et al., 1994). Understanding these factors can help practitioners in designing more effective intervention programs.

Female Batterers

A common and harmful misconception about domestic violence is that it is somehow solely perpetrated by men against women and within heterosexual relationships. This is simply not true. Studies indicate that the percentage of arrested female batterers in different jurisdictions range from 16% (Feder and Henning, 2005) to 35% (Miller, 2005). This data clearly encompasses a large range, but the overall point is that there is a nonnegligible population of female batterers, and their past experiences and vulnerabilities help us to understand the roots of their abusive behavior. While estimates of male violence in intimate relationships are alarming, indicating that up to 95% of spousal assaults are perpetrated by men (Douglas, 1991), and that a stunning one in four men will resort to violence against their partners in their lifetimes (Paymar, 2000), the female dimension of IPV perpetration is substantial enough to merit a full discussion.

Female IPV offenders often have tragic and traumatic lives prior to becoming batterers. A significant proportion of female battering is a response to male violence directed against them (Swan et al., 2008). Additional research that was conducted with female members of a batterer's intervention program suggest that most female participants had either been abused as children and/or witnessed violence between their parents (Seamans et al., 2007). Furthermore, most female participants of the program had left their childhood homes before age 18, did not have a substantive relationship with their mothers, and had been abused by at least one prior partner (Seamans et al., 2007). Therefore, theorists have asserted that male and female IPV perpetrators seem to have different motivations. Male offenders appear to be primarily motivated by maintaining control over their partners, whereas female offenders appear to be motivated by either retaliation for past violence or self-defense against current violence (Seamans et al., 2007). In the next section, the motivations of IPV perpetrators will be discussed more in-depth as we examine the different typologies of batterers.

LGBTQA+ Batterers

It is important to mention the increasing problem of IPV in the LGBTQA+ community. Domestic violence in this population will be discussed in considerable depth in chapter 9, but for our purposes here, it is important to highlight the significant proportion of IPV aggressors among its members. In fact, research indicates that IPV occurs in approximately 12% of same-gender relationships, which represents roughly similar numbers as compared to heterosexual relationships (Rohrbaugh, 2006). Experts conclude that the violence inflicted by same-sex violence perpetrators may be less severe (Rohrbaugh, 2006) than its counterparts.

MOTIVATIONS AND BEHAVIORS OF BATTERERS

Researchers have conducted extensive work with IPV perpetrators and have discerned that not all batterers have the same thoughts and motivations. This seems like an intuitive finding, especially when abusive intimate partners are treated like a monolith. It is important to specifically note that batterers share the trait of being abusive in intimate relationships, but beyond that, there are some significant differences. Researchers have examined specific factors, including the severity of the violence, whether it is only directed at their partner or at others, and the presence of psychopathology and/or personality disorders (Holtzworth-Munroe and Stuart, 1994). As a result, three distinct typologies of batterers were identified initially: family-only batterers, borderline batterers, and generally violent batterers who have elements of antisocial personality disorder (Holtzworth-Munroe and Stuart, 1994). Subsequent research identified two other distinct batterer typologies: sexually violent batterers and psychologically violent batterers (Chiffriller et al., 2006).

Batterer Typologies

In terms of understanding these typologies, researchers have found that family-only batterers confine their violence only to those within the family, especially their intimate partner, and resemble nonviolent individuals in many ways (Holtzworth-Munroe et al., 2000). The family-only batterer exhibits lower levels of physical and psychological violence against their partner and presents a lower risk for criminal activity (Carbajosa et al., 2017). Borderline batterers demonstrate high levels of jealousy and dependency (Holtzworth-Munroe et al., 2000), much like sufferers of personality disorders, and are more likely to exhibit depression, substance abuse, more serious IPV, and more generalized criminal activity than family-only batterers (Carbajosa et al., 2017). Generally, violent batterers have the highest level of violence, substance abuse, and association with criminal peers (Holtzworth-Munroe et al., 2000) and exhibit pronounced traits of antisocial personality disorder (Carbajosa et al., 2017). Finally, both borderline and generally violent batterers showed significant impulsivity, a lack of social skills, and high levels of hostility toward women (Holtzworth-Munroe et al., 2017). In terms of the newly established subtypes of batterers, sexually violent batterers are characterized by their use of often severe sexual coercion against their partners (Chiffriller et al., 2006) while psychologically violent batterers use serious indicators of emotional abuse, including threats, humiliation, verbal abuse, and intimidation (Chiffriller et al., 2006) to exert control and dominance in the relationship.

Significantly, research has also focused exclusively on females as batterers, and from this, researchers have been able to delineate three distinct types of female abusers: victims, aggressors, or those in mixed violence relationships. The research indicates that almost all women in the study had been abused by their male partners and were often victimized by sexual injuries, physical injuries, and coercion (Swan and Snow, 2002). In the study, 34% of female batterers were classified as victims, 12% were categorized as the aggressor in their relationship, and 50% were classified as being in mixed relationships, that is, mutual abuse between partners (Swan and Snow, 2002). Accordingly, researchers consider the typologies of female batterers to have male violence as the genesis of their violence. In contrast, the evidence is strong that male batterers are motivated by a variety of factors, but that their violence is generally not in relation to female aggression. In other words, male perpetrated IPV is most often not done in response to abuse from a partner; the batterer himself can have a variety of motivations behind it and factors that affect his conduct.

AMENABILITY TO REHABILITATION

A common misconception about IPV is that once an abusive partner has engaged in this destructive conduct there is no chance of rehabilitation and that abusive partners only go to treatment because they are trying to please a court and/or an abused partner (Cadsky et al., 1996). In colloquial terms, the layperson may conclude that batterers who attend a treatment programming are shamming the system and their victim. However, when we examine the literature, it can be concluded that this is a concerning oversimplification, and that in fact, there are IPV perpetrators who are highly willing to engage in treatment. Past research that studied the attrition from a brief two-week treatment program for IPV offenders found that there was considerable attrition rate (75%); however, it is important to note that 25% of those offenders did complete the program (Cadsky et al., 1996). Researchers were able to identify specific factors that are helpful/harmful to a batterer attempting to complete a rehabilitation or intervention program. Historical research indicates that offenders who drop out of these programs exhibit higher rates of lifestyle instability, including unemployment, lower income, less education, substance use, and relationship separation (Hamberger and Hastings, 1989).

Recent research has sought to further identify factors that are correlated with receptiveness to treatment. One study found that, not surprisingly, employed offenders have a higher likelihood of successfully completing treatment programs because they have more to lose professionally (Petrucci, 2010). Research has also studied the impact of typology of batterer on willingness to complete treatment. Perhaps unsurprisingly, in general, violent batterers attend the fewest intervention and treatment program sessions and have the highest dropout and recidivism rates (Carbajosa et al., 2017). Family-only batterers exhibited the highest attendance and completion rate and the lowest dropout rate, with borderline batterers in the middle (Carbajosa et al., 2017). Accordingly, because batterer typology so closely predicted amenability to treatment, completion, and recidivism rates, experts have suggested that treatment programs should conduct assessment testing to categorize each participant, and the program curriculum should be tailored to reach each typology accordingly (Carbajosa et al., 2017).

For example, appeals about the moral wrongfulness of domestic violence and its impact on victims may not make an impression on a generally violent batterer with antisocial tendencies and less capacity for remorse. Instead, an effective treatment curriculum tailored to that population's needs could attempt to harness some characteristics of antisocial personality disorder in an advantageous way. In other words, in general, violent batterers may not be motivated to engage in treatment because they care about their victims and want to change; they tend to do so because they have narcissistic and selfish traits and want to minimize their legal and professional consequences, which cause them discomfort. A curriculum that focuses heavily on possible consequences for repeat batterers may get their attention because it is about *them* and their future needs.

MASS MEDIA PORTRAYALS OF BATTERERS

We begin this section with a discussion of how domestic violence has been historically portrayed as a private peccadillo on some of the most famous and beloved television shows in the United States. We ask readers to consider the implications of this for impressionable young viewers who learned about the adult world from these shows. A foremost example of this disturbingly casual portrayal is the mid-twentieth century sitcom,

I Love Lucy. The show is beloved by numerous segments of viewers for the masterful physical comedy of Lucille Ball, but concerning undertones are present throughout. Perhaps the most famous example is an episode that ends with Lucy's husband, Ricky, spanking her repeatedly, but an additional episode features more sustained portrayals of purported domestic violence as "no big deal" and something that can be smoothed over with gifts.

"The Black Eye" episode from 1953 is centered around how both the Mertzes and the Ricardos ended up with black eyes, each mistakenly thinking the others' injuries came from their spouses. The fact that this would be acceptable and contextualized as a little spat is alarming, and Fred's counsel to Ricky during the episode is particularly worrisome. Fred tells his longtime tenant and best friend, when he believes that Ricky is responsible for Lucy's black eye, that Ricky needs to send her flowers telling her, "I love you, I love you, I love you." No discussion of the propriety of IPV and visible injuries is discussed; rather, the violence is minimized and depicted as a source for laughs. The suggested solution is elaborate protestations of love and flowers. A final note that adds poignancy to the episode is that the real-life marriage of Ms. Ball to Desi Arnaz (Ricky Ricardo) was notoriously volatile (Parish, 2010). The extent to which art imitated life is impossible to determine, but clearly a standing theme within the sitcom was Lucy's fear of triggering Ricky's volcanic temper.

The portrayal of IPV in American cinema has been similarly problematic, at times. Perhaps the most famous depiction of domestic violence in film occurs within the American classic film *The Godfather* (1972), in which Corleone family brother-in-law, Carlo, is depicted in jarring scenes abusing his wife, Connie, the youngest child in the family and only daughter. Even more disturbingly, Connie is pregnant in multiple scenes depicting her emotional and physical abuse. However, the abuse is not told with her perspective in mind. Rather, the film emphasizes her oldest brother Sonny's rage at his little sister's abuse, and subsequent assault on Carlo, a brutal scene that is emphasized as almost a feel-good moment in the movie. Given the dearth of focus on Connie as an abused person with thoughts and agency, observers often consider domestic violence in *The Godfather* as but one additional example of male retaliation that is a central theme within (Abhilash, 2015). In other words, viewers learn less about the phenomenon of domestic violence from a victim's perspective than they do about revenge and brotherly rage directed toward a batterer.

Almost 20 years later, *Sleeping with the Enemy* offered viewers a fuller picture of the suffering and perseverance of victims of IPV. Laura Burney (Julia Roberts) is portrayed as a horribly abused young wife of a monstrously controlling and older man, Martin. Laura sees no recourse other than faking her death to escape her husband's severe abuse and starts her life anew in a small town. While the film devotes more time to Laura's perspective and resilience as a survivor than previous cinematic works like *The Godfather*, observers still criticize the film for some of its emphases that are not helpful to better understanding domestic violence. In fact, researchers assert that the prolonged portrayals of graphic violence directed against a young Julia Roberts's character amount to an "eroticization" of violence, and that Martin's portrayal in the film as an evil, irredeemable monster may obscure more difficult truths that IPV perpetrators are people with complexities and nuances (Shoos and Shoos, 2017).

Finally, 1993's *What's Love Got to Do with It* explores the abusive relationship between legendary singer Tina Turner and her husband and musical partner, Ike. Unlike previous seminal cinematic works, the central focus of the film is on Tina's heroic journey from victim to survivor and her eventual fighting back against Ike in the backseat of a limo is the triumphal climax. Again, unlike previous works, the film explores *how* Tina's strength developed, and her Buddhist faith is depicted as a central factor in this growth in the famous "chanting scene." This film is noteworthy and groundbreaking in its portrayal of the trajectory of an abusive relationship, the complexities that can exist therein, and violence, survival, and empowerment from the victim's perspective. The Turners's musical success is highlighted, as are their children, simultaneously to scenes focusing on Ike's substance abuse and capacity for great violence. Thus, the "Why doesn't she just leave?" question that haunts victims of domestic violence is adeptly answered with a portrayal of a complex relationship that is full of considerable accomplishment but also betrayal and abuse. The film is purely Tina's story of her heroine journey navigating years of IPV while building an iconic singing career. In this way, viewers get a much more comprehensive view of how victims of IPV live their lives while experiencing sometimes horrific abuse, without defining their victimization experience.

CONCLUSION

In this chapter, we have learned how there are significant diversities in the psychology, motivations, and behaviors of IPV aggressors. Implications for effective treatment were discussed, and popular media portrayals of abusive partners were explored. In the next chapter, we will explore victims and survivors of IPV and learn that their realities often differ significantly from common perceptions. Life is complex, and IPV is one of the most confusing crimes to fully understand.

SAMPLE CRITICAL THINKING QUESTIONS

1. What are the major research findings on both male and female batterers?
2. What have researchers discovered regarding the motivations and history of batterers?
3. Are abusive partners able to be rehabilitated? Why or why not? Discuss fully.
4. How has the mass media portrayed batterers?

CONTEMPORARY APPLICATIONS

Sleeping with the Enemy (1991), 20th Century Fox movie directed by Joseph Ruben starring Julia Roberts, Patrick Bergin, and Kevin Anderson.

Figure 4.1.   A meeting of a Batterer Intervention Program. Alaska Department of Public Safety, https://dps.alaska.gov/CDVSA/Services/ForThoseWhoCommitDV.

5

The Victims and Survivors

CASE STUDY

Jade is a married 39-year-old administrative assistant at a hospital. She and her husband, Aaron, have been married for four years. They don't have children yet, though Jade is eager to start a family. Jade has been considering returning to school in order to advance her career but Aaron, a personal trainer, has been discouraging it. He believes that they are not in a strong financial position to either have children or pay college tuition, which hurts Jade. They are both quiet, soft-spoken people and hardly ever argue face-to-face, though texts can be heated.

Early in their relationship Jade considered Aaron to be the gentlest guy she had ever dated. He never raised his voice and seemed to listen closely to her, unlike many of her previous boyfriends. However, once they became intimate, she realized that he enjoyed rough sex, which was not something she was used to or wanted. Aaron is fixated on it and is a voracious consumer of violent pornography. Over time, Aaron increasingly pressures Jade to participate in his fantasies and doesn't seem to care that he has hurt her physically on several occasions. He never lays a hand on her outside of their bedroom, but during sex he has split her lip twice and left her with a black eye. Jade knows that Aaron is fully aware that she doesn't enjoy rough sex and in fact, she has repeatedly told him that she loves their sensual moments and doesn't feel comfortable with abusive sex.

As Jade becomes more assertive about her own wants and needs, Aaron begins to withdraw. He doesn't respond to her texts for hours. When she sends him pictures, he waits several hours to send a one-word reply. He goes to sleep with his back turned toward her and becomes annoyed when she initiates sex. She summons her courage and asks him if he's seeing anyone else. He dismisses her concerns of infidelity as "crazy" before telling her that he resents his integrity being questioned with the accusation of cheating. Jade also feels that Aaron has become increasingly critical of her, especially of her body. One night when she treats herself to a cookie, he comments that "she doesn't need to be eating that." He encourages her to track her intake of food with an app like he does. Each day, Jade starts to wake up earlier to ensure that she has a minimum of one and a half hours at the gym.

However, no matter what she does, Jade senses Aaron pulling away. The only time she feels that he emotionally connects with her is during rough sex. If she lets him engage in the kind of sex he craves (even though he knows she hates it), he will hold her for hours afterward and talk softly to her like he did when they first met as recompense. Jade is very conflicted about the future of her marriage. She wants kids and doesn't want to start over again at 39, and she truly loves her husband. When she looks at him, he takes her breath away. At the same time, she knows that he is manipulating and emotionally abusing her to get his own way sexually, that it's not consensual. Consent involves respect for individual autonomy. The night before her birthday, as Jade is excitedly preparing, Aaron asks her if they can engage in a sexual relationship with one of his female coworkers, which has always been a fantasy of his. Jade is shattered and arranges to see her priest for counseling to explore the future of her marriage.

After an emotional meeting with Jade, her longtime priest urges her to see a friend of his, a psychotherapist, who specializes in working with abused women. The priest tells Jade that he doesn't have the expertise to adequately advise her. After a period of reflection, Jade makes an appointment and visits the therapist. She explains that Aaron has never even raised his voice at her, yet he doesn't seem to care about her own sexual agency and continues to push and manipulate her past her stated boundaries. Jade's therapist encourages her to read several books on domestic violence to learn more about the topic and specifically suggests that she explore resources on battered women's syndrome. To Jade's surprise, her therapist tells her that the cyclical aspect of her relationship with Aaron seems reminiscent of this dynamic.

Jade's story is illustrative of the complex tapestry that describes the lives of victims and survivors of domestic violence. It's fair to say that Jade may defy some stereotypes of domestic violence survivors. She is in middle adulthood, childless, and a professional who has been independent for much of her adult life. Her relationship also seems somewhat different from popular conceptions of how domestic violence is defined, as the abuse she suffers is largely sexually and emotionally based. Thus, the focus of this chapter consists of a full examination of the traits, vulnerabilities, and behaviors that researchers suggest are widespread in survivors and victims of intimate partner violence (IPV). Popular misconceptions about IPV victims and survivors are addressed, as well as the disconnect between mass media portrayals of victims/survivors and empirical conclusions from the available research. In this way, we work our way through assigning thoughts and motivations to domestic violence victims in favor of consistently returning to the research to get the full picture of who the victims and survivors are.

Before we engage in our overview of the literature on victims and survivors of domestic violence, it is helpful to note that there is some controversy over the term assigned to describe the abused partner. An evolving trend within this area of scholarship is to describe abused partners as "survivors," not "victims," because theorists believe that the former term emphasizes their "rationality and agency," while the latter term emphasizes their "emotionality and victimization" (Dunn, 2005). In short, the idea is that "survivor" is a more neutral term that serves to remove any possible stigma from the term "victim" (Dunn, 2005). Both terms are used here simply to emphasize that not all abused partners survive the violence that is perpetrated against them. In fact, one-third of homicides in the United States of female victims are perpetrated by intimate partners (Kyriacou et al., 2017). Accordingly, the terminology used in this book is intended to accurately reflect all aspects of IPV and implies no judgment of abused partners.

WHO ARE THE VICTIMS?

Socioeconomic Characteristics of Victims/Survivors

Just as there is no one, prototypical IPV perpetrator, there is no sole model of a domestic violence victim/survivor. However, some generalities can be made based upon the research to date. Before further discussing socioeconomic risk factors, it is important to note that none of the discussion in this chapter is aimed at victim shaming. Rather, our goal is to accurately describe domestic violence dynamics and focus on the victims' experiences and shared vulnerabilities.

Domestic violence is a phenomenon that touches all sectors of society. No one is too wealthy to be a batterer or a victim (Renzetti, 2009). For example, the affluent Palm Beach sugar heir Nico Fanjul was arrested for serious domestic violence offenses in both April 2023 and January

2024, which garnered considerable public attention (McLaughlin, 2024). However, researchers have found that as a family's financial status rises, the likelihood of domestic violence decreases (Benson et al., 2003). Shockingly, studies indicate that rates of domestic violence victimization are seven times higher for women who annually earn less than $7,500 compared to women who earn at least $75,000 (Rennison and Welchans, 2000). Rates of IPV are highest against women who are homeless or on public assistance (Tolman and Rosen, 2001).

Victims of IPV typically experience difficulties in life. When socio-economic risk factors are assessed, a common finding is that victims exhibit aspects of disorganization in life (Edwards et al., 2014). In other words, there are numerous structural factors in the lives of the victims of IPV that do not appear to be coincidental. Certain themes can be gleaned, and while they do not apply to all victims, research helps paint a picture of a typical victim of IPV.

Research indicates multiple metrics of social disorganization often present in the lives of victims, including lower socioeconomic status and higher levels of substance abuse. In fact, researchers identify significant rates of drug use among females, as well as a high percentage of drug use among residents in domestic violence shelters (Miller et al., 2000). Additionally, research shows a correlation between poverty-stricken women and IPV (Edwards et al., 2014). It is not uncommon for sustained economic struggles to lead to IPV. Rates of IPV are three times higher for women who live in rented homes than those who own their own home. Divorced/separated individuals experience the highest levels of domestic violence (Rand and Rennison, 2004). Finally, women who live in urban areas are also disproportionately likely to be victimized by IPV (Rand and Rennison, 2004).

Unfortunately, research also indicates that the average domestic violence victim is disproportionately likely to be a minority female who is experiencing economic struggle. In fact, police reports of domestic violence were two to three times higher for Black and Hispanic women as compared with White women (Lipsky et al., 2009). Additionally, Black and Native American women are troublingly overrepresented when rates of domestic violence homicides are assessed, as data indicates that those two groups are most often the victims of domestic homicides (Petrosky et al., 2017). Additional research indicates that there are economic and gender disparities in IPV victims, with Black individuals victimized the most, followed by Whites, Latinos, and Asians (Cho, 2012). Older and more affluent individuals are less likely to be victimized by IPV, which supports the economic deprivation and multiple disadvantages model in terms of domestic violence victims (Cho, 2012). Supplemental research indicates that Black women experience IPV at a rate that is 35% higher than

White women, and that Black men experience IPV at a rate 63% higher than White men (Rand and Rennison, 2004).

Given racial and economic disparities and the heavy representation of minority women and/or those suffering from addiction in populations of IPV victims, some theorists have proposed a multiple disadvantages model. Essentially, their thesis is that many domestic violence victims are contextualized as having lives in which they have experienced multiple disadvantages, including trauma, poverty, deprivation, abuse, and neglect (Cheng and Lo, 2015). These disadvantages also act as inhibitors for abused individuals to receive appropriate services and interventions.

As we continue to consider factors that are correlated with higher rates of intimate partner victimization, we turn our attention to pregnant women. Pregnancy is a highly vulnerable time in a woman's life. Sadly, research indicates that between 3% and 9% of pregnant women are victims of domestic violence (Martin et al., 2001). Returning to our multiple disadvantages model to explain some of the lives of domestic victims, researchers have also found that women who are most vulnerable to domestic violence during pregnancy are younger, a minority, in poverty, and single (Tjaden and Thoennes, 1998). Staggeringly, research focusing exclusively on low-income pregnant women found IPV rates upward of 50% during their pregnancies (Bailey and Daugherty, 2007). To succinctly summarize the research on IPV victimization during pregnancy, it appears that the most vulnerable women in society experience the highest volume of domestic violence during one of the most delicate periods in their life. The experience of domestic violence during pregnancy is not exclusive to women living on the margins, but there is certainly a correlation between multiple disadvantages and IPV.

The final area we consider when assessing the most common socioeconomic status of IPV victims and survivors is the prevalence of male abused partners. From a socioeconomic perspective, males are most commonly the abusive partners in heterosexual relationships (Huntley et al., 2019). However, there is research that indicates male victimization: approximately 22% of males suffer physical, sexual, or psychological abuse during their lifetimes (Coker et al., 2002). Additional estimates indicate that one in five men experience abuse within their intimate relationships (Desmarais et al., 2012). We note that when attempting to pinpoint hard numbers on male IPV victimization, research indicates that injured men who present to the emergency room due to physical injuries inflicted by a partner also have high rates of past domestic violence arrests themselves (Muelleman and Burgess, 1998). Accordingly, experts suggest that a proportion of abused men may in fact be the primary aggressors, with violence perpetrated against them in self-defense. However, abuse is more severe when directed at a female partner.

Traits and Behaviors of Victims/Survivors

IPV is a devastating experience that can interrupt all aspects of an abused person's life. For example, the professional life of women experiencing domestic violence is negatively impacted. They miss more days of work, arrive late more often, suffer from physical and psychological problems that damage their productivity, and have difficulty maintaining consistent employment over time (Logan et al., 2007). It also bears mentioning that these abuse-rooted employment challenges also serve as an impediment to both accessing help and ultimately leaving abusive relationships, since unsteady employment limits one's financial resources and future professional marketability. Unfortunately, studies indicate that professional disruptions and limitations for victims can persist for many years after the initial abuse starts (Lindhorst et al., 2007).

Many may wonder why they stay. The barriers model focuses on abused women. It examines how they engage in a complicated calculus about the realities of leaving violent relationships and the obstacles surrounding it such as economic dependence on the batterer, barriers due to socialization and role expectations, psychological symptoms of violence, and barriers from childhood abuse and neglect (Grigsby and Hartman, 1997). An additional behavior that is important to note is the tendency of abuse victims to self-isolate because of shame or not wanting friends/ family to know about the violence, which constitutes a major environmental barrier to leaving an abusive relationship (Ptacek, 1999).

Research specific to the psychological behaviors and adaptations of female victims indicates that they exhibit a variety of concerning symptoms, including depression, anxiety, low self-esteem, consistent feelings of worthlessness and powerlessness, and self-blame (Ptacek, 1999). Women also employ defense mechanisms like minimization, rationalization, denial, and dissociation (Anderson, 2008). These defense mechanisms give victims hope that the relationship will change, and that the abuser will stop their violence, which keeps the abused in the relationship. At the same time, abused partners demonstrate a constellation of concerning mental health symptoms. As a result, abused partners often exhibit a disconnect between their internal feelings, which are full of sadness and anxiety, and their external appearance regarding their intimate relationships, which is often overly optimistic to the part of embodying denial, minimization, and rationalization. Dissociation is often conceptualized as the process in which a traumatized person, or someone going through acute stress, experiences an "alteration in consciousness" in which they become somewhat disconnected from their current reality (Cardefia, 1994). Accordingly, and concerningly, it appears that some IPV victims may find their circumstances so overwhelming, and memories of the abuse so terrifying, that they protect themselves psychologically by going to a different and safer place in their minds, leaving them not fully connected to reality at various points in time (Cardefia, 1994).

Vulnerability Factors of Victims/Survivors

Research has also found that there are lifestyle and circumstantial factors that can increase one's risk of IPV. A study of women injured by IPV who reported to emergency rooms indicated that certain predictive factors, including the victim living with a former partner, are correlated with risk of injury from IPV (Kyriacou et al., 2017). It appears that fraught cohabitation can significantly increase the likelihood of violence. Additionally, research indicates that not only do abused individuals often demonstrate psychiatric symptoms as a result of their victimization, but they also often appear to have preexisting psychiatric disorders that may predispose them to experiencing abuse (Kessler et al., 2001). The connection between family violence in early childhood with depression and early marriage to a partner who also suffers from mental illness and then ultimately experiencing IPV (Kessler et al., 2001) provides powerful evidence that domestic violence has a multifactorial relationship with mental health challenges. In other words, consistent with the multiple disadvantage model, mental health struggles constitute a vulnerability that makes individuals more likely to suffer abuse from intimate partners. Additionally, research indicates that domestic violence has an array of negative mental health consequences for abuse victims and survivors.

A significant additional vulnerability that can predispose one to IPV as an adult is experiencing trauma, neglect, and abuse in childhood. The body of literature on intergenerational transmission of violence indicates that the disproportionate rates of childhood sex abuse for little girls as compared to little boys is one explanatory factor for the disproportionate rates that adult women are victimized by domestic violence (Smith-Marek et al., 2015). In other words, theorists have found that little boys who live in violent households are socialized in ways that may predispose them to violence in adulthood and with their intimate partners, whereas little girls who experience violence with their families of origins are socialized in ways that predispose them to IPV victimization as a woman (Smith-Marek et al., 2015). There appears to be a familial cycle of violence that is helpful in understanding IPV victimization, and that the lives of a significant proportion of IPV victims and survivors are characterized by experiences of considerable levels of trauma in both childhood and adulthood. The development of mental illness because of extreme traumas can make someone more likely to be victimized by an intimate partner and also make it more difficult to leave a violent relationship.

MASS MEDIA PORTRAYALS OF VICTIMS

In the previous chapter, we examined US cinematic and television portrayals of domestic violence and the ensuing perspectives on batterers that different themes and scenes from these sources of media reveal. We now turn our attention to the depiction of domestic violence victims both in international and domestic media. Concerningly, an analysis of the depiction of domestic violence victims in international media indicate a significant amount of victim-blaming and portrayals of IPV sufferers as "bad or mad" (Rollè et al., 2020). Equally alarming, analysis of domestic media sources indicates a similarly pernicious view of IPV victims, with stealthily "conservative" views of IPV being communicated in news reports (Easteal et al., 2015). Essentially, the idea is that news stories that focus on IPV often describe the violence in ways that evoke "mutuality" between the participants, which is a more conservative mode of thought, rather than more feminist conceptions of gendered violence as key to understanding incidents of IPV (Easteal et al., 2015).

This ideologically oriented, possibly misogynistic, depiction of domestic violence can be particularly worrisome when local sources of media are analyzed, because local news accounts can heavily affect readers and exert significant influence over policies that affect all parties involved in violent relationships, including both victims and perpetrators (Kelly and Payton, 2019). The proliferation of social media also has a strong impact on the portrayal of survivors of IPV, with researchers identifying two divergent themes in terms of how these survivors are depicted on the various platforms. Essentially, researchers have identified these two themes as abused females portrayed in a stigmatizing manner as victims and abused females portrayed more neutrally as survivors (Taccini and Mannarini, 2024). The major implication of this social media–based study is that there are numerous irresponsible elements present throughout the platforms, but social media also has the power to convey a positive message about domestic violence survivors to a global audience (Taccini and Mannarini, 2024).

Extensive analysis of media treatment of IPV victims and domestic violence homicide victims has confirmed these troubling findings and indicate that victim-blaming, sensationalism, and framing IPV as a private matter and isolated incidents rather than as symptomatic of larger structural and gender issues in society, are consistent rather than episodic themes in media coverage (Perras et al., 2021). Additionally, an examination of media sources indicates a pronounced lack of focus on same-sex victims of IPV (Perras et al., 2021). Furthermore, analysis suggests that there is significantly less reporting of IPV incidents and homicides in lower-class areas as compared to wealthy, which concerns researchers because this bias in reporting can have real-world implications, misleading readers and viewers to believe that domestic violence is uncommon in wealthy areas to the point that all incidents must be reported on extensively (Perras et al., 2021). While every incident of IPV deserves further societal attention, experts are justifiably concerned that *only* focusing on the victimization of the wealthy can skew public perceptions regarding IPV. The media's focus on sensationalizing victims and heavy emphasis on IPV that occurs with the wealthy also serves to obscure the experiences of other victims and survivors, and accordingly, experts urge that media organizations work to ensure that their stories on IPV are consistent with best practices in journalism (Perras et al., 2021). There is significant room for growth in terms of the media's coverage of IPV and especially of its victims; this includes the call for stronger media commitment to simply inform the public about IPV without crafting a dramatic narrative.

CONCLUSION

While this chapter has explored the traumas and challenges faced by victims of domestic abuse, we devote our discussion in the next chapter to understanding why this crime happens. Specifically, we focus on multiple theories that explain IPV behaviors from both the victim and offender's perspectives. We note that our theoretical explanation and attempt to answer why this takes place does not imply that IPV is ever acceptable. Our goal is to offer possible theories to explain this serious crime. Readers will be able to assess for themselves what theories resonate the most to them.

SAMPLE CRITICAL THINKING QUESTIONS

1. Who is most at risk of being victimized by intimate partner violence and why?
2. How does the mass media portray victims of IPV?
3. What is the relationship between economic struggles and IPV victimization?
4. What is the relationship between past trauma and IPV victimization?

CONTEMPORARY APPLICATIONS

Audacy. (August 16, 2017). *Chris Brown Details Rihanna Assault: She Tried To Kick Me, I Bit Her Arm* [Video]. YouTube, https://www.youtube.com /watch?v=jnJmyw7hxZw.

E. McClafferty (October 13, 2016). Domestic abuse: Survivor calls for change in NI law. BBC News, https://www.bbc.com/news/37643205.

6

Theories on Batterers and Victims

CASE STUDY

Helen is a 55-year-old English teacher. She has been married to her husband Paul, a prominent local pastor, for over 30 years. They have three grown children. Helen is shy and bookish. She smiles to herself in acknowledgment at how much she fulfills stereotypes of those in her profession. She loves meditative activities like cooking and gardening. Her children describe her as gentle. In contrast, Paul is a thunderous extravert who is so gregarious that it seems like he has never met a stranger.

Paul believes that one of his greatest talents is his ability to connect with all of his congregants, but he doesn't realize that many of them find him intimidating. He succeeded his beloved father as the church's pastor, and some members of the church now quietly whisper to each other that perhaps they should have vetted him more closely to see if he truly was a good match for their congregation. Universally, however, they adore Helen. Stories abound about how she has humbly helped many members of the congregation with all manner of problems. Some wonder about Helen and Paul's relationship; they are so different.

Helen grew up in a conservative and religious household where wives must defer to their husbands. For many years of her marriage, Helen tried to do just that. However, she found that nothing pleased Paul and he criticized her in every way. He has always belittled her hair, makeup, clothes, weight, cooking, salary, and many other things, which has slowly eviscerated her self-esteem. In addition, Paul has a dreadful temper, and Helen is often his target. He has never physically

---

hurt her, but he has punched walls and once kicked in their television set when his favorite football team lost a playoff game.

Helen doesn't believe in divorce but feels that her marriage has been dead for many years, and she is now chronically lonely. She immerses herself in her job, reads, and makes a point of finding new recipes so that she has an activity to lose herself in during those evenings when she and Paul are at home together. In fact, she is working on a new Thai recipe when her daughter Kristie, a psychology major and intern at a women's shelter, comes to her to talk. Paul is out for the evening leading a Bible study and her daughter knows that she has a couple of hours before his return.

Kristie tells Helen that she has been learning a lot about domestic violence in her classes and internship. Based on what she has witnessed for years in her parents' marriage, she finally has come to realize that her mother is in an abusive marriage and that there are resources out there for her. Helen softly says that Paul has never hit her, but Kristie points out that intimate partner violence (IPV) includes several behaviors distinct from physical violence. Kristie shares that, in her opinion, Paul's screaming, belittling, and bullying is emotional abuse. Helen falls silent. Kristie tells her mother that she is not trying to pressure her to do anything she is not ready to do, but that she might want to read several books that she picked up from the shelter that might resonate with her. Helen agrees but takes them out to her car so that Paul doesn't see them.

Helen's children are puzzled why a brilliant, talented, and caring woman has been trapped in an abusive relationship for so many years. They are equally mystified how their father, who was called to the ministry at a young age, can preach about adherence and fidelity to God's commands while secretly abusing his wife. The goal of this chapter is to provide a detailed examination of the theories that explain the thoughts, motivations, and behaviors of both victims and abusers. Specifically, the main theories behind IPV, including psychological, social, cognitive behavioral, and family and systems theories are examined. Theories explaining the behaviors of victims and survivors will also be assessed, including learned helplessness, a theory that may have particular applicability to Helen, as well as battered women's syndrome and social learning theory. An additional emphasis will focus on the importance of theoretical understandings of domestic violence that addresses root causes and best practices for interventions, treatment of batterers, and assistance to victims and survivors.

THEORIES THAT EXPLAIN BATTERERS

There are indicators that society has the propensity to assign harmful stereotypes to both abusive partners and domestic violence victims (Harrison and Esqueda, 1999), which is not helpful when trying to understand IPV or formulate effective interventions against it. For example, one study found that when participants were asked to evaluate a hypothetical domestic violence scenario, they judged victims more harshly if they returned to the relationship (Yamawaki et al., 2012). Myths about IPV obscure a full understanding of the causal factors behind this violence and make it more difficult for practitioners to understand how to best help all parties. This chapter explores a variety of theoretical explanations for the actions of both batterers and victims. IPV is a multicausal phenomenon, and the goal of this section is to elucidate several empirically supported theories behind IPV.

Psychological

An examination of the psychological well-being of IPV offenders is often a popular track. For example, researchers have explored the psychological health, or lack thereof, of batterers. Over time, psychopathology, other mental illnesses, attachment issues, and anger management challenges have all been implicated as triggers for domestic violence (Ali and Naylor, 2013). Psychopathology is overused in the public lexicon (e.g., "I don't like this person. They're a psychopath!") given that true psychopaths are thought to only comprise around 1 percent of the population (Sanz-Garcia et al., 2021). Accordingly, it is important to understand that the diagnosis of psychopathology is quite unusual, but there are certain traits within the disorder that describe aspects of an abusive partner's personality. Psychopathology is best described as a serious personality disorder characterized by the inability to feel true emotion, empathy, and/or remorse, as well as the inability to fully distinguish between right and wrong (Sanz-Garcia et al., 2021). A true psychopath often has repeated legal problems and difficulties both professionally and personally, but may also have a certain "glib and superficial" charm that draws people to them (Sanz-Garcia et al., 2021).

Research on psychopaths and IPV indicate that perpetrators of IPV often demonstrate at least some symptoms/behaviors of psychopathology (Chester and DeWall, 2018). In fact, researchers have observed enough connections between symptoms of psychopathology and behaviors of *some* IPV offenders that they have posited that a subgroup of domestic violence offenders exist. Essentially, it is thought that offenders within this subgroup have psychopathic tendencies and are generally more violent and resistant to treatment than other subgroups of batterers and are thought to cause the most severe physical and emotional injuries to their partners (Huss and Langhinrichsen-Rohling, 2000).

However, given the rarity of this disorder within the general population, it is certainly not the only explanation for battering, though research is clear that a subtype of batterers with psychopathic characteristics exist. Another personality disorder that has been studied extensively in relation to IPV is borderline personality disorder (BPD), an illness in which the sufferer struggles from intense fear of abandonment, the inability to regulate emotions, impulsivity, a view of people in black/white terms, and the manifestation of intense anger and grief when faced with the termination of relationships (Green and Browne, 2020). Unsurprisingly, given the emotional instability of a person with BPD, and the intense fear of abandonment and rejection, research suggests that BPD is a significant risk factor for IPV (Green and Browne, 2020). There is a clear connection between BPD and both male and female IPV perpetrators that some researchers have even assigned the borderline subtype within the overall groups of batterers (Johnson et al., 2006). It is also important to note that researchers have also found elements of narcissistic personality disorder in batterers (Calvete, 2008), which includes behaviors of grandiose ideations, lack of empathy, and a strong need for ideation.

Depression is also an important factor to consider when evaluating the psychology of some batterers. Studies suggest that the most common disorder that is found in IPV perpetrators is major depression that is not episodic in nature and that carries with it a high number of threats of suicide (Calvete, 2008). In other words, depression is not simply related to recent domestic incidents, rather, it is enduring. In one study, at least 22% of perpetrators had undergone some manner of mental health treatment according to analyses of the research on the psychology of IPV perpetrators (Calvete, 2008).

Studies have also indicated a link between drug/alcohol addiction and IPV. Research indicates a noticeably high rate of drug/alcohol addiction in samples of domestic batterers (Tilley and Brackley, 2005). In fact, one-quarter of a sample of IPV perpetrators indicate that they had sought drug/alcohol treatment, which is a number that is disproportionate compared to the general population (Gondolf, 1999). While research indicates that cocaine, barbiturates, amphetamines, opiates, and the combination of drugs with alcohol are all factors in IPV (Calvete, 2008), researchers have most recently focused on cocaine as a drug that triggers violence, aggression, and irritability (Calvete, 2008). Interestingly, a study of 500 inmates found that the most seriously violent IPV offenders also used cocaine regularly (Logan et al., 2001).

It should be noted that none of the preceding or subsequent discussion exculpates IPV perpetrators from responsibility for their actions, nor is that the intention. Rather, to have a full and fair examination of the theoretical perspectives that explain battering, we must consider a full array of possibilities based upon the scholarship to date. There is generally widespread societal revulsion for IPV, especially when the abuser is a male and the victim is a female. As a foremost example, Baltimore Ravens Ray Rice assaulted his then-fiancée in an elevator in 2014, which was caught on video and made its way into the public sphere (Christensen et al., 2016). The footage depicted Rice knocking his fiancée out with a punch and then dragging her out of the elevator as she lay unconscious. Public outrage was fierce and sustained, and Rice never played another NFL game. Society is angered by abusive partners, but it should be cautioned that that anger should not blind us to the more pragmatic consideration of reducing IPV.

Social

We begin our examination of domestic violence with a discussion of control theory. Essentially, abusers are motivated to obtain power in their intimate relationships and use violence, fear, coercion, and isolation to intimidate their partners into giving them that coveted control (Goode, 1971). Another critical piece of this theory suggests that victims slowly modify their behavior(s) over time to avoid further violence and threats (Goode, 1971). For example, a control-oriented abuser may initially tell his girlfriend that he wants her to change her hairstyle or her weight. Over time, his behavior escalates to where he is exerting control over her friendships and social calendar. Finally, the abuser may then exercise total control sexually, dominating his partner through fear of being dumped for another, more willing girlfriend.

A more controversial theory that explains IPV is resource theory, which asserts that when women have less resources at their disposal, they are susceptible to abuse, and that men with less resources are more likely to abuse (Goode, 1971), so the odds may increase that one partner resorts to abuse to control the other. In contrast, violence and control become less likely a tool when partners with financial stability have more resources at hand. For example, a wife who is the breadwinner may threaten to cut off her husband's access to their credit cards to induce a change in behavior. Resource theorists are not asserting that violence is strictly the province of lower-class couples because the research on IPV indicates that it transcends economic status and position. Rather, these theorists explain how violence can become a solution for a power-oriented partner who lacks other economic resources.

It is also important to acknowledge the impact of theories that focus on the impact of life stressors on IPV, especially when the abusive partner has had certain experiences that may have predisposed them to violence.

The idea behind the life stressor theory is that traumatic life events like job loss, extramarital affairs, and economic challenges may increase the likelihood of IPV, particularly when one partner has a history of growing up in a violent family environment and is dissatisfied with their relationship overall (Malley-Morrison and Hines, 2004). When a person has grown up in an environment where violence was frequent, they may resort to violence as a normative response, especially when under extreme stress, which is the crux of the life stressors theory, sometimes also referred to as exosystem factor theory.

Feminist

The feminist theory of IPV focuses predominantly on identifying social factors that explain male-on-female violence in heterosexual relationships. It also focuses on the traditionally patriarchal arrangement of families in the United States, which fosters a propensity for male dominance and the willingness to use violence to maintain control (Lenton, 2017). This theory also illustrates that there is fundamental structural gender inequality in society; essentially, that the deck is stacked in favor of male dominance and control (Lenton, 2017) and that this inequality has historically served to constrict abused women's options. Researchers examining the feminist theory of IPV have found that certain types of men are uniquely vulnerable to being inculcated with patriarchal notions: those who have abusive fathers, who have been unemployed, who are in common-law marriages, and in low-income families (Lenton, 2017).

Cognitive-Behavioral

Our next area of focus examines the thought processes of IPV perpetrators and how they're developed. The reactive aggression theory explains that when some individuals experience unpleasant emotions, it results in rage and a desire to hurt those around them. IPV occurs when a deterrence is not present, like another individual from whom the abuser wants to hide violent outbursts from (Berkowitz, 2004). An example of this theory in action is, for instance, an abusive partner who feels deep frustration when his favorite team loses and does not know how to handle that frustration without almost immediately lashing out at his partner.

Social learning theory is a particularly poignant explanation of the cycle of family violence that can occur throughout generations. Essentially, children who grow up in families where violence is common may learn that it's an acceptable means of solving problems and as a result, when those children become adults, they may repeat those behaviors in their own intimate relationships (Kaufman and Zigler, 1987). For example, men who witness their fathers abuse their mothers are more likely to abuse their own wives (Dutton, 1995). We offer the sad story of a little boy who, during his childhood, witnessed his father repeatedly abuse his mother without any consequence like arrest or divorce. According to social learning theory, that little boy may learn that violence solves problems and thus, when he grows into adulthood, may tragically repeat that pattern of violence with his own partner. This theory points to the importance of early intervention with families experiencing a violent member so that intergenerational trauma is not repeated.

Family Systems Theories

There are some similarities between aspects of family systems theories that explain IPV and social learning theory. Family systems theory also focuses on the family and not solely the individual to explain IPV. The idea is that to understand IPV one needs to understand the family unit in which the domestic violence occurs by examining the relationships between members of the family, stressors weighing on it, and the interaction patterns of members (RoDe and RoDe, 2016). Family systems theorists note that, per the research, IPV perpetrators often suffer from low self-esteem and a feeling of inferiority, and that aggression and control are ways that abusive partners attempt to reclaim dominance within the family (RoDe and RoDe, 2016). In a way, violence can be thought of as a form of overcompensation, as a perpetrator who feels "less than" in many ways tries to combat that feeling with the expression of aggression and control. Family systems theorists also examine the behavior of victims within families experiencing IPV. The victim's perspective of IPV is the focus of our next section.

THEORIES THAT EXPLAIN THE VICTIM'S PERSPECTIVE

One of the most misunderstood phenomena in modern relationships is the plight of victims in abusive relationships and how that violence materializes. Unfortunately, research indicates that victim blaming is common (Waltermaurer, 2012), and a lack of understanding for victims of IPV is another obstacle in designing helpful interventions. Accordingly, this chapter focuses on the roots of domestic violence from the victim's perspective, a voice that is all too often ignored. It is important to note that our exploration of the genesis of IPV based on victims' vulnerabilities and experiences is not meant to be exhaustive, but to offer an in-depth description and analysis of three of the major theories: learned helplessness, battered women's syndrome, and social learning theory. "That would never happen to me" is a pernicious but common attitude of victims of

IPV, and it is important to understand that no one is born a victim of it. In fact, as with domestic violence offenders, a complex and multicausal group of factors align before the IPV takes place.

Learned Helplessness Theory

The term "learned helplessness," when applied to IPV victims, connotes a certain pejorative, negative judgment. It is important to start our discussion on the learned helplessness theory with the note that it is an explanation of a complex series of processes and responses on the part of the victim—it is not an expression of judgment toward a victim who is perceived to be unable to change their lives. However, one of the reasons that this theory is viewed as controversial is that it is perceived as an oversimplification of a victim's behavior. If someone is subject to repeated forms of abuse, a psychological adaptation takes place in which the abused person gives up in some manner and appears passive (Launius and Lindquist, 1988). Essentially, the theory posits that from a victim's perspective, if the abuser feels that nothing the victim does is right and there is constant violence in the relationship, the victim stops trying so desperately to avoid the violence and some odd form of acceptance can result (Launius and Lindquist, 1988).

Understandably, this aspect of the theory can be polarizing among domestic violence experts because many abused partners never accept the violence and fight back in various ways, ranging from leaving the relationship to pressing charges against the abuser and even to physically harming the abusive partner (Downs, 1997). The exponential growth of domestic violence shelters nationwide provides evidence that many victims of IPV strongly reject the violence in their relationships and seek help (Glenn and Goodman, 2015). Accordingly, it is fair to say that this theory is an explanation for *some* of the behaviors that are observed in domestic violence victims. Passivity and a feeling of helplessness certainly can be one adaptation to repeated trauma, but it is not the only possible one.

Battered Women's Syndrome

Perhaps the most well-known theory that explains the behaviors of IPV victims is battered women's syndrome. In fact, many individuals may have some familiarity with battered women's syndrome and the behaviors of its victims, such as self-blame, due to its prevalence in the public lexicon. It focuses on the psychological adaptation of battered women (specific to the theory) to the abuse of male partners, regardless of the form of the abuse (Walker, 1979). It is crucial to note that the violence and abuse does not have to be physical in nature for an abused female partner to develop this syndrome (Walker, 1979). The key tenets of battered women's syndrome are that abused women demonstrate PTSD-like behaviors, thoughts, and beliefs, and may develop a variety of serious issues because of this chronic abuse. These behaviors can range from suicidal ideation to substance abuse to isolation from friends and family (Walker, 1979). Additionally, victims can develop certain PTSD-like beliefs regarding their abusers particularly, including that they're more powerful than they are, and that the violence is the victim's fault and must take on the responsibility to change (Walker, 1979).

An additionally important aspect is the cycle of abuse in the relationship, which takes place in recurring phases. While there are different events and emphases in abusive relationships, battered women's syndrome includes a generalized description of a violent intimate relationship. In the first phase, tension between the victim and abusive partner builds and ultimately explodes into violence (Walker, 1979). After the abusive incident, which does not have to be physical in nature, the abusive partner fears losing the victim and professes deep remorse and that such an occurrence will never happen again. Unfortunately, and possibly inevitably in abusive relationships, the "honeymoon stage" does not last. There may be a sustained period of what feels to the victim like bliss and healing following the abusive incident, but according to battered women's syndrome, it will not last, tension will start to build between partners, and the only question is *when* the next abusive incident will occur. An example of an abusive relationship that is cyclical in nature is one in which a wife senses increasing tension with her husband, who is snappy and belittling to her. One night, he explodes over a minor dispute and slaps her. He immediately apologizes, cries, and begs her forgiveness. He showers her with gifts over the next few weeks and the connection between them feels to her like it did in the early days of their romance, when she was completely besotted. However, this feeling does not last. Her husband's verbal denigration slowly resumes. He frequently raises his voice. He punches the wall. The cycle of violence has begun anew.

Social Learning Theory

The final theory that we examine is social learning theory. While we previously discussed this theory within the lens on IPV perpetrators, we now concentrate on the explanatory power of social learning on the mentality of victims. Sadly, but perhaps unsurprisingly, just as some abusive partners learn from their childhoods that violence is an acceptable means of solving conflicts, other children witness violence perpetrated by role models and take from that violence as a normal part of a relationship. In fact, research on battered women indicates that up to 40% of them witness violence in childhood (Okun, 1986). This finding supports the idea that violence can be intergenerational for both abusive partners and victims, and further emphasizes the urgent need for early intervention. This finding also provides some support for learned helplessness as a theory, because it appears that repeated exposure to violence both as a child and as an adult may result in the victim's feeling that there is no hope to escape the violence.

Here's an example of how social learning impacts victims of IPV: A girl grows up in a patriarchal household in which her father rules the family with an iron fist and frequently strikes and verbally abuses her mother. Despite the violence, her mother frequently praises her father to the children as a wonderful protector. She herself was a daddy's girl and idolized her father, despite his rages. This girl, now an adult, is in a marriage in which her husband frequently berates her and throws things at her when he is angry. She tries to explain the violence to herself in the quiet moments and rationalizes it as her husband "letting off steam." She reasons that all couples argue, and that her husband is just more demonstrative than others. He always insists that "yelling isn't the worst thing in the world," and she thinks to herself that he must be right. After all, her daddy, her favorite person in the world even now, screamed at her mother all the time. Some husbands are just more tempestuous than others, she decides. Everything must be fine because her parents are still married, after all, and her mother experienced the same thing. Totally normal, she tells herself.

CONCLUSION

This chapter has focused on possible root causes and overall explanations of IPV. It was retrospective in nature, as a way to understand the impact of past experiences on both the victim and the perpetrator. In the next chapter, the scope becomes more future-oriented and seeks to understand the variety of interventions for IPV that can aid both victims and perpetrators, as well as the efficacies of these various interventions.

SAMPLE CRITICAL THINKING QUESTIONS

1. What are the psychological theories of IPV?
2. What is the social theory of IPV?
3. What is the feminist theory of IPV?
4. What is the family systems theory of IPV?

CONTEMPORARY APPLICATIONS

Ray Rice (former Baltimore Ravens football player) and his then-fiancée and now-wife Janay Palmer's violent altercation in an elevator in which Rice knocked Janay out with a punch, galvanized national attention, led to legal charges for Rice, and prompted significant speculation about both of their mindsets (Maaddi, 2014).

Actress Emma Roberts was arrested in Canada in July 2013 for domestic violence against her boyfriend in a hotel room (Bacardi, 2019).

7

Contemporary Interventions against Intimate Partner Violence

CASE STUDY

Casey and his girlfriend Jessica are both 35 years old and have been together for six years. They met on a dating app shortly after both had completed a stint in rehab (in separate states). They were well-versed in the traditional guidance that recovering addicts should not get into a relationship their first year of sobriety, but they disregarded that in favor of their strong connection and attraction. Alcohol is the drug of choice for both, and perhaps predictably, they both relapsed within a month of starting their courtship.

They both currently work as waitstaff but at different restaurants. Jessica holds a master's degree and is extremely frustrated with her current circumstances. When she gets home from work each night, she drinks to self-medicate and to numb her sadnesses. In contrast, Casey often goes out after work with his coworkers, and drinks to party. Both Casey and Jessica experience profound difficulties when under the influence—over the past 10 years Casey has gotten three DUIs and Jessica has gotten one. Additionally, their fights have become loud, personal, and recently, physical.

Their last altercation creates a seismic shift in their relationship. Casey returns home from clubbing, while Jessica is highly intoxicated after several hours of drinking alone on their sofa. Alcohol makes them both irritable and jumpy, and an argument ensues quickly. They angrily debate over who will sleep in the bedroom and who will sleep on the sofa. As Casey makes his way into the bedroom, he grabs Jessica and throws her across the room, causing her to hit her head on the coffee table. The neighbors, concerned by the commotion, call the police, who arrive very quickly.

Jessica is dazed, in pain, and already has a huge knot on her forehead. Law enforcement has no problem determining that Casey was the primary aggressor and arrest him for domestic violence. First responders escort Jessica to the hospital, where doctors determine that she has a concussion, among other injuries. Given the severity and potentially life-altering nature of her injuries, authorities opt to upgrade Casey's charges to felony level domestic violence.

Given the seriousness of the facts and clear medical evidence of Jessica's injuries, Casey's lawyer advises him to plead no contest and essentially throw himself on the mercy of the court. Initially, Casey is adamant that his lawyer assert that Jessica brought about her own injuries in a drunken stupor, but his lawyer explains to him that all that will do is aggravate the judge and increase his chances of incarceration. His lawyer goes on to tell Casey that the judge appreciates when offenders take responsibility for their actions and express willingness to enter treatment. The lawyer anticipates that Casey will receive a variety of conditions as a part of his sentence, including strict alcohol/drug monitoring, substance abuse counseling, at least two years of supervised probation, and participation in a year-long batterer intervention program (BIP). The lawyer explains that in the state in which they live, BIPs are much tougher on offenders than a straight jail sentence and that it is quite difficult to fake one's way through it. He tells Casey that if he has no intentions of exploring his past behavior and the root of his violence, as well as overcoming his substance abuse, he guarantees Casey will end up in jail serving a lengthy sentence.

Casey's impending experience with BIP indicates the increasingly robust stance the US legal system and wider society have been taking against domestic violence. Whereas slaps on the wrist and minimal treatment once characterized the national approach to domestic violence, twenty-first-century American society takes a much more assertive posture. Accordingly, this chapter examines both the current legal and community interventions against intimate partner violence (IPV), as well as an analysis of the empirical evidence of their efficacies. Assessments of various contemporary batterer intervention programs will be discussed, as will contemporary treatments and therapies for victims and survivors. The necessity for any intervention effort to prioritize the safety and well-being of the survivor will also be covered. First, we offer a brief history of IPV interventions in the United States.

HISTORY OF INTIMATE PARTNER VIOLENCE
INTERVENTIONS IN THE UNITED STATES

Both legal and community interventions against IPV in the United States are inextricably linked to the burgeoning feminist movement of the 1960s and 1970s. They urged that IPV be treated with appropriate legal severity for perpetrators and public support measures for victims (Walker, 2015). Essentially, these interventions became two paths to a similar goal, one that thoroughly attacks IPV from multiple angles. In short, while feminist leaders successfully lobbied then-president Ronald Reagan to establish the Office on Violence Against Women in the Department of Justice and urged congressional leaders to use the power of their committees to address IPV, psychologists and therapists were also intensely focusing on developing helpful treatments for both perpetrators and victims (Walker, 2015).

LEGAL INTERVENTIONS AGAINST DOMESTIC VIOLENCE

One issue that the feminist leaders rallied against was the informal approach to the criminalization of IPV. As a result, domestic violence experts asserted that it was essential that law enforcement change that approach. For example, for therapeutic interventions to have an impact, many domestic violence experts believed that abusive partners needed to be under the watchful supervision of the judicial system to ensure their diligent attendance at treatment programs (Walker, 2015). It is important to note that feminist leaders urged law enforcement to have measures in place in order to have abusive partners removed from the home because data reflected that IPV, particularly directed against women, was pervasive throughout society (Walker, 2015). Feminist advocacy for aggressive law enforcement and appropriate legal measures was not rooted in a punitive approach or a retaliation against perpetrators. Rather, the data collected on IPV in the 1970s and 1980s, as well as the fact that domestic violence shelters were full of abused women and children, showed that treating IPV as private family matters, which was the standard for much of the nation's history until the late twentieth century, had done nothing to truly address violence between intimate partners. To protect abused partners and address this crime, feminist leaders (supported by many IPV experts) successfully advocated for a variety of legal and community interventions against IPV.

Mandatory Arrests

One recommendation in which feminist leaders and numerous IPV experts agreed upon was the importance of mandatory arrest policies. The

Minneapolis Domestic Violence Experiment, conducted by the Minneapolis Police Department and the National Policing Institute in the early 1980s, indicated that mandatory arrest, not informal measures like couple's counseling from the police or removing the aggressor from the home for several hours, was most helpful in reducing IPV recidivism (Sherman and Berk, 1984). The significant publicity that the study garnered put pressure on police departments to adopt mandatory arrests, which meant that officers were required to make an arrest when probable cause for IPV existed (Sherman and Cohn, 1989). In fact, within the first seven years after the publication of the research, one-third of US police departments had instituted policies of mandatory arrest for IPV aggressors (Sherman and Cohn, 1989) and numerous states passed laws in support of them.

Police agencies had additional pressures placed on them from other external events that prompted their move toward more aggressive law enforcement measures. In 1983, the Tracy Thurman case in Connecticut served as an impetus for departments to alter their policies and adopt a more proactive stance. Thurman had been repeatedly abused by her husband, only to be met by police indifference. During one horrific attack—being stabbed by her husband and kicked in the head—the police looked on (Goodmark, 2018). Thurman's successful lawsuit incentivized police departments to address suspected domestic violence more aggressively, as did the attorney general's 1984 Task Force on Family Violence report, which designated IPV as a crime and asserted that the default police strategy toward IPV should be the arrest of offenders (Goodmark, 2018). Mandatory arrest policies became so popular among policymakers that the 1994 Violence Against Women Act required jurisdictions receiving federal funding to enact these policies.

While these policies were aimed at removing the offender from the home and promoting accountability for aggressive partners, the evidence for their efficacy is complicated. Federal data from 2006–2015 indicate that police made an arrest in 39% of domestic violence cases (Reaves, 2017). Increased police proactivity can be a helpful measure in promoting both accountability and general deterrence. Mandatory arrest policies result in decreased rates of *nonfatal* IPV in the states that have these laws on the book, but there are significantly heightened rates of intimate partner homicides in those same states (Çelik, 2013). Essentially, experts in IPV have concluded that mandatory arrest policies are helpful deterrents against future violence in many IPV cases, but the caveat is that for some perpetrators, it creates rage toward the victim and raises the risk that the perpetrator will inflict fatal violence upon the victim in retaliation (Çelik, 2013). As a result, it is essential that law enforcement understand the risk/reward nature of mandatory arrest policies, which can have a helpful impact in reducing nonfatal IPV but can also trigger homicidal rages in some abusive partners. It is important to note the plausible concern that mandatory arrest policies may strip some agency from victims by not considering their wishes, in any substantive way, to not proceed with the prosecution of their abuser (Barata, 2007).

One solution to some of the issues with mandatory arrests for IPV is *preferred arrest policies*, in which the police are encouraged to make arrests for IPV but are not absolutely required to (Goodmark, 2018). These policies address some concerns from victims that their voices are not considered at all within mandatory arrest policies. Additionally, allowing police officers to use some level of discretion, while still conveying the message that IPV is a serious crime and that arrests are encouraged, can be helpful in addressing situational dynamics within abusive relationships (Goodmark, 2018).

No-Drop Prosecutions

No-drop prosecutions constitute a significant tool within legal interventions against domestic violence. Historically, IPV prosecutions were very difficult, with many victims unwilling or unable to participate in the litigation against their abusers, which made it difficult for the prosecution team to move forward (Goodmark, 2018). The rules to no-drop prosecution evolved from these difficulties and mandated that regardless of the victim's participation level, the prosecution would not drop the cases and would participate using other evidence, such as medical records, 911 calls, and photographs of injuries (Goodmark, 2018). The rationale behind the adoption of these policies was multifactorial: they were thought to protect the victims from further abuse and coercion from the perpetrator. Victims no longer had decision-making power over whether their abusers were persecuted or not. Therefore, abusers were less likely to bully their victims to drop charges now that the state held that role (Goodmark, 2018). Additionally, proponents of no-drop policies believed that these policies sent a message that victims mattered, that their abuse mattered, and that the criminal justice system took both seriously. Finally, it is important to note that there was some level of discretion within some no-drop jurisdictions: soft no-drop jurisdictions encouraged victim participation but did not subpoena them or require their testimony under oath, as was the case in hard no-drop jurisdictions (Goodmark, 2018).

In terms of the efficacy of these prosecutorial policies, the evidence is mixed, with some researchers concluding that no-drop policies led to a much higher conviction rate for IPV (Smith and Davis, 2004). On the other hand, others concluded that there was no difference in recidivism in no-drop jurisdictions versus those without such mandates (O'Sullivan et al., 2007). The research further reveals that prosecutors are less likely to drop

IPV prosecutions with minority defendants than for White defendants (Henning and Feder, 2005). It can be concluded from the mixed evidence that, not surprisingly, there are pros and cons to both prosecutorial strategies, no-drop, and discretionary. What is key is that prosecutors continue to encourage victim cooperation and emphasize the criminal nature of IPV and the importance of their safety, as well as the endeavor to foster trust with victims.

Restraining Orders

The aim of restraining orders as a legal intervention within IPV is to legally prohibit the perpetrator from harassing or further abusing the victim, or in many cases, even being in their presence. If offenders violate a legal restraining order (RO), they are then subject to a variety of sanctions, including rearrest and incarceration, as well as a higher bond (if they have already been arrested for IPV offenses). The idea is that ROs are an additional measure that can safeguard the victim, but the global evidence for their efficacy is mixed. In fact, a study in Sweden concluded that ROs were effective in reducing recidivism for low-to-medium-risk offenders, but perhaps unsurprisingly, did not deter the behavior of high-risk offenders (Strand, 2012).

While the parameters of ROs can vary by state and jurisdiction, every state allows for these civil protections for victims (Wolf et al., 2000). Research indicates that victims who seek protective orders are more likely to be employed, married, over 24 years old, and less likely to be involved with the perpetrator at the time of the alleged incident (Wolf et al., 2000). Experts have formed general conclusions based on the findings that victims who seek ROs are more likely to be financially independent than victims who are not (Wolf et al., 2000). This finding has implications for the efficacy of civil protection measures for victims and indicates that the most vulnerable victims (from a financial and safety standpoint) may not be seeking ROs. This is especially concerning given data that indicate that individuals who apply for a two-year protective order report significantly reduced levels of subsequent violence, regardless of whether their applications are granted (McFarlane et al., 2004). Experts in domestic violence have posited that restraining order applications serve as a protective factor for many victims because they indicate to perpetrators that the victim is sharing their abuse with the criminal justice system (McFarlane et al., 2004). Some victims are silent no longer and it appears that in many cases, perpetrators have adjusted their behavior in response to this "loudspeaker" effect (McFarlane et al., 2004).

COMMUNITY INTERVENTIONS WITH
INTIMATE PARTNER VIOLENCE PERPETRATORS

Batterer Intervention Programs

While BIPs are most used in conjunction with legal sanctions for battering, the therapeutic nature of these treatment groups makes them somewhat distinct from legal interventions. In this section, we will characterize them as a therapeutic intervention within the community. From the mid-1980s on, research indicates that BIPs are the most popular treatment program used by the courts following a perpetrator's guilty plea to IPV or conviction (Hotaling and Sugarman, 1986). These programs are psychoeducational in nature and are predicated on the idea that treatment for abusive partners will help to reduce future incidents of violence (Price and Rosenbaum, 2009). BIPs exist in most states, and while they differ in treatment and approach, there are some commonalities that can be observed (Price and Rosenbaum, 2009).

Many BIPs are predicated to some degree on the Duluth model of treatment, which postulates that power and control are at the root of IPV and that batterers should be educated about this dynamic so that they can begin to change their maladaptive behaviors (Pence and Paymar, 1993). Research aimed at delineating common characteristics of BIPs indicates that besides the Duluth model, other popular treatment modalities include CBT (cognitive behavioral therapy) and the incorporation of certain feminist concepts, like confronting patriarchal models of relationships (Price and Rosenbaum, 2009). Additionally, researchers found that the typical length of a BIP was around 40 hours (Price and Rosenbaum, 2009), and that shorter programs are associated with higher completion rates and lower recidivism rates (Edleson and Syers, 1991). One possible implication of this finding is that it is important to meet abusive partners where they are currently at in their lives, not necessarily where we wish them to go. Many perpetrators may be experiencing severe disruption in their lives during the legal process, and it is possible that shorter, highly targeted programs reflect empathetic understanding of this dynamic.

Concerningly, 90% of surveyed BIPs indicate that they don't incorporate different typologies of batterers (a concept discussed in chapter 4) into their treatment plan; rather, they employ a one-size-fits-all approach, which may not be advisable given the different treatment needs of the various types of abusers (Price and Rosenbaum, 2009). Also, the training for program leaders/trainers/educators appears to fluctuate wildly from program to program, as only 27% of surveyed BIPs had staff leaders with PhDs or PsyDs (Price and Rosenbaum, 2009). Program excellence is not wholly dependent on a proliferation of staffers with high-level degrees, of course, but that presence can indicate a certain standard of education and training.

Positively, over 50% of surveyed BIPs appear to incorporate alcohol and substance abuse modalities into their curriculum (Price and Rosenbaum, 2009). Experts in the field support this inclusion, given the documented link between IPV and substance abuse (Stuart, 2005). Conversely, some experts have raised concerns about the fact that 76% of surveyed BIPs included anger management in their curricula (Price and Rosenbaum, 2009). While some might think that anger is an important aspect of abuse that should be addressed, others caution that IPV is about power and control and that "abuse is a controlled behavior, not an anger response" (Price and Rosenbaum, 2009). Essentially, the incorporation of anger management in BIP curricula can serve to mislead abusive partners about the fundamental nature of abuse; they might think that the major issue is that they have bad tempers when in most cases abuse is about control, not tempestuousness.

The empirical evidence for the efficacy of BIPs is complicated by the sheer size and dramatic increase in the programs in the last 35 years (Stuart et al., 2007). Nonetheless, several studies have found that male batterer participation in BIPs is correlated with lower numbers of rearrests and self-reported growth and progress in victims' lives (Gondolf, 2004; Bennett et al., 2007). At the same time, experts caution that this optimism should be tempered by the finding that around 20% of batterers are treatment-resistant and will not be helped by any program (Ferraro, 2017). They also advise that there is no one-size-fits-all approach to BIPs and thus cannot recommend a standardized one, but important core elements include holding abusive partners accountable for their actions, explaining the power and control aspects of IPV, and addressing their rationalizations and minimizations (Ferraro, 2017). Additionally, it appears to be important for treatment practitioners to not treat the abusive partner population as a monolith and to conduct batterer typology assessments that provide the highest level of care (Ferraro, 2017).

Other Therapies for Perpetrators

Group therapy approaches have also been employed in treatment interventions for abusive intimate partners. These therapeutic settings are often cost-effective and flexible in their psychoeducational program. Their leaders/facilitators help in mentoring abusive intimate partners to improve their problem-solving abilities and to develop anger management and stress management techniques (Nicholls, 2006). Group programs can be grounded in CBT approaches in which counselors help participants develop enhanced communication skills and address cognitive biases and/or more psychotherapeutic approaches, in which leaders help participants to safely address past trauma (Saunders, 1996). Experts in this area find that a positive peer encouragement aspect of these groups can be beneficial (Yalom and Leszcz, 2020), but that there is also the potential for the group setting to normalize aggressive behaviors among participants (Saunders, 2008).

TREATMENTS FOR VICTIMS AND SURVIVORS

Battered Women's Shelters

It is estimated that in the United States annually, approximately 300,000 abused women and their children seek refuge at domestic violence shelters (Jonker et al., 2015). These shelters have multiple aims, including providing for the safety of abused families, stopping the abuse, improving quality of life for victims, providing enhanced social support and community, providing increased access to helpful resources, and reducing symptoms of depression and PTSD (Jonker et al., 2015). Given the breadth of services offered in shelters to what are oftentimes the most severely abused women, it is not surprising that the research supports the efficacy of shelter-provided services (Ben-Porat and Sror-Bondarevsky, 2021). Researchers have found that the longer a woman stays in a shelter, the more likely she is to leave the abusive relationship (Ben-Porat and Sror-Bondarevsky, 2021).

Counseling and Therapy

Researchers have found that therapeutic treatment options for victims of IPV are diverse, which is important given the toll that the violence takes on survivors. Experts note the prevalence of therapy, counseling, and advocacy programs for IPV survivors (Condino et al., 2016). CBT is commonly used with survivors (Condino et al., 2016), as are targeted therapies specifically addressing their trauma experiences and PTSD symptoms through education, stress management, and exposure therapy, among other measures (Kubany et al., 2003).

Interpersonal therapy (IPT) also has a demonstrated efficacy in reducing depression in survivors of IPV (Condino et al., 2016), which is a promising finding. Additionally encouraging IPV treatments for survivors include culturally competent support groups (Kaslow et al., 2010), social support groups (Constantino et al., 2005), and even grief therapy (Condino et al., 2016). Another therapeutic intervention that demonstrates a helpful impact on IPV victims' healing is the assignment of paraprofessionals to help battered women in making the transition from the shelter back to the community. These paraprofessionals are tasked with advocating for the welfare of women returning to the community after stays in a domestic violence shelter and appear to significantly aid in improving the quality of life for survivors who are just leaving the shelter environment (Sullivan and Bybee, 1999).

Perhaps one lesson learned from therapeutic and counseling interventions for IPV survivors is that just like with interventions for perpetrators, there is no one-size-fits-all approach. Rather, what seems clear is that therapies that address certain common factors among survivors, like targeting trauma and PTSD symptoms, addressing the social isolation that can trigger depression, and the need for assistance in transitioning back into the community, can be quite helpful in encouraging healing in victimized individuals. The courage of survivors who are attempting to heal from often-unspeakable victimization and serial trauma is admirable, and it is essential that professionals with extensive subject matter expertise can offer multiple services to survivors of IPV. No one is an island nor should they be alone as they try to navigate the world after experiencing severe trauma and pain.

CONCLUSION

This chapter has explored the increasingly proactive legal and therapeutic interventions within IPV, actions that reflect the larger theme that society no longer views it as a private family matter. Rather, it is commonly understood to be a serious crime and one that requires treatment for both perpetrators and victims. The efficacy of these treatments is still a matter of some controversy, but we note that only around 20% of batterers are classified as treatment-resistant, which means that much of this population is amenable to treatment. However, it is crucial that interventions be empirically grounded and targeted appropriately. Similarly, experiencing violence from an intimate partner does not have to consign victims to a life of sadness and anxiety. It is essential that they receive the necessary help and resources to address their trauma and overall needs, but with care, survivors can move on to enjoy thriving and healthy lives. In the next chapter we explore IPV globally and will learn that, sadly, some of the legal and therapeutic interventions we have discussed in this chapter have not yet been incorporated in some countries and regions of the world.

SAMPLE QUESTIONS FOR CRITICAL THINKING

1. What are the roots of legal interventions within IPV?
2. What is the efficacy of mandatory arrest policies for IPV?
3. How should experts assess the effectiveness of BIPs? What are the main components of BIPs?
4. What are the common therapies for victims of IPV?

CONTEMPORARY APPLICATION

MedPsych Health Services advertises a counseling group therapy session for IPV survivors. See https://medpsychmd.com/group-therapy-for-domestic-violence-victims-and-perpetrators/.

8

The Global Struggle against Intimate Partner Violence

CASE STUDY

Alejandra Chub, 32 years old, lived in a remote village in Guatemala. She was in a relationship with a married man who abused his wife and Alejandra (Beck and Mohamed, 2021). In fact, Alejandra and the man's wife had formed an unlikely friendship based upon their shared abuse (Beck and Mohamed, 2021).

Alejandra's partner exhibited extreme jealousy. His wife reported him to local authorities for abuse, but village law enforcement took no action, which violates Guatemalan law that requires authorities to investigate all cases of violence directed against women and girls, even if the complainant tried to walk back an initial report (Beck and Mohamed, 2021). This dereliction of duty would prove to have torturous results for Alejandra.

Alejandra came home one evening to a furious partner who was convinced she had been having an affair, even though she said she was visiting her sister. Her partner held her down, and when he discovered that she was not wearing underwear, he used a machete to brutalize her. He cut her face with it, disfiguring her, and severed her hands (Beck and Mohamed, 2021). Because of the remoteness of the village, Alejandra was forced to wait over half an hour for help to arrive, during which time she passed away from injuries. However, as she lay terrified and dying, she experienced a final indignity. Her neighbors, who had heard her screaming during the attack, discovered her brutalized in the aftermath. Rather than offer words of comfort and solace, an unidentified neighbor chose to exploit her, filming a graphic video of her on the bed, terribly disfigured and moments from death (Beck and Mohamed, 2021).

The video spread quickly on social media platforms (Beck and Mohamed, 2021), culminating with multiple YouTube creators hosting discussions and viewings of it. Alejandra was given a sadistic nickname based on her mutilation: Ms. Pacman. Mocking the appearance of a murder victim is appalling and a probable violation of those platform's rules, but the ongoing presence of the videos indicates that no such violation had been invoked. Alejandra's brutal murder is an indication of Guatemala's and the local authorities' grievous errors in the handling of her case, but her dehumanization is global. Even her name was stripped from her after her death.

The October 2018 murder of Alejandra Chub by her jealous boyfriend and the ensuing social media response is a harrowing display of how domestic violence and dehumanization are a global phenomenon. While there are differences in domestic violence rates by country, the underlying issues that can lead to it are strikingly similar. Alejandra's horrific murder, and the ensuing response over social media, illustrates that prurient behavior and victim-blaming attitudes exist globally and transcend regional differences on intimate partner violence (IPV) rates.

Alejandra's haunting case indicates the depth of the challenges faced by millions in the global fight against intimate partner violence (IPV). This chapter focuses on the pervasiveness of global IPV, examining both peer nations to the United States as well as less privileged, economically struggling countries. The prevalence of lifetime estimates of IPV and disparities therein between the West (Europe and the United States, as examples) and countries in the Middle East and parts of Africa and Asia are described and assessed. Disparate global laws addressing IPV are also considered, as are global implications for intimate partner relationships. Specific global changes in the prevalence of domestic violence in the wake of the COVID-19 pandemic are specifically addressed in chapter 14; therefore, this chapter concentrates on consistent global themes in IPV. These themes can be considered as a more "stable" cohort of the key factors that can lead to domestic violence worldwide, not temporal factors triggered by crises.

DOMESTIC VIOLENCE IN EUROPE

European countries are often lauded for their progressive policies and the perception that their citizens live well. Theorists point to the "modern cosmopolitan intellectual tradition" (Bhambra and Narayan, 2016) that is thought to dominate policy and practice throughout Europe. However, there are certain indicators that suggest that this progressivism and liberal thought does not shield European countries from the hardships caused by IPV. Research within the past decade indicates that approximately 20% of women in Western Europe have experienced IPV (Devries et al., 2013). This concerning finding was echoed in more expansive research throughout European Union member states. In 2014, the European Union's survey on violence against women (EU-VAW) revealed that some of these nations, particularly Nordic countries, have a higher-than-expected problem with IPV (Gomez-Casillas et al., 2023). This finding is known as the Nordic Paradox.

The EU-VAW conducted a survey in 2012 indicating that a startling one in three women in European Union countries had been a victim of partner violence (Humbert et al., 2021). Rates were disproportionately high in Nordic countries, with 46% of surveyed Swedish women, 47% of Finnish women, and 52% of Danish women reporting that they had been victimized by IPV (Humbert et al., 2021), a finding that surprised researchers because of perceived higher levels of gender equity in those nations. There is not a clear expert consensus that explains those findings, though multiple research works have engaged in an analysis of the EU-VAW.

Another finding indicates that Greece, Italy, Romania, the Czech Republic, and Cyprus have the highest rate of violence directed against women (Humbert et al., 2021), which helps provide a roadmap for policymakers and practitioners in implementing target intervention. In the United Kingdom, researchers found that ethnic minority women were hesitant to report IPV because of specific deterrents. They conclude that the most daunting barriers for abused women to overcome to report their abuse to health practitioners include (but are not limited to) fear, shame, the presence of the abusive partner and the ability of that partner to manipulate health service authorities, language difficulties, and religious practices (Heron et al., 2021). These findings indicate that culturally competent training for health authorities can facilitate enhanced reporting rates for IPV in the United Kingdom specifically, and throughout the European Union more generally.

DOMESTIC VIOLENCE IN MEXICO, CENTRAL AMERICA, AND SOUTH AMERICA

Mexico has long been considered a patriarchal society in which IPV against women flourishes, but there are indications that the country is proactively addressing this serious societal concern. The statistics are alarming and show that a staggering 44% of women in Mexico have experienced IPV at the hands of their partners (Gordon, 2018). Research has consistently implicated machismo culture, in which men actively oppress women by embracing violence, aggressiveness, and authoritarianism, as a prime factor behind the significant levels of IPV directed against women there (Olivera, 2006). It is also important to note that Mexico is a deeply religious and overwhelmingly Catholic nation, and some researchers have found indicators that women endure abuse because they don't want to break up their families and believe in the sanctity of marriage (Bauer et al., 2000).

An analysis of IPV in Mexico is not complete without discussion of the overwhelming cartel violence that threatens all segments of its society. Researchers have found strong evidence that indicates that rampant societal stressors like poverty, unemployment, high crime, and narcotics violence have overextended Mexican authorities to the point that they can no longer respond effectively to IPV cases (Ertürk, 2006). While the current high levels of IPV in Mexico may seem almost intractable given the other types of serious violence that are endemic in the country, observers assert that a two-pronged approach could be helpful in addressing these concerns: attacking the problem both culturally and legally.

Social observers suggest the implementation of educational programs that directly challenge both the subjugation of women and machismo culture itself (Joseph, 2017). The thought behind the import of challenging some of these fundamental tenets is that while authorities can tighten the laws on IPV and encourage more vigorous enforcement action from policing authorities, there will be no fundamental change until the ingrained beliefs that facilitate this violence are directly confronted (Joseph, 2017). Additionally, it is heartening to note that in recent years, pieces of legislation specifically targeting violence against women have been passed, and early evidence indicates that even *weakly enforced* legislation has had an impact on reducing rates of domestic violence and diminishing attitudes that condone it (Htun and Jensenius, 2022). This is a crucial finding because the performance of Mexican police has been heavily scrutinized in recent years, with the suggestion that numerous officers have been corrupted by the cartels (Aldana et al., 2022). Public perception based on this belief has resulted in a diminished legitimacy and moral authority for Mexican policing in general (Aldana et al., 2022). The importance of the findings that there are laws in Mexico put in place to protect women suggest that the fight against domestic violence does not depend *strictly* on the performance of the police, which may be at a crisis level depending on the state. Continuing to challenge patriarchal cultural norms, as well as having strong anti-IPV laws on the books, appears to be effective in slowly diminishing the high rates of IPV in Mexico.

Similar challenges exist throughout Central and South America. The tragic case of Alejandra Chub in Guatemala is, sadly, not an isolated incident but representative of a much larger issue that exists throughout Central and South America. The World Health Organization has found that at least 25% of Latin American women ages 15–49 have been abused by an intimate partner (Pispira et al., 2022). Even more concerning numbers are found in Ecuador, where approximately 43% of women have experienced violence at the hands of their intimate partners (Pispira et al., 2022). The numbers are equally troubling in Argentina, as data indicates that at least 45% of women have experienced IPV (Pispira et al., 2022).

We caution that even with these deeply concerning data points, the actual number of abused partners throughout Central and South America may be even higher because of high rates of nonreporting. Research suggests that a shocking 88% of women in Ecuador who had experienced psychological abuse and threats from a current or former partner never reported the incident(s) to authorities and almost 32% of women in Argentina never told anyone, much less involved a formal institution (Pispira et al., 2022).

Researchers examining pervasive IPV throughout Central and South America have posited that while countries throughout these regions have many differences, there is some manner of shared culture that still is predicated on the expression of male dominance over women, and this culture is both ingrained in relationships and key to understanding why high rates of domestic violence persist (Di Marco et al., 2021). Observers also point to research that suggests that part of patriarchal culture is to objectify women in a way that allows men to claim sexual and physical dominion over them (Pispira et al., 2022). The harrowing case of Alejandra Chub is indicative of a culture where men believe that they own and/or completely control their partners.

The objectification of women in macho, patriarchal cultures is not simply politically incorrect or offensive; rather, it represents a grave threat to the safety of women throughout Central and South America because it both legitimizes and facilitates violence against women and girls. IPV is, unsurprisingly, a central part of patriarchal countries throughout Central and South America. It is crucial that harmful and misogynist beliefs be confronted before violence ensues, as it did in Alejandra's gruesome murder. Knowledge is power, and educational programming is key in allowing people to explore limiting beliefs that they may have internalized from very young ages. Domestic violence is *not* inevitable, even in countries that have traditions of patriarchal, sexist, misogynistic cultural beliefs.

DOMESTIC VIOLENCE IN AFRICA

Multiple countries on the African continent have experienced a myriad of challenges over the past several decades, including war, famine, rampant racism and oppression from colonial powers, societal inequalities, and extreme levels of poverty (Langan, 2018). While observers often heatedly debate the causes of these rampant instabilities, these countries have also experienced concerning levels of IPV, most often directed at women. Recent research concluded that over 30% of married women in Ghana had experienced IPV, and that certain factors reflecting societal stability/instability were highly predictive of experiencing domestic violence (Owusu Adjah and Agbemafle, 2016). The risk of domestic violence was 41% higher for women who grew up in a home in which their fathers beat their mothers (Owusu Adjah and Agbemafle, 2016). It was also found that women who had a male partner who had a higher level of education significantly reduced their chances of being a victim of domestic violence. Women whose husbands had more than a secondary level of education were 48% less likely to experience domestic violence than women who were married to men with no formal education (Owusu Adjah and Agbemafle, 2016). Substance abuse is a strong predictive factor for domestic violence. Women whose husbands drank alcohol were two and a half times more likely to experience domestic violence than women whose husbands were nondrinkers (Owusu Adjah and Agbemafle, 2016).

These findings point to markers that indicate that social stability (education, a violence-free childhood, and minimal use of substances) serves as a helpful factor in preventing IPV in Ghana, which can be used to planners' advantages as they combat IPV throughout Africa. Research suggests that African women hold a more favorable/less unfavorable attitude toward domestic violence than men (Alesina et al., 2020). This finding suggests that in addition to other social, religious, and economic factors throughout the continent that could serve as risk factors for IPV, one significant area of concern that perpetuates domestic violence is African women's attitudes toward it.

Additional research has sought to identify predictive/risk factors in other countries throughout the continent, given that the rate of domestic violence directed against women is so high. South African–based research indicates that 50% of men who participated in the South African Demographic and Health Survey in 2016 committed IPV in their households (Fapohunda et al., 2021). Just as alarmingly, 50% of murdered women in South Africa were killed by their intimate partners (Fapohunda et al., 2021). This means that in South Africa, four women per day are killed by their intimate partners (Fapohunda et al., 2021). The research team investigating South African domestic violence additionally offered the concerning caveat that as high as the rates of IPV are, it is likely that the official numbers reflected a significant underreporting of the actual numbers.

As a result of the intensive investigation into South African society and the factors that can perpetuate IPV, the research team recommended that the government focus on female empowerment in general, enhancing early education for girls, and concentrating on job creation for women. This holds true for countries in Africa that are significantly less stable than South Africa. For example, research in Ethiopia indicates that rates of IPV are high, particularly and tragically, during a woman's pregnancy (Semahegn and Mengistie, 2015). The research team concentrating on Ethiopia concluded that among other factors, including alcohol consumption, religious beliefs, and family history of violence, the lack of education was a significant predictor of the likelihood of experiencing IPV (Semahegn and Mengistie, 2015). It is crucial that policymakers throughout the African continent take note of the intense research on IPV in Ghana, South Africa, and Ethiopia, and address societal substance abuse and religious/cultural beliefs that could be favorable toward domestic violence, while also striving to empower women and girls through enhanced educational and professional opportunities.

DOMESTIC VIOLENCE IN THE MIDDLE EAST AND ASIA

Intimate Partner Violence in the Middle East

Perhaps the most concerning region, when one considers both women's rights and IPV, is the Middle East. Many observers conclude that the Middle East is the hub for cultural and religious subjugation against women, which has resulted in considerable concerns about their welfare throughout all sectors of society. Practices such as forced marriage, female genital mutilation, and the persistence of honor killings have prompted ongoing fears about the plight of women in the region (Kisa et al., 2021). There are considerable religious and cultural boundaries in the Middle East that prevent women from participating in civic life, gaining an education, participating in the labor market and politics, and rising out of poverty (Kisa et al., 2023).

Collectively, there are numerous societal features in the region that also are highly predictive of increased rates of IPV. A comprehensive meta-analysis of abuse-focused studies conducted in countries throughout the Middle East conclude that among other risk factors, large families, childhood exposure to violence, substance abuse, lower socioeconomic status, marriage without the woman's permission, younger age at marriage, impaired mental health, a large age difference between partners, and past genital mutilation were predictive factors for IPV (Kisa et al., 2023). Younger women with less education and a lower income level who lived in rural areas with less educated husbands had a higher risk of experiencing domestic violence (Kisa et al., 2023).

In some Middle Eastern countries, an additional risk factor for high levels of domestic violence is the overwhelmingly accepting attitude toward IPV. For example, research conducted in Egypt and Jordan indicates that upward of 90% of women who had ever been married accepted at least one reason that justified IPV (Boy and Kulczycki, 2008). Researchers conclude that wife-beating was "widely accepted" throughout the Middle East (Boy and Kulczycki, 2008). While media attention has been given to the efforts of some governments throughout the Middle East (perhaps most notably Saudi Arabia's), considerable concerns remain (Aldossari and Calvard, 2021). There are many brave women and men who are campaigning against IPV throughout the Middle East, but significant religious and cultural factors serve to perpetuate systematic subjugation of women and widespread acceptance of domestic violence, at least in some circumstances.

Intimate Partner Violence in Asia

Patriarchal societies are pervasive throughout Asia, domestic violence is often excused, mental health treatment is lacking, and not surprisingly, IPV remains a vexing social issue. Per the research, the highest levels of IPV occur in Africa and Southeast Asia, as well as a considerable level of social acceptance toward domestic violence (Koirala and Chuemchit, 2020). Recent research indicates the pervasiveness of IPV in Asia even during pregnancies and the resultant high levels of depression found in new mothers (Koirala and Chuemchit, 2020).

Research from multiple countries throughout the continent indicate a common acceptance of domestic violence directed against wives and a culture of silence, which allows the violence to continue. For example, a study in Tibet concludes that the only context in which participants expressed significant disapproval of IPV directed toward wives was when they were engaged in helping their families (Rajan, 2018). For example, beating a wife who is the caregiver for her parents would be frowned upon because it would keep her from her familial duties. In a way, it serves to emphasize the precarious position of women in countries in Southeast Asia. Based on that study, it appears that both men and women in Southeast Asia may have internalized inherently objectifying views toward women and struggle to see that they have any agency outside of serving their families of origins and their husbands.

Research in India also emphasizes the extent to which there is a culture of silence around the topic of domestic violence. The National Family Health Survey in India, which was completed over 2014–2015, suggests that only 1% of abused Indian women actually sought help from a medical professional (International Institute for Population Sciences, 2007). This is a stunning finding that indicates that regardless of the level of injury, Indian women remained overwhelmingly silent about IPV. Crimes flourish in secrecy, and it appears that a culture of secrecy still largely reigns in parts of Southeast Asia.

There are multiple countries in Asia that have experienced modernization, increased female empowerment, challenges to patriarchal structures, and diminished rates of IPV. For example, research in South Korea indicates a dramatic fall in domestic violence rates from almost 40% in 2010 to only approximately 12% in 2016 (Han and Choi, 2021). The research team concluded that this impressive improvement could be largely ascribed to national economic growth, higher wages, the influences of some aspects of westernization, and measures of female empowerment (Han and Choi, 2021). The South Korean experience provides a blueprint for countries throughout Asia that continue to struggle with high rates of IPV, as there is clear empirical data that supports the power of economic growth, the democratization of family roles, and the empowerment of women.

GLOBAL TRENDS IN LAWS AGAINST DOMESTIC VIOLENCE

According to a 2018 Global Bank study, almost one billion women globally live in nations that lack formalized laws against domestic violence (Tavares, 2018). While many of those countries are in the Middle East and sub-Saharan Africa, it is inaccurate to portray domestic violence as an epidemic *only* in those countries. However, there is substantial room for growth in the fight against domestic violence in North Africa and the Middle East, where only one in three countries have formal laws against domestic violence (Tavares, 2018). Specific legal reforms in Belarus, Algeria, Kenya, Saudi Arabia, Lebanon, and the Netherlands target domestic violence and increased protections for abused partners (Tavares, 2018). These reforms indicated that the share of nations globally without domestic violence protections went from 29.1% to 24%. In South Korea, progress against IPV offers a heartening blueprint for continued gains against domestic violence. Work still needs to be done. Globally, the needle continues to move in the direction of reform and enhanced laws against domestic violence improve as we move through the twenty-first century.

CONCLUSION

No society can succeed when IPV is widespread. National economic growth cannot happen when half of the workforce is systematically degraded, abused, and subjugated, as is sadly the case in multiple countries around the globe. However, it is also a Western ethnocentric misnomer to ascribe domestic violence largely to "other places." While there are certainly an array of legal protections against domestic violence in Western countries, it still persists in stubbornly high numbers. In the next chapter, we will explore domestic violence in marginalized populations, which is a troublingly pervasive phenomenon.

SAMPLE CRITICAL THINKING QUESTIONS

1. What are the causes of IPV in Central and South America?
2. What are the causes of IPV in the Middle East?
3. Do you think domestic violence is a more serious issue globally than it is domestically? Why or why not?
4. What are the current trends in the global fight against domestic violence?

CONTEMPORARY APPLICATIONS

Anti IPV-campaigners in Beirut, 2015: MEE and agencies (October 5, 2017), Violence against women hurts Arab economies, UN says. Middle East Eye. https://www.middleeasteye.net/news/violence-against -women-hurts-arab-economies-un-says.

Five Thirty Eight illustrates general trends in global IPV: Chalabi, M. (April 17, 2014), How Violence Against Women in the U.K. Compares to Stats Across the World. FiveThirtyEight, https://fivethirtyeight.com /features/how-violence-against-women-in-the-u-k-compares-to-stats -across-the-world/.

9

Domestic Violence and Marginalized Populations

CASE STUDY

Justin is a 30-year-old physical therapist who lives with his longtime partner, Cade. He is passionate about his career and derives great satisfaction from helping the injured. He has been with Cade for six years. They have lived together for the past two years. Cade was recently let go from his job as a server and is currently working as a delivery driver, which has been a recurrent theme—Justin remains steadily employed whereas Cade has been fired multiple times from a variety of jobs. Justin loves his partner but is increasingly conflicted about what to do about the relationship.

In addition to employment issues, periodic violence and substance abuse is also present in their relationship. Justin has barely had a drink since college and has never used illicit drugs. Cade, on the other hand, is a daily drinker and pot smoker, and occasionally uses cocaine at parties. Cocaine makes Cade angry and aggressive, and when he combines it with alcohol (as he generally does), he focuses his attention on small targets. He has been arrested for a bar fight, but his behavior is even worse at home; he frequently screams, throws objects, and punches walls.

Cade is tremendously frustrated with his stalled career. His substance abuse has made him paranoid, and he believes that Justin looks down on him and actively seeks a new partner, no matter how many times Justin reassures him that's not true. Violence in the relationship began when Cade demanded to look through Justin's phone and insisted that Justin give him his email passwords. When Justin refused on grounds

---

of privacy and tried to calm him, Cade pushed Justin for the first time. Since then, Cade has been physically violent with Justin, punching him and causing injury so that he has to call out of work with "the flu."

Unlike Cade, Justin is a peaceful and gentle person. His family has not accepted his sexuality yet, so he keeps most relationship details to himself, concentrating instead on telling them about what they love to hear; that is, about his successful career. He is aware that his friends dislike Cade and he doesn't want to give them any further reason to disapprove of someone he loves. Justin has recently begun therapy through his employee assistance program. He has opened up about the abuse but has inner conflict because he loves Cade even though he suffers from his abuse. Intellectually, Justin knows that Cade's control and violence is escalating, but Justin worries about kicking Cade out of their condo because he's ill-prepared to support himself. Justin tells his therapist that he is concerned that breaking up would constitute kicking Cade when he's down. As with other challenges Justin has faced in his life, he's determined to persevere and overcome the issues in his relationship. His therapist has encouraged him to listen to audiobooks on domestic violence dynamics and has suggested that they create a safety plan. Justin goes back and forth frequently on what he wants to do and feels overwhelmed and isolated.

Justin's concerning and volatile situation epitomizes the challenges faced by millions of domestic violence victims and survivors who come from traditionally marginalized communities and whose plight sometimes seems ignored by both society and the criminal justice systems. As a gay man and a victim of serious domestic violence, Justin has justifiable concerns that the police and courts will not take his situation as seriously as they should. While he knows that he is economically privileged and an educated professional who owns his own condo, he also knows that society pictures someone else entirely when the words "victim of domestic violence" are beamed into the public lexicon. Accordingly, this chapter focuses on victims and survivors of marginalized communities who are experiencing domestic violence. As we move through the chapter, we will consider the challenges faced by members of the LGBTQA+ community, male victims and survivors of domestic violence, minority females (especially Asian, Black, and Latina), and individuals experiencing both poverty and domestic violence simultaneously. The disproportionately high rates of domestic violence within certain communities and the factors driving those rates, including poverty, social isolation, social stigma, and reduced access to community resources, will be discussed.

INTIMATE PARTNER VIOLENCE AND THE LGBTQA+ COMMUNITY

Intimate Partner Violence and Gay Men, Lesbian Women,
and Bisexual Individuals

As previously discussed, it is important to note that some seminal films that feature domestic violence focus upon heterosexual relationships with male offenders and female victims, notably *The Godfather* and *Sleeping with the Enemy.* That aspect of intimate domestic partner violence (IPV) is quite common and deserves extensive study, but it is essential to note that there is a considerable volume of domestic violence that is not based in heterosexual relationships. There are studies that indicate that violence takes place in gay male relationships. In 2013, domestic violence was the third largest health crisis for American gay men (Letellier and Island, 2013). The data indicates that approximately 26% of men in same-sex relationships are victimized by IPV, as compared to around 29% of heterosexual males (Rollè et al., 2018). Additionally, research suggests that almost 50% of gay men and 75% of gay women have been victimized by psychological IPV, with over four million gay and lesbian individuals having experienced IPV in their lifetimes (Walters et al., 2013).

Research suggests that gay men and lesbian women are at a heightened risk for *severe* relationship violence, with almost 30% of lesbian women and 16% of gay men experiencing it, compared to 24% of heterosexual women and 14% of heterosexual men (Walters et al., 2013). Even more alarmingly, it appears that bisexual individuals are at a considerably heightened risk of experiencing both IPV and severe IPV. Research indicates that over 60% of bisexual women and over 37% of bisexual men experience IPV at some point over their lifetime and almost 50% of bisexual women experience severe IPV over the course of their lives (Walters et al., 2013).

Given the high rate of IPV in gay, lesbian, and bisexual relationships, one would think that IPV in this community has been extensively studied, but the opposite is true. In fact, only around 3% of the literature on IPV focuses on the gay, lesbian, and bisexual population (Edwards et al., 2015). Researchers have concentrated on specific social stressors found in LGBTQA+ communities that include enhanced challenges to physical and mental health, social exclusion, employment barriers, and increased rates of poverty, many of which stem from societal biases (Perales and Todd, 2018).

The explanation for these high rates of violence is based on data studied by researchers who assert that IPV is more likely to take place in homosexual and bisexual relationships, as well as experiencing unique stressors, because of their sexual minority status (Messinger, 2011). Researchers have found that a "culture of silence," which is born out of fear of further stigmatization and that victims will be treated as stereotypically "weak," has characterized IPV within the gay, lesbian, and bisexual community (Ristock, 2003). Researchers conclude that victims may fear that by reporting abuse it could fuel those who already harbor negative views toward them. Additionally, lesbian, gay, and bisexual victims of IPV are fearful that if they come forward, they will be reduced to unfounded stereotypes, such as gay male victims of domestic violence will be treated as "less masculine" or that they will not be taken seriously because some people think female aggressors cannot seriously hurt someone (Ristock, 2003). Of additional interest is the finding that some prominent feminists have discouraged reporting of IPV from within the lesbian community out of the fear that such reports may contradict the fact that most domestic violence is perpetrated by men against women (Ristock and Timbang, 2005).

Another stereotype that the LBGTQA+ community has faced regarding reporting IPV is the "mutual combat" fallacy. In other words, society has garnered some level of acceptance toward men using violence to solve conflicts with one another and as a result, there is the perception that men are equal in strength and, therefore, there can't be abuse in relationships between gay men (Rohrbaugh, 2006). Obviously, this idea is erroneous as there are many relationships, both heterosexual and same-sex, in which one partner has dramatically more physical strength than the other. However, unlike heterosexual relationships in which there is widespread societal condemnation of generally larger men abusing generally smaller women, the "mutual combat" myth has persisted and served as a disinclination to victimized gay men who are considering coming forward. If gay men are just going to be told to "fight back," that they are "strong men," they may feel that their abuse has fallen on deaf ears.

One final aspect that is important to consider when assessing IPV in the gay, lesbian, and bisexual community is the impact of heightened rates of HIV within this segment of the population. It is heartbreaking to think of someone who is living with HIV also experiencing IPV, but sadly, researchers have found evidence that supports this (Merrill and Wolfe, 2000). Additionally, there is empirical evidence that suggests that HIV-afflicted individuals in the lesbian, gay, and bisexual community stay in relationships over fear of dying alone or struggling to date successfully with HIV (Merrill and Wolfe, 2000). Researchers also point with concern to data that indicate that IPV may increase the risk of transmission of HIV within gay relationships. The unequal power dynamic that characterizes abusive relationships may make it difficult for abused partners to assert their sexual boundaries and request monogamy, condom usage, and/or additional measures that could reduce the chance of contracting the virus (Nowinski and Bowen, 2012). As we assess IPV within sexual minority communities, it is important to consider experiences beyond those of lesbian, gay, and bisexual individuals. Next, this chapter explores the trans experience with IPV to illuminate an often-misunderstood phenomenon within an often-misunderstood community.

Intimate Partner Violence and the Transgender Community

Research conducted within the trans community continually points to high levels of personal and employment discrimination (Miller and Grollman, 2015). Experts note that trans people, unlike other sexual minorities, stand out more visually as "different," and thus are constant targets than other members of the LGBTQA+ community (Miller and Grollman, 2015). Unsurprisingly given the array of obstacles that the trans community currently faces in society, research is clear that trans individuals are at an alarmingly disproportionate risk of being victimized by IPV.

The hard numbers are stunning, as the research indicates that trans individuals have a lifetime physical IPV prevalence of around 37% (though some studies put the risk as high as around 50%) and a lifetime sexual IPV prevalence of 25%. This means that trans people are 1.7 times more likely than cisgender people to experience any form of IPV, 2.2 times more likely to experience physical IPV, and 2.5 times more likely to experience sexual IPV (Peitzmeier et al., 2020). Trans people suffer sexual IPV at disproportionate rates as compared to cisgender individuals. Antitrans rhetoric and attacks on the community have had a tangible impact; these attacks have made it easier for abusers to sexually violate and degrade their trans partners and sexual partners. Words matter, and based on these disproportionately high rates of IPV victimization, we posit that political rhetoric that constantly points to the trans community as some sort of danger may unconsciously give abusive partners the idea that wider society and law enforcement won't care about trans people as victims. For example, the Proud Boys hate group stages public protests against drag and gender nonconforming events (Silverman, 2023). This demonization of the trans community has culminated in shocking levels of IPV directed against this population.

MALE VICTIMS/SURVIVORS OF DOMESTIC VIOLENCE

As mentioned in earlier chapters, it is important to note that research is consistent in its findings that women experience IPV, stalking, and sexual violence in relationships in greater numbers than men do, and that men are more commonly perpetrators than are females (Huecker et al., 2023). Scholars and practitioners certainly must be wary of any attempt to twist or manipulate the data that in cisgender relationships men are more commonly perpetrators and women are more commonly victims. Intentional distortion of the clear weight of the evidence that men are more commonly perpetrators of IPV may also serve to obscure valid concerns about the ingrained misogyny that can facilitate IPV. At the same time, it is essential for any comprehensive discussion of IPV to consider the less statistically common scenario: men as victims and women as perpetrators.

Research indicates that while women are significantly more likely to experience sexual or physical IPV than men, approximately 22% of males suffer physical, sexual, or psychological abuse during their lifetimes (Coker et al., 2002). Approximately 800,000 physical assaults are perpetrated against male partners each year (Huecker et al., 2023). Men are also victimized sexually, financially, and psychologically (Huecker et al., 2023), which must be acknowledged and taken seriously. The lived experiences of all victims of IPV matters.

It is important that structural and societal barriers to male victims seeking help be addressed and confronted so that survivors can access much-needed resources. Researchers have identified cultural reasons why abused males seek help at lower rates than abused females, including the fact that men are socialized to be tough and self-sufficient, and that they may feel that reporting a female partner is damaging to their masculinity (Mahalik et al., 2003). Others note that male victims have historically been reluctant to come forward out of fear that they would be wrongly painted as the aggressor (Huntley et al., 2019) and arrested. Lastly, and perhaps most troublingly, researchers have found that many male victims are completely unaware that there are services available to them (Hogan et al., 2021). It is quite concerning to note that male survivors of female-perpetrated IPV often report being treated in a disrespectful manner when they courageously report their victimization (Walker et al., 2020). Given that male and female victims of IPV suffer many of the same long-term impacts on their physical and mental health (Lysova et al., 2019), it is imperative that male survivors be informed about the resources that are available to help them, and when reporting the abuse, they are treated with full respect and dignity.

MINORITY FEMALE VICTIMS/SURVIVORS OF INTIMATE PARTNER VIOLENCE

Research indicates that ethnic/racial minority females (i.e., Black/African American, Asian American, Hispanic/Latina, and Native American women) are at a disproportionately high risk of experiencing IPV (Stockman et al., 2015). Historically, research has found heightened rates of domestic violence within Black/African American relationships (23% of respondent relationships) and Hispanic/Latino relationships (17% of respondent relationships) as compared to White-coupled relationships (approximately 11% of respondent relationships) (Caetano et al., 2017). Unfortunately, there are pronounced systemic barriers against many Black women victimized by IPV that prevent them from trusting the system enough to fully access resources. Many Black women have such a serious history of oppression-based experiences within the criminal justice system and at the hands of law enforcement that their trust in the process has been significantly diminished (Hampton et al., 2008). Even though Black women are disproportionately at risk for IPV, they are less likely to involve themselves in the formalized criminal justice system by making a report.

Research into Native American populations on reservations suggests that IPV against them is endemic (Matamonasa-Bennett, 2015). Some studies have found that IPV directed against Native American women is significantly higher than IPV found in any other ethnic group (Jones et al., 2021). Distressingly, Native American women appear to be victimized more than non-Native women, and *more severely*. For example, 56% of Native American women's injuries from IPV require medical attention/supervision, as compared to White women's injuries from IPV (Bachman et al., 2010).

Domestic violence has also continued to be a significant area of concern for Asian American females. Researchers posit that possible causes include language barriers for Asian immigrants who do not speak fluent English, immigrant issues, racial discrimination, and a lack of prioritization from the overall Asian American community (Wang, 1996). Researchers have identified a lack of cultural competence as a significant impediment in properly examining IPV in the Asian American community (Yick and Berthold, 2005). This is an important obstacle to overcome to fully understand all aspects of IPV within this community.

In terms of possible causes for the increased violence in minority relationships one major research finding is that there is a strong presence of alcohol in these abusive relationships, both on the part of abusive male and female partners (Caetano et al., 2008). Additional research focusing on Native American populations and IPV found that the ongoing effects of historical oppression (e.g., reservations that resulted from ethnic displacement are now characterized by high poverty, violence, and unemployment) are key causal factors behind high rates of IPV in this community (Burnette, 2015).

It is also important to note that there is evidence that suggests that victimized minority women suffer greater levels of enduring trauma than nonminority victimized women, perhaps because of cultural differences, as well as other systemic factors. Studies of trauma responses of abused Latina women as compared to non-Latina women indicate that IPV-victimized Latina women exhibit significantly greater trauma responses, higher levels of depression, lower levels of self-esteem, and higher levels of parental stresses than non-Latina abused women (Edelson et al., 2007). These findings point to the importance of increasing and targeting culturally competent intervention services for minority victims of IPV, as well as marginalized victims overall.

POVERTY AND DOMESTIC VIOLENCE

The last marginalized/underrepresented community we consider in relation to IPV is individuals who are living in poverty or economic deprivation. IPV is a phenomenon that transcends class, economic status, gender, race, sexuality, occupation, or political inclination. There are multiple factors about poverty and economic deprivation that act as catalysts for domestic violence, which makes low-income women uniquely vulnerable to IPV (Slabbert, 2017). Research indicates that women in the poorest neighborhoods experience IPV at the highest rates, perhaps because of the relationship between poverty and social disorganization and familial fractures, as well as intense everyday stress (Bonomi et al., 2014). Data indicates that women who have an income significantly below the poverty level endure the risk of being victimized by IPV, which is five times more likely than economically comfortable women (Zawitz, 1994). It is also important to note that low-income females who have less access to, or availability of, liquid funds have less options for leaving their abusers. Thus, economic deprivation plays an active role in leaving them trapped in a cycle of abuse.

While low-income women tend to be disproportionately victimized by IPV, research is also clear that lower-income victims of IPV are consistently treated with disregard both interpersonally and institutionally (Cheek et al., 2023). Researchers have uncovered something known as the "thick skin bias," which suggests that low-income women are less harmed by domestic violence than they are by other stressors in their lives caused by the challenges of ongoing economic deprivation (Cheek et al., 2023). This means that when an abused, low-income woman comes forward to get help, she is often treated in a way that suggests she is uniquely equipped for enduring victimization, and thus less touched by it. Such notions serve to deny both her experiences and humanity.

CONCLUSION

This chapter has examined IPV in a variety of marginalized and/or misunderstood populations. It is crucial that the societal barriers that place individuals from these communities at unique risk for IPV victimization and/or decreased access to resources be fully addressed. As we have discussed, some members of the LGBTQA+ community are at a disproportionate risk to experience IPV, yet societal stigmatization and discrimination make many abused individuals less likely to come forward. Male abuse within heterosexual relationships is an ongoing and concerning problem, yet men seem to be treated in a degrading fashion when they come forward. Other male victims are unaware altogether of the helpful resources out there. Women living in poverty are at an increased risk for experiencing IPV and being assigned characteristics that deny the importance of their experiences. Minority heterosexual women have a heightened risk of IPV victimization for a variety of reasons, but institutionally, the criminal justice system and society at large have not aggressively addressed those factors. Today, the societal and institutional treatment of marginalized victims and survivors of IPV serve to emphasize why IPV remains a hidden phenomenon.

SAMPLE CRITICAL THINKING QUESTIONS

1. What are the aspects of IPV in the LGBTQA+ community?
2. What are the aspects of batteries against male victims?
3. What is the relationship between poverty and IPV?
4. What suggestions do you have for how society (not simply antidomestic violence professionals) can act as resources for IPV-victimized individuals within marginalized communities?

CONTEMPORARY APPLICATIONS

Arkansas Valley Resource Center, a crisis intervention agency: https://arkansasvalleyresourcecenter.org/2020/10/27/domestic-violence-in-the-lgbtq-community/.

Figure 9.1. NYC Mayor's Office End Domestic and Gender-Based Violence graphic, posted on X. https://x.com/nycendgbv/status/1313550498763546626.

10

Policing Strategies and Domestic Violence

CASE STUDY

Carolyn is a 65-year-old senior executive at her company. She has been married to her second husband Greg, a professor, for the past decade. On the surface they have it all: a beautiful house, four children from their past marriages, a vibrant travel schedule, and thriving professional lives. Behind the scenes, however, their marriage is strained because of financial difficulties and disagreements. Greg has purchased several cars using their shared accounts, dines at lavish steakhouses weekly, and has amassed serious credit card debt. In contrast, Carolyn has been a saver her entire adult life, driving a 15-year-old car and bringing no debt into the marriage.

Recently, arguments about their finances have become explosive. Furious over yet another collection call, Carolyn decided to lock Greg out of their bedroom. In turn, he attempted to force his way in. Carolyn responded by slapping him in the face twice, splitting his lip in the process. Stunned, Greg retreated to the guest bedroom where he placed a call to 911. When the police arrived at their residence, they immediately noticed red marks on Greg's cheek and his split lip. Despite Carolyn's protests, they arrested her on domestic violence charges.

By the time Carolyn is handcuffed and placed in the back of a police cruiser, she is despondent and tells the police that a serious arrest like this will threaten her job and ruin her life. She begs her arresting officer to reconsider and says that she is willing to go to a hotel for the evening. She promises that, going forward, they will not receive calls for service to their house, and pledges to enroll in anger management and individual counseling. The arresting officer realizes that Carolyn is unfamiliar with police treatment of domestic violence cases and explains to her that it is there to automatically arrest offenders of domestic violence when a primary aggressor can be determined. The officer further explains that Greg's split lip and bruised face indicates that Carolyn was the aggressor, and therefore, she must be arrested. He tells her politely, but clearly, that the arrest cannot be reversed.

Carolyn struggles to process what is happening to her. Despairingly, she points out her long history of being a model citizen and exemplary professional. She tells the officers that surely hers is a case that demands the utmost discretion and sensitivity, rather than subjecting her to a humiliating arrest. This time, with a sharper tone, the officer informs Carolyn that it doesn't matter who she is or what her background is, none of those things make her above the law. The officer emphasizes that mandatory arrest for primary aggressors in domestic violence cases is their department's policy and law enforcement will be dispensed accordingly. Carolyn asks what will happen to her after she is processed at the jail, assuming that given her clean record, she will immediately be released on her own recognizance. The officer tells her that the procedure is more involved in domestic violence cases and that Carolyn cannot be released until she has appeared before a judge. Therefore, she should expect that she will not be leaving the jail anytime soon. Additionally, the officer informs Carolyn that a temporary restraining order will be issued on Greg's behalf to protect his safety once she is released.

During the ride to the station, Carolyn is shellshocked. She tells the officer that all this "drama" is harrowing to her and not what she expected. She shares with the officer that, during her childhood, she remembers her aunt and uncle having domestic incidents. The police would frequently be called, but no one ever went to jail. Generally, the situation was resolved with her uncle being sent to his parents' home for the night. Carolyn acknowledges that she made a huge mistake this evening, one for which she is remorseful, but again asks the officer why she and Greg can't just be separated as her warring aunt and uncle had been. She arrives at the station and continues to protest to anyone who will listen that she is one of their town's leading citizens and resents being treated like a threat to public safety. She demands to speak with the on-shift supervisor, who also tries to explain departmental policy to her to no avail.

Carolyn's legal predicament illustrates police policies and procedures regarding domestic violence cases, the evolution of which will be traced over the course of this chapter. We analyze the laissez-faire approach and informal policies that characterized law enforcement's response until the latter part of the twentieth century, when more formalized intervention strategies and mandatory arrest policies were instituted. The impact of rate changes of intimate partner violence (IPV) is assessed, as is the relationship between the police and marginalized communities, which has often hindered survivors' efforts to get help. We also consider the implications of high rates of IPV found among police officers themselves and what takes place as a result.

POLICING'S LAISSEZ-FAIRE APPROACH TO DOMESTIC VIOLENCE

In the United States, the police's approach to domestic violence was best characterized as noninterventionist, casual, and often uninformed. In fact, prior to the 1970s, it was quite common for the police to avoid arrest in cases in which they had probable cause (Black and Reiss, 1967). The prevailing societal view, reflected within police departments, was that IPV was a family matter, and the police should not interfere. Instead of arresting perpetrators, officers traditionally took to alternative and less aggressive responses, referring families to counseling and/or perpetrators to alcohol abuse treatment (Bard and Zacker, 1974). These referral policies did not necessarily reflect pervasive maliciousness or willful dereliction of duty, though they certainly existed within some departments; rather, research indicates that police often expressed the belief that IPV overwhelmingly resulted from one or both of the parties having had too much to drink (Bard and Zacker, 1974). Contemporary research tells us that IPV dynamics are considerably more complicated than that.

The Minneapolis Domestic Violence Experiment (Sherman and Berk, 1984) was a seminal moment in research that helped to fundamentally alter US police policies regarding IPV. The research team examined the impact of mandatory arrest (for the primary aggressor) in misdemeanor domestic violence cases as compared to the impact of less formal approaches, that is, counseling, or barring one partner from the home for eight hours (Sherman and Berk, 1984). The results of the study indicated that mandatory arrest policies were most effective in reducing recidivism. Throughout the 1970s leading into the 1980s, police were hamstrung by overly onerous arrest policies for IPV. In fact, police in most states could not make an arrest for misdemeanor domestic violence unless they personally witnessed the crime (Houston, 2014). A tangible impact that resulted from the research in Minneapolis was that police agencies garnered the support of both experts in the field and the burgeoning feminist movement (Wermuth, 1982) to institute more aggressive arrest policies to combat IPV. While subsequent studies were unable to replicate the mandatory arrest findings in Minneapolis (Leisenring, 2008), one of the most crucial legacies of the Minneapolis research is that it disrupted the status quo and suggested that passive police policies toward domestic violence merited serious reexamination.

It is also important to note that the police received heavy criticism from some segments of society as they increasingly pivoted to a more interventionist model for IPV. Some theorists harshly criticized heightened arrest policies, asserting that the police were inserting themselves into private family matters and even undermining the family unit (Wermuth, 1982). A takeaway from this criticism is how fraught the discussion of IPV can get, and how the police are often caught in the middle of competing policy interests. Feminist organizations criticized the police in the latter years of the twentieth century for nonintervention and urged the adaptation of mandatory arrest policies (Leisenring, 2008). However, when police agencies shifted their IPV strategies, they received heavy criticism from other observers for perceived interference within the family structure, indicating that they cannot make everyone happy in the implementation of their policing, which should not even be the goal. Rather, it is imperative that police executive leadership teams continually review the relevant literature on IPV, with the goal that their IPV strategies are grounded in best practices suggested through research. Domestic violence is a dangerous and destructive phenomenon that must be confronted with an eye always fixed on the empirically established information.

THE INCEPTION OF MORE FORMALIZED INTERVENTION STRATEGIES AND THE IMPACT OF THE EVOLUTION OF POLICING'S APPROACH ON DOMESTIC VIOLENCE RATES

Research on much more aggressive policing with domestic violence suggests that agencies are making considerable progress in their approach to it as well as the seriousness with which they treat the offense. Federal data from 2006–2015 indicates that the police responded to domestic incidents in 10 minutes or less in 64% of cases and made an arrest in 39% of reported cases (Reaves, 2017). Both of those metrics (response time and arrest decision) point to the seriousness with which contemporary police departments treat IPV. Another encouraging statistic is that officers generated formal reports in 78% of reported cases (Reaves, 2017). The calls are clearly being treated as a priority in most departments and arrest rates suggest that offenders are being taken into custody when the available evidence gives officers the necessary probable cause.

Also heartening was the finding that 90% of police departments operating in cities with 250,000 citizens or more had a dedicated domestic violence unit (Reaves, 2017), which is an indication that large departments are overwhelmingly committed to best practices and specialized interventions for IPV calls. A federal study from 2006–2015 also concluded that there were basic commonalities between these specialized domestic violence units, even with understandable variation from department to department. Generally, the units included detectives, counselors, and social workers, with unit goals centering around investigation of IPV crimes, assisting victims, educating and training police, the community, and victims about IPV, and working with local agencies and organizations to assist with treatment and prevent further acts of violence (Reaves, 2017).

At the same time, the findings indicated that there were some pronounced disparities in police treatment of domestic violence, likely intensified by harmful but widespread attitudes among officers. For example, police appear to be more proactive in addressing IPV offenses when the victim is female rather than male (e.g., the police followed up with 43% of female victims who had sustained minor injuries, as compared to only 28% of similarly injured male victims) (Reaves, 2017). Additionally, researchers have found that there is a patriarchal culture among many departments, a symptom being that many officers tend to hold "problematic" views about IPV and victims of IPV (Lockwood and Prohaska, 2015). These potentially misogynistic viewpoints are what researchers find to be an "oversimplification" of IPV dynamics—victim-blaming and shaming; overall patriarchal views toward women; and an assumption that victims would not cooperate (Lockwood and Prohaska, 2015). Research indicates that these attitudes affect policing, with more patriarchal and "traditional" officers being more likely to accept IPV than more "progressive" officers who support community policing and understand the complex dynamics behind IPV (DeJong et al., 2008). Officers that are more traditional and patriarchal in their views regard IPV calls as a nuisance, while more progressive officers approach IPV calls as serious and deserving of care and compassion (DeJong et al., 2008).

Studies have shown additional bias in law enforcement performance in IPV calls. Researchers have found that police incorporate both legal and nonlegal factors into their arrest decisions in IPV cases (Avakame and Fyfe, 2001). While the data indicates that police *mostly* rely on factors like the quality of the evidence in their calculus about making an arrest, it also suggests that police prioritize some IPV victims more than others (Avakame and Fyfe, 2001). The police are more likely to arrest perpetrators when the victims were White, female, older, wealthy, and resided in the suburbs (Avakame and Fyfe, 2001). Interestingly, it appears that there is little difference in how White officers handle IPV cases as compared to minority officers, and that formal academy training on IPV appears to have little impact

(Stalans, 2007). However, there is a clear difference in how male and female officers approach IPV, which is not necessarily manifested in arrest decisions, but rather the overall approach that male officers have as compared to female officers. Research suggests that female officers approach IPV calls with fewer preconceived notions about the victim and tend to demonstrate more empathy while on scene (Stalans and Finn, 2000).

At the same time, it would be an oversimplification to say that female officers differ substantively with their male colleagues in relation to arrest decisions. Research indicates that when police officers are analyzed early in their careers, both female and male officers appear to heavily rely on the degree of injury to the victim when making arrest decisions (Stalans and Finn, 2000). Over time, female officers who grow their careers and attain seniority become more confident in assertive approaches to IPV (Stalans and Finn, 2000). It is also possible for female officers to become enmeshed in a department's patriarchal culture and internalize norms that can be victim-blaming and antifemale (Stalans and Finn, 2000). The idea that female officers are more sympathetic to the predominantly female victims of IPV is overly sweeping and not supported by the data, though there are demonstrated differences between genders in their expressions of empathy while on the scene.

Given the ongoing presence of factors besides case-related issues (e.g., a difficult victim), in some officers' arrest decisions, experts on IPV continue to suggest that mandatory arrest policies within departments can remove the specter of discrimination becoming an issue in domestic violence cases (Lockwood and Prohaska, 2015), though there are some concerning ramifications in some types of violent relationships that must be noted. In general, domestic violence researchers and professionals generally assert that not only do mandatory arrest policies result in decreased rates of nonfatal IPV and overall recidivism (Çelik, 2013), they also serve to make arrest decisions as legally grounded and objective as possible.

The concerning caveat to these findings is that states with mandatory arrest policies also demonstrate significantly heightened rates of homicides committed by intimate partners (Çelik, 2013), which indicates that violent retaliation from offenders must be carefully considered, and victim safety must be paramount. Mandatory arrest policies are intended to act as deterrents for future acts of domestic violence, and while these policies appear to succeed in many IPV cases, they also can prompt deadly levels of rage from abusive partners in the most aggressively abusive relationships. Mandatory arrest policies can act as crucial and helpful interventions in "less" abusive relationships in which the abusive partner is possibly open to change. On the other hand, the humiliation and stress of an arrest appears to serve as a strong trigger for the most violent partners, one that can sadly lead to homicidal violence.

Accordingly, it is fair to conceptualize mandatory arrest policies as one tool in combating IPV recidivism, but successful policing in this area also depends on implicit/gender bias training for the police and the continued emphases on generating reports in which they explain their arrest/nonarrest decisions. It is not fair to expect patrol officers to automatically and correctly assess all nuances of a relationship to try to gauge the risk level posed by mandatory arrests; however, it is essential that officers receive the most updated information and research on IPV. When officers and police departments understand the complexities of IPV, they are more likely to communicate and coordinate with each other and with other potentially helpful agencies and entities in their next steps following IPV arrests. As we have previously emphasized, arrest is not a magic cure for IPV, and officers must not expect problematic relationships to transform or end once the abusive partner has been arrested. As discussed in this chapter, in some relationships, arrest can trigger much more intense violence, and police need to be aware of and prepared for this eventuality. Police agencies need to understand that while arresting perpetrators can be a powerful tool in combating IPV, it is not the only answer because it carries serious risks for some abused partners. As a result, other measures are also necessary.

THE RELATIONSHIP BETWEEN POLICE AND MARGINALIZED COMMUNITIES/CITIZENS IN COMBATING DOMESTIC VIOLENCE

Police and the LBGTQA+ Community

Research consistently demonstrates the importance of police officers, as first responders, receiving culturally competent training to effectively deal with traditionally marginalized victims of IPV who may have historical distrust of policing as an entity (Barrett, 2015). The LGBTQA+ victim community is one such example. Findings suggest that individuals who identify as sexual minorities are significantly more negative toward the police than other minority groups (Owen et al., 2018). Reasons for this include historically discriminatory policies by police, though some departments have recently begun aggressive outreach efforts (Owen et al., 2018). Experts have identified major issues with how police officers perform their duties when dealing with sexual minorities and suggest that the police are not sufficiently supportive in helping when LGBTQA+ individuals are victimized. In contrast, however, the police are often overly aggressive when policing gays and lesbians and other sexual minorities in "places of leisure" (Dario et al., 2019). Additional research suggests that a considerable proportion of police officers engage in harassing behaviors toward sexual minorities (Hodge and Sexton, 2020). Unsurprisingly, these actions have dramatically undercut LGBTQA+ people's confidence in police legitimacy and performance (Dario et al., 2019).

Researchers conclude that despite outreach and education efforts made by some police departments, the official law enforcement response to IPV in the older LGBTQA+ community is often inadequate and insensitive (Hillman, 2020). Additional research substantiates that there remains widespread problems with the police response to IPV throughout the LGBTQ+ community (Messinger, 2020). These concerns are even more pronounced when assessing the lived experiences of transgender victims of IPV, because police discrimination against this group appears to be uniquely high (Hodge and Sexton, 2020). For example, draconian police arrest policies target trans women carrying condoms as "soliciting," which has a negative impact on trans individuals' willingness to report when they are victims of IPV (Guadalupe-Diaz, 2016). A significant percentage of community members indicated that when they reported IPV victimization to police, they were confronted with "hostile" and/or "indifferent" officers (Tillery et al., 2018). To improve the police-LBGTQA+ relationship and foster a higher likelihood of criminal reporting, experts suggest that police departments educate their officers regarding homophobia, bigotry, and toxic masculinity (Mallory et al., 2013). High standards of training and selection will continue to help officers bridge this trust gap with this community.

Police and Minorities

Another concern is the often-fraught relationship between police and minorities, which also negatively impacts the experience of minority IPV victims. Researchers have found that minority survivors of domestic violence often avoid formally reporting their experiences to law enforcement because of their mistrust of the police, and instead seek help from family, friends, and community advocates (Bent-Goodley, 2007). Women of color who have witnessed police discrimination against minority males may not report IPV because they believe it reinforces the societal mass incarceration of minority males (Kim, 2012).

Research consistently indicates that Black women face high rates of excessive force and different forms of violence from police, as compared to women from other ethnicities (Crenshaw et al., 2015). In terms of how the police deal with IPV perpetrated against minority women, as discussed previously in this chapter, police are most likely to make an arrest for wealthy, White, older victims. Given disproportionately high rates of IPV experienced by Black and Hispanic women as compared to White women (Lipsky et al., 2009), as well as its impact on women with low incomes, experts believe that disparities in arrest rates send a message that they value the lives of some victims more than others.

Studies researching the attitude of law enforcement indicates that White police officers exhibit more racial resentment, are more likely to see Blacks as violent as compared to Whites, and tend to minimize anti-Black discrimination (LeCount, 2017). These attitudes impact how officers treat IPV when the victim is an individual of color in a way that further damages their relationship with minority female victims. It is essential that police departments continue to emphasize antiracism training in their curricula and that they screen out potentially bigoted applicants. Policing holds a powerful weight, and individual officers have tremendous powers of discretion, as well as the ability to do significant good for and considerable harm to individuals whom they encounter. There are opportunities for police to improve their relationships with sexual, racial, ethnic, and other minorities, which increases the likelihood of a positive collaboration within IPV cases.

Police and Male Victims of Intimate Partner Violence

Lastly, it is important to discuss the lived experiences of male victims of IPV within heterosexual relationships with female perpetrators. Experts have identified a sexist and "macho" culture within policing that can be pervasive even with the presence of female officers (Miller, 2021). Unfortunately, this culture of machismo and perhaps even toxic masculinity can negatively impact the experiences of male domestic violence victims. Abused men are less likely to report their experiences due to fears of emasculation and perceptions that men are bigger and stronger than women and more likely to be the aggressors (Dutton and White, 2013). Research indicates that these concerns are well-founded, as police often engage in ridiculing male victims or even wrongfully arresting them as the primary aggressors (Cook, 2009). Concerningly, some men report that the police do not even respond to their calls for service (Cook, 2009). To improve service and responsivity to this population of victims, it is critical that departmental training emphasize antigender bias and that a full picture of IPV dynamics is offered to trainees before they are inculcated into the wider policing culture.

POLICE AS INTIMATE PARTNER VIOLENCE PERPETRATORS

Studies show troubling data that suggests higher rates of domestic violence between police officers and their partners (Cheema, 2016). Domestic violence rates in marriages where one partner is an officer stands at 24% (Cheema, 2016). Additionally concerning is the fact that many victimized partners are too intimidated by their abusive partners' law enforcement status to formally report IPV (Cheema, 2016).

Police officers face significant stressors because of their profession, in-cluding heightened risks of alcoholism, divorce, and even self-harm (Lott, 1995), which are contributing factors in IPV perpetrated by police officers. Further, negative aspects of the policing subculture can contribute to these concerning statistics on IPV (Blumenstein, 2009). Researchers have identified several negative traits that are pervasive within this subculture, including authoritarianism, distrust and cynicism toward the public, as-sessing people in terms of threat level, and a general feeling of burnout (Westley, 1970). While norms of this subculture can vary over time due to the changing demographics of the police, including retirement, a general thread within the policing community is the approval of these negative traits (Blumenstein, 2009).

Certain aspects of this subculture (e.g., authoritarianism) can be pres-ent in other areas of officers' lives, including their intimate relationships, in ways that can contribute to IPV (Terrill et al., 2003). Research indicates that exposure to violence coupled with excessive alcohol use, excessive authoritarianism, and burnout can combine to increase risks of domestic violence within these relationships (Johnson et al., 2005).

It is critical that these harmful aspects of policing subculture are ad-dressed and not ignored, and that officers are encouraged to seek psycho-logical help to cope with their traumatic experiences. Researchers have concluded that police officers may underutilize the resources available to them because of the stigmatization that accompanies psychological assistance (Barker, 2019). Stress, trauma, alcoholism, isolation, burnout, depression, and so on, must be properly addressed in a constructive way so they don't negatively affect police officers' personal lives.

CONCLUSION

The policing sector is only one component of the criminal justice system. Lowering rates of IPV depends on a comprehensive collaboration between all sectors of the justice system, along with the private sector. The police response to IPV has been problematic, but they cannot do it alone. Offend-ers must also be held accountable in the courts, and laws must reflect the seriousness of their crimes. In the next chapter we examine the US court system and domestic violence, exploring how the courts treat domestic violence cases and where improvements in processes are needed.

A FORMER OFFICER'S PERSPECTIVE

My department's policy on domestic violence was incredibly strict and meant to hold to the letter of the law. Section 19.2-81.3.B orders that police "having probable cause to believe that a violation of

§18.2-57.2 [Simple Domestic Assault] or 16.1-253.2 [Protective Order Violations] shall arrest and take into custody the person . . . [they] believe was the predominant aggressor unless there are special circumstances." My department was adamant about prosecution as a future deterrent, and sometimes it worked. We frequently encountered the same couples where disputes would arise but never to the level of a crime. As soon as there was a shred of probable cause for arrest, we made one.

I can't recall a time when there wasn't a huge emotional tension between two parties in intimate partner violence (IPV) situations. Rare was the call when I would arrive and the victim party was immediately forthright with information that would quickly lead to an arrest. One aspect of this, that I never realized until reflecting upon it, was the potential effect of the parties having a trauma bond, known as an emotional bond arising from a cyclical pattern of abuse. Experiences of poverty, financial dependence, rough childhoods, tough situations in adulthood, and even near-death experiences that both individuals weather together can create intense bonds of connection that override the threat of death or great bodily harm at the hands of the other person. Not that I'm a psychiatrist or a supercop, but I know that I was one of the few who cared to learn the law and concern myself with the lives of those I interacted with during IPV cases. I'm sure that the concept of trauma bonding was lost on many officers. Too many times I would see officers mishandle a situation and lose rapport with the victim of IPV when they simply couldn't figure out why the victim wouldn't leave their abuser. In my experience, that position comes from a place that reveals the officer's worldview and background. Coming from an environment without the violence and abuse that many poor and minority females face can color their perspective, and if they don't learn to look past it and attempt to understand the victim's mindset, it will prevent them from developing rapport. They'll wonder why victims don't cooperate and are always failing to follow through with court appearances or emergency protective orders (EPOs).

I never felt contempt or hate toward a victim who called us to stop her from being hurt or killed but didn't want us to do anything further. However, that doesn't mean I never felt frustrated. The mandatory arrests that my department implemented weren't to punish the victims for calling but to hold ourselves to a high standard according to the law. That doesn't mean I didn't hear officers tell victims, "Well, if you didn't want him arrested why did you even bother calling us?" That's a really quick way to completely deflate a victim and tank rapport. It can also turn what could be a domestic violence incident into a murder in the future. We did start obtaining failure-to-appear warrants on victims who refused to come to court after IPV calls/arrests because we had several cases nolle pros'd, meaning the charges were dismissed by the prosecutor. While I generally agree that we should be ensuring that police resources aren't wasted, I understand how this would create a mindset in some victims to refuse to call 911 the next time. I think that a case-by-case basis would work best with the understanding between someone who *can't* make it to court and someone who *won't*.

I consider deterrence through arrest to be the most effective, especially when coupled with a strict and enforced EPO. Domestic violence calls are some of the most dangerous for police to respond to. Calming the situation down through arrest not only saves the victim but also officers from having to come back to an escalated situation later. I remember plenty of domestic violence calls where officers from a previous shift "passed on" a situation that they simply didn't want to work and articulated (weaseled) their way out of making an arrest. Later, if the parties hadn't cooled off, the situation worsened and became even more dangerous. I remember several times offenders telling me, when I responded to the same call location after being passed a domestic from a previous shift, "Well, so and so came here earlier and told me that I was fine or that I'd be okay if I just leave for an hour." That makes the police look like they don't know what they're doing, and flip-flopping on the law and what is expected of them. What's wild is that, eventually, longtime offenders catch on and try to outwit officers they think will be susceptible to a no-arrest, no-paperwork solution to an IPV.

My arrest decisions came down to the letter of the law. Like I said before, my department had pro-prosecution policies they expected us to uphold. In order to arrest someone, I would first determine if physical contact had been made or if the victim had been placed in reasonable fear that they would be assaulted. Then I would decide if that contact was unlawful. Finally, I would establish who the predominant aggressor was—which could be simply blocking access (like standing in front of someone purposefully threatening them), threatening with a weapon, or using extreme force like striking, shooting, or stabbing—and take them into custody. Another policy my department held was that for every simple domestic arrest, you also were required to obtain an EPO. I think that is a great policy because it allows officers and victims a simple remedy for when the offender tries to reengage. We were also required to complete lethality surveys and provide victim/witness information cards. The surveys determine the likelihood of future assaults, and the cards identify various local resources available to the victims like shelters, free clinics, food pantries, and mental health providers. As part of annual domestic violence training, we were able to tour several of the facilities to get a better idea of what/who we were recommending to victims.

SAMPLE CRITICAL THINKING QUESTIONS

1. What are the strengths and weaknesses of both historic and contemporary police performance as it relates to IPV?
2. How do some aspects of police subculture potentially alienate police from victims of interpersonal violence?
3. Why are there high rates of IPV among those in law enforcement and what are some possible solutions to lower those rates?
4. What are mandatory arrest strategies? How are they effective in preventing further IPV?

CONTEMPORARY APPLICATIONS

Figure 10.1. The Newport News Police Department shares information about their special Domestic Violence Unit. https://www.nnva.gov/2494/Domestic-Violence -Awareness.

Figure 10.2.   Officer Breann Leath, from the Indianapolis Police Department, was killed during a domestic violence call in 2020. From "Man charged with killing IMPD officer Breann Leath found guilty but mentally ill" by WFYI Indianapolis, 2024, https://www.wfyi.org/news/articles/breann-leath-elliahs-dorsey-klling-guilty-verdict.

11

Domestic Violence and the Courts

CASE STUDY

Kate and her wife, Chelsea, have been married for two years. Kate is 26 years old, a recent college graduate, and preschool teacher. Chelsea is 10 years older than Kate and works as an actuary. Kate comes from a loving and close-knit family but dares not share with them her growing concerns about her marriage. Kate loves going out to bars and clubs with friends, whereas Chelsea is much more of an introverted homebody. Initially, Kate brought fun and excitement to Chelsea's regimented life, while Chelsea acted as something of a professional mentor to Kate, dramatically overhauling her resume and coaching her on her first series of interviews. Now that they are well past the honeymoon stage, Kate increasingly fears that she and Chelsea are too different, that they won't be able to last, but neither partner has filed for divorce.

Kate wouldn't necessarily describe Chelsea as tempestuous, but she notices that Chelsea can exhibit rage in more subtle ways. For example, Kate goes out with her friends every Friday night while Chelsea finishes up her weekly paperwork. One recent Friday night ended with Kate banging on their apartment door for several minutes before Chelsea, who had deadbolted it, "woke up." She claimed to have been exhausted from a busy work week, but Kate suspects that her wife was punishing her for staying out late. Christmas is fast approaching. Kate enjoys decorating elaborately, something she learned from her family as a child. After another Friday evening out, Kate returns only to find that two of her childhood Christmas tree ornaments have been shattered, and Chelsea is vague about how she managed to "trip" into their

---

tree and fall into what she knew were Kate's favorite two ornaments. No other ornaments were damaged.

Kate has now reached her breaking point. After a night of drinking, she begins screaming and says that she wants a divorce, that she no longer loves Chelsea and is sick of her trying to control and change her. As Kate heads to their guest room to sleep, she hears a *thud* and turns to the wall to her left. Chelsea launched her expensive phone at the wall, and the screen is now shattered. The combination of screaming and the phone hitting the wall sparked their neighbors' attention and concern, and multiple calls are made to the police. When the officers arrive, they observe no bruises or obvious injuries on either woman before their attention turns to the hole in the wall and the shattered cell phone, now resting on the sofa. Chelsea admits that in a moment of frustration after Kate's request for a divorce, she threw her own phone but insists that she did not mean to hit Kate with it.

The officers confer and place Chelsea under arrest for domestic violence. Chelsea is confused because neither partner has ever physically abused the other, but the officer informs Chelsea that her actions in breaking Kate's ornaments and then throwing a phone in Kate's general direction fall under the rubric of domestic violence. A couple of weeks after Chelsea's arrest, Kate phones the prosecutor's office and informs them that she doesn't want to proceed with the charges against Chelsea. She shares that Chelsea has apologized profusely and has enrolled in counseling to address her anger. Kate is not sure about the future of their relationship, but she is sure that prosecuting Chelsea will do more harm than good. The prosecutor gently tells Kate that as they are in a "no drop" state, this is not her decision to make. The prosecutor's office has the final decision-making power on whether the case moves forward. He informs her that one major reason for the adoption of this policy is because abusive partners pressure and threaten their victims to drop charges. Placing the power in the prosecution's hands is one way to address this dynamic. The prosecutor tells Kate that he will take her request into consideration, but that at this point, he plans to proceed prosecuting Chelsea.

Chelsea's legal woes illustrate the major principle of this chapter—the dramatic transformation in the courts' treatment of domestic violence in the twentieth century. An exploration and assessment of the trajectory of IPV court cases will be explored. That wife battering was only made illegal in the twentieth century, and the difficulty in prosecuting and obtaining convictions in IPV cases is discussed in detail. IPV as a hidden crime with reluctant complainants is explained, and the efficacy of current civil court measures like protective orders, firearm protections, and supervised child custody exchanges/visitation is evaluated. Additionally, specialized domestic violence courts are discussed. However, the main focus of the chapter centers on the growth in proactive and innovative measures with which US courts now treat IPV.

THE TRANSFORMATION IN COURT TREATMENT OF INTIMATE PARTNER VIOLENCE IN THE UNITED STATES

Historical Court Stances Toward Intimate Partner Violence

In chapter 3, the transformation in laws regarding IPV in the United States was discussed. The consideration of engaging in a brief review of that chapter in concert with this one is encouraged. While the courts treat issues within the boundaries of strict legalities, it should be noted that judges are people too and their decisions may reflect their own societal sensibilities as much as their interpretation of the laws. An example of how broader societal forces can impact the legal system, states like Maryland, Delaware, and Oregon criminalized IPV in the latter part of the nineteenth century into the twentieth century (Gregory, 2002). Yet at that time, with some notable exceptions, patriarchal notions prevailed within the courts, as IPV was widely considered to be a private family matter worthy of judicial intervention only when the level of violence spiraled (Hafemeister, 2010), a stance that would largely prevail until the 1970s, when the voices of feminist advocates for battered women grew into a crescendo.

However, it is important to note that the all-male judiciary of the early twentieth century also upheld patriarchal notions of marriage and intimate relations in a way that *helped* abused women, sometimes vigorously. As part of the maintenance of the patriarchal ideal, some judges harshly punished abusive male perpetrators for violating notions of manhood with their brutality, while assisting female victims who embodied the "ideal" of womanly dependence and vulnerability (Katz, 2014). The corollary to this judicial patriarchy was that judges often ridiculed male victims of IPV as unmanly for not being able to control or defend themselves against their physically abusive wives (Katz, 2014). Accordingly, it is fair to say that early to mid-twentieth century jurists did not engage in the protection of victims as much as they did a protection of what they thought should be the societal status quo: strong, nonabusive husbands who ruled the households and their demure and genteel wives.

When abusive men violated these norms and appeared before certain judges, the response was often thunderous, with punishments including fines, whipping, and incarceration (Katz, 2014). In 1907, in a shocking breach of judicial ethics, Pennsylvania-based judge D. A. McKelvey furiously announced to defendant Louis Sambolia that he would give him the punishment he deserved for IPV and proceeded to personally haul the defendant outside the courthouse, handcuff him to a post, and whip him repeatedly as the victim looked on with "evident satisfaction" (Katz, 2014). Assertive judicial punishments for IPV were common throughout the early part of the twentieth century because of the belief that men who abuse helpless women are "the meanest of cowards" (Katz, 2014), not because the nation was ready to fundamentally reexamine its treatment of intimate partner relations.

Legal scholars have found that these interventions were "intermittent" in nature, not thematic, and that the posture of the US court system toward IPV was largely noninterventionalist and minimizing, rather than treating it as a serious crime and in a manner consistent with other cases of assault and battery (Siegel, 1995). In essence, up until the 1970s, judicial goals with IPV cases in the United States were predicated on the promotion of "domestic harmony" by allowing for informal dispositions for abusive husbands (Siegel, 1995). In this way, the US judiciary could be credibly viewed as enabling IPV for much of the twentieth century, with many judges unable or unwilling to treat these cases as crimes.

As discussed in chapter 3, despite the growth of anti-IPV laws in the early part of the twentieth century, arrests and prosecutions of batterers were selective in nature. Social observers continued to wrongly characterize IPV as a practice limited to the lower classes, and historical records indicate that judiciary enforcement of IPV laws was most robust in cases where the defendants were immigrants and Black men (Siegel, 1995). In fact, the proliferation of the whipping post as a method to punish convicted batterers (with 12 states and the District of Columbia allowing it on abusive husbands until 1906) is now understood in the broader historical context to "break" minority and poor men (Siegel, 1995). Thus, the harshest of societal punishments for IPV in the twentieth century had very little to do with revulsion toward IPV; rather, they were a continued manifestation of racial and class biases reinforced by the judiciary.

The development of family courts in the early twentieth century also served to complicate the judicial response to IPV (Tsai, 2000) because the goal was the "reunification" of the family, which meant that family court personnel were focused on measures of "compromise," rather than enforcing recent state laws that criminalized IPV (Tsai, 2000). Essentially, the trend of putting IPV cases under the auspices of family courts indicates that elements of the judiciary continued to prefer treating IPV cases as a family matter rather than a crime. We note that criminal matters are disposed of in criminal courts; family cases are heard in juvenile and domestic relations courts. The fact that for much of the twentieth-century IPV cases were based in family courts demonstrates the prevailing judicial mentality toward domestic violence overall.

Assessment of Contemporary Court Treatment of Intimate Partner Violence

Today, US courts have dramatically shifted in their posture toward IPV as discussed in chapter 2. The success of the feminist movement's partnership with conservative lawmakers in the criminalization of IPV prompted a sea change in the treatment of IPV. The "get tough" collaboration resulted in the criminalization of IPV in 47 states and federally (Fagan, 1996). Accordingly, judges now, under increased legislative and judicial pressure, take these cases seriously, which illustrates that they view IPV as a crime. Over the course of the 1990s leading up to the twenty-first century, experts have termed the judiciary response to IPV as vigorous (Mills et al., 2013).

The increasingly aggressive judicial actions toward IPV, with moves toward mandatory arrests, no-drop prosecutions, and heightened conviction rates, fueled experts' concerns that just like with IPV punishments in the early part of the twentieth century, stronger enforcement actions were disproportionately targeted toward poor and minority abusive partners (Coker, 2001), in addition to multiple other concerns. For example, experts have observed that strong court actions against IPV appear to also lead to mothers being "punished" for being abused. For example, court actions have increasingly broadened the definition of "child abuse" to include witnessing violence, that is, residing in a home in which children are exposed to IPV between their parents or other household members (Coker, 2001). This means that contemporary court treatment of IPV also seems to have resulted in abused partners being further punished by the Child Protective Services (CPS) investigations and/or the removal of their children from the household. Finally, heightened scrutiny of IPV in the judiciary system also seems to have endangered abused women who are involved in forced criminal activity with their abusers, like drug trafficking or prostitution (Coker, 2001). Mandatory minimum sentences for drug offenses give judges little leeway when sentencing abused women. This discussion is not meant to undercut the importance of judiciary enforcement of IPV laws; rather, it's to share the scholarship on IPV in the court system from a variety of perspectives to illustrate what a complex phenomenon this is. There are no easy answers. Enhanced court protections for some victims do not necessarily transform the lives of victims across the board, and in some cases, may complicate matters.

At the same time, other experts conclude that US courts set the standard globally in the development of its "court practices and treatments" to address IPV (Mills et al., 2013). Throughout the 1980s into the early years of the 1990s, judges worked both independently and in cooperation with prosecutors to establish creative ways to respond to IPV cases, including specialized IPV prosecution units, specialized IPV violence courts, victim/witness advocacy programs, and court-community partnerships (Peterson and Dixon, 2005). Specialized IPV courts are a particularly interesting innovation and are consistent with the overall trend in US jurisprudence to address difficult offenses.

Specialized Domestic Violence Courts

The goal of specialized state courts to address IPV is to consolidate and coordinate the response, with judges, prosecutors, court personnel, and other resources all working together to improve the efficacy of judicial treatment of IPV (Tsai, 2000). These courts are predicated on "therapeutic jurisprudence" and provide comprehensive services to offenders enrolled in the court (Tsai, 2000). The significance of these courts is that without any legal sanction for IPV, both batterers and society receive the message that it is not a crime or even a lesser crime (Tsai, 2000). However, a court model where offenders take accountability, offered treatment, held to high standards for program completion, and given both consequences and help seems to address IPV dynamics from multiple angles. IPV is not a crime addressed *solely* by arrests and convictions, and specialized domestic violence courts represent a positive contemporary judicial strategy of administering justice while offering treatment.

Some researchers also note that specialized domestic violence courts, in which judges generally trained in IPV dynamics work closely with participants over a sustained period, is a helpful reform measure given the often-cursory treatment with which the judiciary has often treated IPV. Experts observe that "judicial efficiency" is key to perceptions of judicial ability, and a prime barometer of a judge's performance is the speed with which they manage the courtroom caseload (Tsai, 2000). One major problem with that philosophy is that IPV cases are generally complex and do not commonly offer an "easy" solution.

Recall our previous discussions about the complications of IPV and the intense consequences that often haunt survivors (Condino et al., 2016). Victims' finances are often intertwined with abusers, with whom they may reside and share children. Pressure on the judiciary to run a "rocket docket," as legal experts observe, may be helpful in resolving cases more quickly, but is likely counterproductive and possibly unhelpful in IPV cases. A judge's attempt to manage an IPV case by browsing some court documents and then moving on to the next case is not likely to yield a contemplative decision. Specialized courts for IPV allow for enhanced training for all judicial personnel and facilitate an ongoing relationship with abusive partners. This allows judges to monitor offenders over time, which can also address a continuing weakness within the criminal justice system: its inability to predict which IPV offenders' violence will escalate to homicides (Matias et al., 2020). Specialized IPV courts allow judges to spend dramatically more time with offenders as they monitor their progress and observe them in different situations. While no one expects the judiciary to know the future, it is also fair to note that specialized IPV courts afford judicial personnel the opportunity to get to know offenders as people and not simply as names on a page of a court record. This deeper knowledge can be helpful in identifying abusive partners who are not amenable to treatment and who are likely to escalate their violence.

THE DIFFICULTY OF PROSECUTING/OBTAINING CONVICTIONS IN INTIMATE PARTNER VIOLENCE CASES AND COORDINATED COMMUNITY RESPONSES

Despite heightened judicial efforts in addressing IPV, significant obstacles remain in terms of holding abusive partners accountable in the courts. Good-faith efforts from the police and the judiciary, including mandatory arrests and no-drop prosecutions (discussed in chapter 7), do not fully address the dynamics behind an abused partner's connection to their abuser. Many victims fear retaliation from their abuser for their continued participation in the court's prosecution of them (Cerulli et al., 2014) and as a result withdraw their charges, which complicates the process of holding an offender legally accountable.

Research data suggests that certain factors are key to understanding why victims want to proceed to trial; for example, the more severe the injury, the more willing the victim is to go to trial (Hare, 2010). Almost 70% of IPV victims support the initial decision to bring charges against their abusers, yet less than 40% want to proceed to trial (Hare, 2010), which indicates that victims feel unsupported at some stages of the process, particularly after charges are filed. Enhanced victim support during the pretrial and trial process may promote increased levels of victim cooperation.

Coordinated community responses (CCRs) to IPV, in which judges, the prosecution, and other agencies work together to respond to IPV, appear to be helpful in offering enhanced assistance and support to victims (Visher et al., 2008). CCRs began in several localities in the 1990s, including Alexandria, Virginia, and DuPage County, Illinois (Visher et al., 2008). Research into their efficacy indicate that increased funding for victim services agencies as well as coordination between government agencies and nonprofits, enhances victims' ability to access needed resources during the trial process (Visher et al., 2008). Additionally, coordinated responses from victims' rights agencies, including early contacts made with victims, the generation of safety plans for victims, and ongoing delivery of services, are key to improving victims' experiences in the formal justice system (Visher et al., 2008), which can also increase their willingness to proceed to trial. Past research has indicated that between 50% and 80% of victims attempt to interrupt the prosecution of their alleged abusers, either by requesting that charges be dropped or by not appearing in court (Ford and Regoli, 1993). Enhancing victims' trust in the courts through efforts like CCRs are integral to rates of participation.

CURRENT CIVIL MEASURES

The issuance of civil protection orders in the courts is an additional tool in the ongoing fight against IPV. Civil orders generally prohibit contact between victims and abusers (abusive partners who violate these court orders are arrested) and are official elements of the judicial response to IPV in all 50 states (Keilitz, 1994). Additionally, the standard of proof in civil court is by the preponderance of the evidence rather than beyond a reasonable doubt, which is helpful for victims (Ko, 2001). The initial rationale behind these orders is that they offer the victim enhanced safety without participating in the criminal justice system (Durfee, 2009). Theoretically, the victim is in control of the process—they initiate the proceedings by filing a petition and have the power to terminate it if they want (Durfee, 2009). In the criminal justice system, law enforcement initiates the process by arresting the abuser, which is mandatory when probable cause exists. No-drop prosecutions may further make the victim feel that their voice is being lost in the criminal process.

However, there are significant concerns that the civil protection process often departs from its intended purpose of fostering equality and providing justice to victims who are seeking protection. For example, when victims appear pro se, representing themselves, it can put them at a significant disadvantage when their abusers are represented by knowledgeable counsel (Murphy, 2001). This imbalance in power is further magnified by the fact that many victims of IPV cannot afford experienced attorneys (Tjaden and Thoennes, 2000). As a result, experts have voiced fears that structural inequalities can undermine victims' attempts to seek civil protection.

Also of concern is the exclusion of members of sexual minority communities from the protection order process. For example, LGBTQA+ individuals are excluded from protective orders in South Carolina and Montana (American Bar Association, 2008), and in other states the statutes remain unclear, which means that courts assess restraining order petitions on a case by case basis (Potocznick et al., 2003). Troublingly, a recent study of 14 states and two Canadian cities indicated that over 50% of civil protection orders requested by LBGTQA+ individuals were turned down (NCAVP, 2010). This finding suggests that entire segments of the victimized population remain unprotected by restraining orders, which is ironic because these orders were originally intended to be available to petitioners on an equal access basis.

Examination of the effectiveness of protective orders indicates that there are particular risk factors that are key to understanding potential violations of the orders. For example, meta-analyses of research on restraining orders suggest that violations were less likely in relationships where couples had a medium to high income, when perpetrators had not previously engaged in stalking behavior, and when perpetrators had not previously been arrested for IPV (Cordier et al., 2021). It appears that restraining orders exercise the most control over perpetrators who are low risk; that is, they have not stalked their victims before, and their relatively high incomes may further incentivize them to respect the protective order process and not risk incarceration and possible job loss by incurring subsequent violations and arrests.

Domestic violence restraining orders can also be issued as part of the criminal court treatment of IPV when an offender initially appears before the judge (Ko, 2001). Oftentimes, these orders are conditions of the offender's bail, and violations of them are understood to result in the offender's arrest with a lower likelihood of a pretrial release at that time (Ko, 2001). Criminal protection orders are considered a part of the typical case management of IPV; they are not necessarily "independent vehicles to protect victims" (Ko, 2001).

Exhaustive studies of the efficacy of restraining orders indicate that they are still the primary protective mechanisms for victims (Ko, 2001). Evidence suggests that restraining orders are effective in reducing future violence, but much more so for women who had experienced "less severe" abuse (Grau et al., 2018). Seasoned and committed abusers who are fixated on controlling their victims are less likely to adhere to the terms of a protective order and more likely to view such orders as "just a piece of paper," as some law enforcement, victims, and victims' advocates believe (Logan and Walker, 2010). Accordingly, some observers believe that mandatory arrests and enhanced penalties for violations of court orders are crucial measures that can encourage heightened compliance, even with perpetrators who pose a higher threat level. Research also indicates that stalking is a uniquely concerning behavior that is predictive of a lack of adherence to the terms of restraining orders, which means that legal protections for stalking victims need to be stronger at an earlier stage. By the time stalkers are placed under restraining orders, their behavior may already be completely beyond legal control. The threat level to victims in these instances is considerable.

CONCLUSION

Throughout the course of the chapter, we have explored the uneven historical court treatment of IPV, ranging from almost complete nonintervention to patriarchal manifestations that did not challenge the underlying issue of IPV, to a more assertive posture that largely addressed the conduct as criminal. The efficacy of various court innovations was examined, including specialized domestic violence courts and coordinated community response, as well as the civil protection process. Structural inequalities remain throughout the court process, which means that some victims are still not being protected. In the next chapter, the focus is on the impact of firearms on domestic violence and the impact of court cases on this vital issue.

SAMPLE QUESTIONS FOR CRITICAL THINKING

1. Up until the 1970s, how was IPV treated by the courts?
2. How do specialized domestic violence courts in the judicial system combat IPV?
3. How do coordinated community responses help encourage victim participation in the judicial process?
4. What is the importance of civil protection orders in the judicial fight against IPV?

CONTEMPORARY APPLICATION

Singer Chris Brown appears in court with counsel after his 2009 arrest for beating his then-girlfriend, fellow singer Rihanna (Seabrook, 2016).

12

Guns and Domestic Violence

CASE STUDY

Erika was a 37-year-old homemaker with two children. She had been married to her husband, Tom, for over a decade, and they had one daughter together. She was loved in her small town for her tireless community work, and up until the final months of her life, it seemed that she had the perfect life with the perfect marriage. Tom owned his own contracting company, which entailed working long hours away from home. Six months before her death, one of Tom's multiple mistresses called their house to tell Erika everything. Erika felt there was no turning back—the marriage was over. However, despite her resolve and eagerness to look to the future, Erika's pain only grew in the months to come.

The circumstances of Erika's death are shocking to her family. She was found dead in her home, shot twice in the head. Based upon information that the police uncover, they quickly arrest Tom for the murder, which leaves her family reeling. To better understand her twin's life, Emily decides that she must read Erika's journals. She deeply respects the privacy of journals, but when she finds multiple diaries in Erika's safe-deposit box, she decides that the information could be helpful to the police and also help her family learn everything they can, no matter how painful.

From the journal entries, Emily is stunned to discover years of abuse her sister endured. For many years she had thought that her twin had the perfect life and was heartbroken to learn that Tom had physically abused Erika on numerous occasions. To Emily's horror, Erika had used her journal to document her growing fears that Tom would hurt her and recounted harrowing incidents of violence. Tom's serial infidelity

---

was the last straw, and she quickly filed for divorce. However, Emily learns that Tom's behavior became even more alarming in the months before her sister's death. Erika recounted in her neatly penned journals repeated incidents of Tom stalking her, and she openly debated getting a restraining order. However, the journals reveal that she agonized over Tom's close relationship with their daughter, something she feared a restraining order would interrupt. She desperately wanted to keep a sense of normalcy for the young girl and thus opted against going to the authorities and having Tom arrested.

Emily becomes convinced that Erika intentionally left a road map in case anything happened to her. She had documented each abusive incident in detail and had carefully enclosed pictures of her bruises. Emily had known that her brother-in-law was a firearms enthusiast, but she knew nothing of the violence her sister endured. Emily is haunted by the idea that she could have somehow prevented her sister's death. As Tom's initial court date approaches, Emily learns more about the role of firearms in domestic violence and is stunned to find out that two-thirds of women who are killed by intimate partners are killed by gun violence. While she couldn't save her sister, she knows that there are people out there whom she can help to save, and she contacts her senators to see how she can help in the fight against gun violence.

Erika's tragic story is a searing example of how guns can significantly intensify the risk of domestic violence fatalities. As stated in the case study, two-thirds of women who are killed by intimate partners are via a firearm. In this chapter, a full examination of the research on gun ownership and domestic violence will be explored, including the significance of US Supreme Court cases like *U.S. v. Rahimi* (a Supreme Court case decided in 2024 that focused on whether the government can bar gun possession for those who have domestic violence restraining orders). Gun ownership policies can be a heated, polarizing topic in the United States. It is important to note that the goal of this chapter is not to take a position on that topic, but to narrow the focus as we strive to present the relevant scholarship on guns and domestic violence to provide as much information as possible so independent conclusions can be made. Broader discussions of the Second Amendment are both interesting and necessary, but that is not within the purview of this book. There are many views regarding the propriety and advisability of guns. We encourage all to keep an open mind as we review and contextualize the scholarship on firearms and intimate partner violence (IPV).

THE UNITED STATES AND GUNS: THE DATA

Statistical Information

Before moving on to an examination of guns and IPV, it is necessary to first explore guns in the United States because the statistics on firearms are markedly different here than its peer nations around the world. Violent crime rates in the United States are seven times higher than other "high-income" countries worldwide. This violence is correlated with a gun homicide rate in the United States that is a stunning 25% higher than its peer nations globally (Grinshteyn and Hemenway, 2016). When the United States was compared to 23 other countries (which included Canada, the United Kingdom, Australia, Italy, Japan, France, and Spain) it accounted for 82% of all firearm-related deaths. Further, 90 percent of all women worldwide who were killed by firearms were United States residents (Grinshteyn and Hemenway, 2016). This stunning disparity was also consistent when applied to children less than one year old to14 years old who had been killed by firearms and youth aged 15–24 who had been killed by firearms (Grinshteyn and Hemenway, 2016).

Additional statistics on firearm violence in the United States are equally jarring. From 2003–2012 over 300,000 people died from gun-related injuries. Overall historical American deaths at the hands of firearms are higher than all US combat losses from World War II and combined combat fatalities from *all* wars in our nation's history (Wintemute, 2015). The economic toll from gun violence is also extraordinary, with an estimated $174 billion in costs to society (in terms of justice and health costs, among other considerations) in the year 2010 alone (Miller, 2012). This figure was over 1% of the United States' entire gross domestic product for that year. As of 2018 in the United States, at least one mass shooting with four or more victims took place *every day* (Galea et al., 2018).

Disparities in Violence Rates

Alarmingly, there are pronounced disparities in the firearm death toll in the United States. Researchers have found that firearm violence was the leading cause of death for Black males aged 15–24 in 2012 and was the second leading cause of death for Black females aged 15–24 years old in 2012 (Grinshteyn and Hemenway, 2016). When firearm homicide rates were calculated for all males aged 20–29 in 2012, the data indicated that young Black males had a homicide rate that was five times higher than Hispanic males and 20 times higher than White males (Grinshteyn and Hemenway, 2016). Gun violence, therefore, can be considered a hazard to Black male teenagers and young men. However, the data changes significantly when researchers examined middle-aged men. Research indicates that for men aged 60–64, more than 90% of firearm deaths have White males as the victims (Grinshteyn and Hemenway, 2016).

Nationally, there are geographical disparities in gun violence. Researchers were able to draw some general conclusions, as they found that states with low rates of gun-related homicide and suicide tended to be in New England (Grinshteyn and Hemenway, 2016). States with high suicide rates from guns but low homicide rates were in the Northwest, and troublingly, Southeastern states demonstrated high rates of gun-related homicide *and* suicide (Grinshteyn and Hemenway, 2016). Given these sobering facts, many may wonder what the causes are behind the disproportionate firearm-related violence in the nation—they're complex, multifactorial, and controversial.

The United States, Causes of the Violence, and Gun Culture

A popular contention among some segments of the population is that mental health concerns are at the root of the gun violence epidemic and that, essentially, guns are secondary to the much larger problem of mental illness. However, the body of the research indicates that this assertion is not supported by the evidence. In fact, a comprehensive gun violence study indicates that gun access is the "primary culprit" for gun-related violence (Lu and Temple, 2019). The data indicates that individuals who have gun access are 18 times more likely to threaten someone, after mental health factors are considered (Lu and Temple, 2019). Researchers concluded from this study that regardless of one's mental health diagnosis or other demographic information, the key factor behind gun violence was rather simple and came down to the individual's access to or ownership of a firearm. This debate between mental illness and gun access as a primary cause of gun violence is known as the "dangerous people versus dangerous weapons" argument (Gostin and Record, 2011) and remains highly polarizing despite the weight of the research supporting it.

Perhaps one reason why a sizable segment of the US population discounts many of the hard numbers on gun violence is because of "gun culture." Many US citizens view firearms differently from those of other nations. Gun culture in the United States evolved from frontier and colonial citizens viewing gun ownership as a "necessity" to gun owners enjoying their firearms for hunting and shooting to today, where there's a strong emphasis on maintaining an armed citizenry for reasons of self-defense, as well as a considerable population of gun range hobbyists (Yamane, 2017). Estimates from 2007 indicate that there were over "270 million" civilian-owned firearms in this country (Yamane, 2017). In short, the United States has more guns in circulation than any other country in the world. Furthermore, because many US citizens have an emotional attachment to firearms as an expression of "personal values" (Yamane, 2017), this complicates discussions of gun control measures that could prove helpful in combating the high rates of firearm violence. This unique attachment to and proliferation of firearms in the United States has proven to have considerable implications on IPV.

FIREARMS AND DOMESTIC VIOLENCE FATALITIES

Statistics on Firearms and Intimate Partner Violence

The correlation between firearms and negative outcomes in violent intimate relationships is clear throughout the body of literature. Access to firearms or past threats to partners with firearms are the strongest predictive factors for fatal IPV, and firearm ownership is associated with a five times higher risk of intimate partner homicide (Gold, 2020). Tragically, over 1,800 people are killed each year by their intimate partners and about half of these are perpetrated with firearms (United States Department of Justice, 2011). Research indicates that around 85% of victims of intimate partner homicide (IPH) are women, which means that IPH is the cause of around 50% of all female homicides each year (Parks et al., 2014). Research on how guns are used in violent episodes of IPV suggests that in almost 70% of these incidents, guns are used to threaten the victim (Sorenson, 2017), which is clearly an infliction of psychological terror upon an abused partner.

Pregnancy and Firearm-Related Intimate Partner Violence

A particularly alarming subset of firearm-related IPV violence is directed against pregnant women. Researchers have found that the presence of a firearm on the part of the abusive partner is correlated with more severe levels of violence perpetrated against the pregnant partner (McFarlane et al., 1998). Research indicates that pregnancy is a dangerous time for abused women, and that homicide may well be the leading cause of maternal death (Chambliss, 2008). IPV during pregnancy is already associated with a variety of negative health outcomes, including higher stress for the victim, a higher likelihood that the victim engages in substance abuse, a higher risk for premature delivery and low birth weight, an increase in pregnancy complications, and a decreased likelihood of seeking prenatal care (Chambliss, 2008).

When pregnant women in abusive relationships are further endangered by the presence of a firearm, the health implications intensify and significantly increase the odds of a fatal outcome for mother, baby, or both. Researchers examining this area of IPV, sometimes known as intimate partner physical violence (IPPV) generally find that pregnant women are at a heightened risk of IPH. One study has found that firearms were used in over 63% of IPHs of pregnant women (Keegan et al., 2023). As a result, experts conclude that it is crucial that pregnant women be screened for IPV at their prenatal appointments, which can be opportunities for early intervention.

Nonfatal Firearm-Related Intimate Partner Violence

Risks from firearms are not simply limited to homicides when we consider IPV. Abusers with firearms have the potential for enhanced dangers that are separate from murder. Perpetrators can use guns to coerce their victims more easily and to abuse them more severely (Lu and Temple, 2019). They can also use firearms and the threat of them to keep victims from leaving.

There is also the potential for nonfatal injuries resulting from the use of a firearm. In July 2020, rapper Tory Lanez kicked his intimate partner, celebrated hip-hop artist Megan Thee Stallion, out of his car in Los Angeles, California, after they attended a party together. He then shot her in the feet (Roberts, 2021). Megan was naked when she was ejected from the vehicle, adding to her vulnerability and humiliation. She later recounted that Lanez had tauntingly instructed her to dance before opening fire. Megan later noted in her written victim impact statement at Lanez's sentencing that she felt "terrorized" and had not experienced a day's peace since the shooting (Herstik and Coscarelli, 2023). This event verifies that firearm violence within an intimate relationship can have lifelong impact even if it is not fatal. Lanez used his firearm to traumatize, injure, and humiliate Megan. Her pain was compounded by the online harassment and lies she later endured at the hands of his fans and supporters (Odusola, 2023). It is important that academics and practitioners consider the full ramifications of firearm violence within an intimate relationship and not focus *only* upon the worst-case scenario of IPH. Significant attention must be paid to homicides of any kind, but we cannot lose sight of the fact that guns play a disturbing role in abusive relationships in multiple ways, and they carry threats that are not limited to fatalities.

THE EMPIRICAL EVIDENCE FOR GUN CONTROL TO PREVENT INTIMATE PARTNER HOMICIDES

In 1968, a law prohibiting firearm ownership for any individual who had been convicted of a domestic violence-related felony was passed in the

United States (Vizzard, 1999). As part of increasingly aggressive legislation targeting IPV, it was expanded in 1996 to preclude firearm ownership by anyone who had been convicted of a misdemeanor IPV crime (Polan, 2017). Further, the 1994 Violence Against Women Act expressly forbade firearm possession by anyone who was subject to a permanent IPV-related restraining order (Maloney, 1996). However, there is a significant caveat that is crucial to understanding the impact of this legislation. The federal enforcement of these laws has been uneven, meaning that states have largely been left to their own devices, specifically as it relates to firearm relinquishment cases (Diez et al., 2017). As of 2016, 11 states have legislation mandating that individuals convicted of IPV-related misdemeanors surrender their firearms, and 15 states require that all individuals subject to an IPV-related restraining order relinquish their firearms for as long as the order is in effect (Diez et al., 2017). As of 2024, that prohibition on firearms for domestic violence offenders extended to the federal level with the Supreme Court decision in the aforementioned *Rahimi* case (Dwyer, 2024).

The lack of states with explicit firearm relinquishment laws is concerning when we examine studies that suggest how effective such measures can be. Research indicates that states that have laws prohibiting firearm ownership and mandate firearm relinquishment for persons under IPV-related restraining orders, demonstrate almost 10% lower total IPH rates and 14% lower firearm-related IPH rates as compared to states without these prohibitions (Diez et al., 2017). This indicates that when governments take proactive measures to separate IPV offenders from firearms, there is a substantial reduction in future violence.

The use of firearms in domestic violence cases is terrifying. States can prohibit domestic violence offenders from their firearms, but what about other weapons like fists and knives? It must be kept in mind that other tools of violence can be used in IPV. However, guns have a singular ability to inflict widespread and fatal violence very quickly. The statistics on gun violence in the United States and in IPV are sobering. We cannot prohibit or ban perpetrator ownership of every conceivable weapon that might be used to inflict harm, but as a society, we can place limits on offenders' abilities to acquire the most lethal tool of destruction.

GUN OWNERSHIP FOR INTIMATE PARTNER VIOLENCE VICTIMS

For much of the chapter we have concentrated on the impact of firearm prohibition laws for IPV offenders as a helpful measure in reducing IPV and IPH. We now turn our attention to the impact of gun ownership for abused women specifically as a tool for self-defense. Research conducted with 215 women from multiple domestic violence shelters indicated that 10% of abused women in the sample reported owning a firearm, were White and employed, and had previously been threatened with a gun and had a higher likelihood in engaging in gun ownership (Lynch, 2020). No Black women in the sample owned a firearm, but Black women tended to express higher levels of belief than other women that owning a gun would make them safer from future incidents of abuse (Lynch, 2020).

An example of an increasing legislative push to arm victims occurred in Kentucky in 2014, when it enacted a law that expedited the application process for concealed-carry permits when applying for a domestic violence protective order (Lynch, 2020). Experts caution, however, that the empirical evidence for guns providing enhanced victim safety in these cases is limited and that there are concerning aspects about introducing a firearm into an IPV situation. Researchers note that the presence of a firearm in the home and the abusive partner's access to it dramatically increase the chances for a fatal outcome. There is certainly the possibility that a victim's introduction of a firearm in the household could provide a lethal tool to the abuser, who can gain access to it through deception, force, or coercion and then use it against the victim (Lynch and Logan, 2018). Accordingly, experts have urged lawmakers to reconsider laws that are likely well-intentioned but that result in a higher likelihood of a firearm's presence in an already-volatile household, which significantly increases the likelihood of terrible violence to take place.

Lastly, we broach the concern that laws attempting to streamline the process to arm victims of IPV may be more ideologically oriented than empirically grounded and as such, reflect an incomplete understanding of IPV dynamics on the part of policymakers and legislators. As discussed early in this chapter, firearms as tools for protection and the importance of an armed citizenry are ideas that are emphasized heavily within the current incarnation of US "gun culture." It is crucial that victims and survivors be protected from IPV, but given the research on the myriad dangers that firearms pose in domestic violence, there is a real question whether adding another gun to the equation will help the victim.

If an individual is already being severely abused and the abusive partner is exerting significant control over every facet of the victim's life, it may be naïve to think that the abuser has no knowledge of the firearm, no access to its storage place, and no ability to commandeer it from its rightful owner. We certainly understand how, in the abstract, the idea of providing firearms to severely abused IPV victims could be attractive, and even could appear to be a life-saving tool. Unfortunately, domestic violence dynamics do not lend themselves to easy solutions. They often involve complex processes of control, a recurring cycle of love, tension, violence, and passion.

Giving a lethal weapon to one of the parties involved in such a painful cycle may carry with it unjustifiable risks of intensified violence.

CURRENT CASES AND TRENDS

The recently decided case of *U.S. v. Rahimi* represented a significant opportunity to better understand how the increasingly conservative Supreme Court chose to address intimate partner cases as they relate to firearm regulations. The case itself involved a test of the Fifth Circuit's invalidation of the federal law that prohibited individuals from firearm possession while under a domestic violence–related protective order (Al-Rawi, 2023). The case centered around Zackey Rahimi, a Texas man who perpetrated a stunning level of violence against his girlfriend and a witness in December 2019 (Murakami, 2024). Rahimi and his girlfriend got into an altercation in a parking lot, which culminated in Rahimi physically forcing her into his vehicle, injuring her in the process (Murakami, 2024). Rahimi further fired a shot at a bystander who witnessed the assault, and then threatened to shoot his girlfriend if she told anyone about what happened (Murakami, 2024).

A Texas court concluded that Rahimi was likely to commit IPV again, issued a protective order against him, and barred him from owning weapons (Murakami, 2024). Rahimi then filed a court challenge and cited a purported violation of his Second Amendment rights, which became the basis of the case that made its way to the Supreme Court (Kumar, 2023).

This case had tremendous implications nationwide, especially for those who are in violent intimate relationships. As we have discussed throughout the chapter, there is a strong relationship between the presence of firearms and the escalation of violence within a relationship, as well as a significantly increased likelihood of fatal outcomes. We also have discussed the positive impact of legislation aimed at placing restrictions on the ability of IPV offenders to access firearms. Had the Supreme Court decision struck the federal legislation that enacted such prohibitions, there would have been clear reasons to be concerned for IPV-affected individuals, regardless of one's personal position on firearm ownership. A liberalization of gun rights for individuals who have been found guilty of domestic violence–related offenses and/or have been subject to civil protection orders for domestic violence–related offenses would likely have resulted in a dramatic increase of IPV-related firearm violence and IPV-related homicides. In an opinion that reflected understanding of these concerns, the high court ultimately opted in an 8–1 decision to uphold the longtime federal ban on gun ownership for domestic violence offenders (Dwyer, 2024).

CONCLUSION

This chapter examined gun culture in the United States and the resultant rates of disproportionate firearm-related violence and homicide, as well as the concerning role that firearms play in escalating the violence in domestic violence situations. Many of the injuries sustained by victims of firearm violence, even if they are not fatal, are life-changing and is the focus of our next chapter. Next, we will examine IPV through the lens of its enduring impact and assess the various physical and emotional traumas that victims and survivors endure to better understand the sustained impact that IPV has throughout the lifespan of a victim/survivor.

SAMPLE QUESTIONS FOR CRITICAL THINKING

1. What roles do guns play in IPV?
2. How does gun culture in the United States correlate to firearm-related IPV?
3. How do you feel that the Second Amendment should be weighed compared to a prospective gun buyer's possible record of domestic violence?
4. How do you think the Supreme Court should decide in the *Rahimi* case and why?

CONTEMPORARY APPLICATIONS

Everytown Support Fund, "October is Domestic Violence Awareness Month," https://everytownsupportfund.org/october-is-domestic-violence-awareness-month/.

TMZ shows a graphic image of the July 2020 shooting of Megan Thee Stallion, TMZ (July 15, 2020), MEGAN THEE STALLION: I WAS SHOT IN THE FOOT!!! New Vid Shows Bloody Footprints. https://www.tmz.com/2020/07/15/megan-thee-stallion-shot-twice-foot-tory-lanez-arrest-glass-injury/

13

The Enduring Impact of Intimate Partner Violence

CASE STUDY

Monica, a 38-year-old mother and white-collar professional, experienced abuse during childhood as well as relationship violence as a young adult. She has consulted with numerous therapists over the years because she feels deep inside of her that something is "off," that her feelings and actions are often confusing, even to her. She had multiple serious relationships over the past 10 years, none of which were physically abusive, but two were full of infidelity on both sides. She realizes that she tends to idolize her boyfriends, regardless of what is happening in the relationship. She finds herself desperate to please them physically, emotionally, and sexually, even if it involves doing things that she would prefer to avoid. Even though she is deeply religious and believes that sex is a sacred part of relationships, she often engages in it very early in her relationships and before she is ready. Additionally, she struggles with nightmares, flashbacks to her abusive relationship, periodic binge drinking, compulsive spending, and when under extreme stress, "goes elsewhere," something she finds hard to explain to her friends and therapists. To her, it feels like she is disconnected from reality in those moments, and that she has floated off elsewhere. It is common for this to happen in moments of sexual intimacy with her new boyfriend Alan.

Alan is a contractor in the intelligence community who is 20 years older than Monica. He is capable of being quite fun and charismatic, but like Monica, he is a binge drinker and is often moody and unpredictable. Monica finds herself desperate for his affections and his favor. In a way, his mood determines hers. She senses that she is not the only woman he is actively seeing, but she struggles to talk to Alan about her fears. He can be snappy and yell, which is something that she avoids at all costs. As a result, their relationship status remains unclear to Monica, but she is too anxious about possibly losing Alan to seek further clarity. After a couple of years of hot and cold, erratic behavior from Alan, he abruptly breaks up with Monica, offering the most cursory of explanations that his life is complicated, and he needs to find himself before he pursues another serious relationship.

Monica is crushed and experiences weeks of intense depression and hopelessness. At the recommendation of a counselor friend, she visits a specialized trauma therapist for a consultation. After multiple in-depth discussions, her therapist diagnoses her with C-PTSD, or chronic post-traumatic stress disorder that's related to her past abusive relationships. She is also diagnosed with anxiety, depression, and substance use disorder. Her therapist recommends further evaluation for trauma-related dissociation, as she sees multiple signs that Monica dissociates when she feels vulnerable or scared. Monica is stunned by her diagnoses and is eager to learn more about her treatment plan. She realizes that her abuse left emotional scars, but she had no idea that things were so serious. She acknowledges that she needs to prioritize intense mental health treatment so that she can face her trauma and not let it control her life.

Monica's story epitomizes the intense struggle that survivors of intimate partner violence (IPV) often face as they attempt to heal from their traumatic experiences. While it is possible for many survivors of IPV to move forward successfully with their lives, it is important to note that the body of domestic violence literature is clear—survivors are, sadly, at a heightened risk for a variety of negative physical and emotional outcomes. The legacy of the violence can be seen in the survivor's physical and emotional health for many years after the conclusion of the relationship. There is still much for society to learn about trauma and its impacts; therefore, the focus of this chapter is on the lasting nature of IPV traumatization. IPV need not be a determinative factor in a survivor's future, but the weight of the evidence thus far supports the idea that numerous physical and emotional obstacles can block the survivor's path toward healing. The goal of this chapter is to promote a deeper understanding of these obstacles and the root causes behind them.

DOMESTIC VIOLENCE SURVIVORS AND POST-TRAUMATIC STRESS DISORDER AND COMPLEX POST-TRAUMATIC STRESS DISORDER

Post-Traumatic Stress Disorder and Domestic Violence Survivors

The most acknowledged and understood disorder that survivors of violence face is post-traumatic stress disorder, or PTSD, which is characterized by a post-trauma response that consists of heightened fears and responses, intrusive thoughts, and relationship disturbances, among other concerning symptoms (American Psychiatric Association, 2013). Such is the prevalence of PTSD among survivors of IPV that it has been termed the most common psychological complication that survivors face, with researchers estimating that roughly 30% to 80% of survivors exhibit symptoms of PTSD (Golding, 1999; Kelly, 2010). Therefore, conservative estimates indicate that survivors of IPV face a serious risk of experiencing PTSD.

Not only does PTSD appear to be the most common psychological complication that survivors of IPV face, but it also results in more sustained PTSD symptoms and a lengthier period of suffering before remission, as compared to less personal forms of trauma (Chapman et al., 2012). On an intuitive level, these research indicators make sense. When an intimate relationship is characterized by abuse, it is not hard to imagine that the victim experiences an ongoing series of heartbreaking betrayals, fear, violence, and threats to self-esteem. These traumas take a strong toll over time, and unfortunately, PTSD is a common obstacle that survivors face as they attempt to heal from the violence.

At the same time, even by the most dramatic estimates of the prevalence of PTSD in survivors of IPV, not all survivors exhibit diagnosable symptoms of this disorder. Thus, a logical question is why some survivors, but not others? What are the protective factors among survivors who are not diagnosed with PTSD as compared to survivors who are? Do they possess special traits of survival? Researchers have explored these questions in-depth and have concluded that resilience and the possession of positive coping strategies in the face of life's challenges are particularly important factors in determining whether a survivor of IPV develops PTSD. Researchers have been able to tangibly quantify this dynamic. Studies indicate that fewer coping strategies are associated with the manifestation of increased PTSD symptoms among survivors of IPV (Sullivan et al., 2018). Therefore, someone who enters a traumatic interpersonal experience emotionally healthy may likely have a more successful recovery than someone who has experienced repeated traumas even before enduring relationship violence.

Complex Post-Traumatic Stress Disorder and Domestic Violence Survivors

At this juncture, it is necessary to explain how CPTSD differentiates itself from PTSD, given the higher rate of CPTSD than PTSD in survivors of IPV. CPTSD is a relatively new diagnosis and differs from PTSD in a couple of substantive ways. CPTSD refers to a series of experienced traumatic events, often beginning in early childhood, some of which have a sustained duration (Herman, 1992). CPTSD can be treated as a more serious and treatment-resistant version of PTSD. This is especially concerning when one analyzes the prevalence of both disorders in survivors of IPV. Recent research indicates that the prevalence of CPTSD in domestic violence survivors is twice as high as that of PTSD (Fernandez-Fillol et al., 2021).

What is different between survivors who develop CPTSD versus those who "merely" develop PTSD? That is, what is the difference between survivors who develop a trauma-based disorder from those who develop a much more complex version of that same disorder? According to researchers, a key difference between IPV sufferers of CPTSD versus IPV survivors of PTSD is that those who develop CPTSD appear to have less ability to emotionally regulate (Fernandez-Fillol et al., 2021). The same research team also concluded that high levels of avoidance among survivors are also associated with higher levels of emotional maladaptation and a higher likelihood of the development of CPTSD. While treatments for survivors are discussed in much greater detail in other sections of this book, it is important to note here that these contemporary findings have implications for treatments of IPV survivors and that it might be essential to target avoidant and emotionally volatile behavior and instead focus on helping survivors to develop increased levels of resilience.

DOMESTIC VIOLENCE SURVIVORS AND MENTAL HEALTH DISORDERS

Domestic Violence Survivors and Depression

While PTSD and CPTSD are particularly worrisome challenges for many survivors of IPV, it is important to note that they are not the only psychological hurdle that survivors face. Indeed, the sustained nature of this interpersonal trauma can result in a host of emotional maladies for survivors, ranging from depression and anxiety to thoughts of suicide and actually committing it. Not surprisingly, international studies into domestic violence have found that there is an association between the experience of this violence and the development of depression in survivors (Chandan et al., 2020). Violence and abuse beget pain and suffering, and depressive disorders are among the most challenging for clinicians to treat. Isolation is a key factor in prolonging both depression and IPV; therefore, it is essential that clinicians encourage survivors to maintain ties to supportive family, friends, and peers.

Domestic Violence Survivors, Anxiety, and Additional Psychiatric Issues

When one considers how sustained abuse likely fosters repeated fear responses over time, domestic violence is linked to high levels of anxiety and other negative emotional outcomes for survivors. For example, research has found that in addition to depression, anxiety, and PTSD, IPV also has been linked to psychosis, a lower level of trust, self-harm, and numerous other serious psychosomatic illnesses in survivors (Stewart and Vigod, 2019). There are certain risk factors for more intense psychiatric symptoms in survivors, one being the use of survivors' children in IPV. That is, when the abuser chooses to incorporate the survivor's child or children into the abuse, perhaps by threatening to kidnap them or to manipulate them in other ways, this serious emotional abuse is harrowing for the victim at the time of the abuse and seems to significantly increase the survivor's anxiety and display of PTSD symptoms (Clements et al., 2022).

The use of children in IPV is quite common. One study examining the dynamics of domestic violence for survivors with young children concluded that around 90% of abusers had used or attempted to use the children as a control tactic, and that predictive factors for this type of manipulation included the abuser being the biological father of the children, court-ordered visitation being in place, and the survivor attempting to exit the relationship (Beeble et al., 2007). These findings suggest that when IPV survivors receive therapy or mental health treatment, screening questions should consider the role that the survivor's children played in the violence, among other factors. It is imperative that the unique trauma of having children involved in IPV manipulations be comprehensively addressed so that survivors can substantively heal.

Domestic Violence Survivors and Borderline Personality Disorder

Studies have shown a connection between surviving domestic violence and the presence of borderline personality disorder (BPD) symptomology. BPD is a serious psychological condition that is characterized by a pattern of unstable relationships, emotional volatility, and intense fears of abandonment and rejection (Bozzatello et al., 2021). It causes intense suffering for those who are afflicted and can result in serious disruption in multiple types of functioning. Experiencing severe trauma is one risk factor for the development of this illness. Unfortunately, and not surprisingly, there appears to be a significant relationship between psychiatric struggle in women, IPV, and the manifestation of BPD.

Researchers examining female psychiatric inpatients concluded that there was a staggeringly high correlation between IPV victimization and BPD. Over 90% of hospitalized women who had a history of domestic violence exhibited clinically significant measures of BPD, compared to only around 65% of nonabused hospitalized women (Sansone et al., 2006). Trauma is a central part of domestic violence and can be an impetus for the development of various trauma-related disorders like PTSD and BPD, and that IPV has a clinically significant relationship to BPD. This connection is particularly ominous for the healing of IPV survivors because BPD is notoriously difficult for clinicians to treat. In fact, some practitioners even refuse to take on patients who have it because those patients are resistant to treatment. Clinicians with specialized training in the disorder are viewed as the only ones skilled enough to handle its treatment (Alfonso, 2008). The lack of treatment and stigmatization of BPD can certainly play a role in the delayed healing for IPV survivors who exhibit symptoms of BPD. No one in therapy should be assigned some form of scarlet letter because of trauma, especially when one considers how much stigma IPV victims face from police, family, and friends during their abuse.

Domestic Violence Survivors and Suicidal Ideation/Completion

The tragic saga of legendary actor Marlon Brando's daughter Cheyenne illustrates one particularly wrenching threat to the healing of victims of domestic violence—that the demons and pain from long-term victimization can lead to suicidal ideations and even completion. In a harrowing real-life tale that was disturbingly reminiscent of a major plotline in Brando's Oscar-winning turn in *The Godfather*, that of the abuse of youngest Corleone sister Connie and her older brother's volcanic response to it, Cheyenne's lover Dag Drollet assaulted her in 1990 at the famed actor's California residence when she was seven months pregnant. Her older brother Christian then fatally shot Drollet before Brando attempted CPR on the fallen man (Malnic, 1995). What followed was a series of tragedies for the entire Brando family. Christian later pleaded guilty to voluntary manslaughter and received a sentence of 10 years in prison (Malnic, 1995). Cheyenne returned to her native Tahiti to give birth to her baby before she went into a spiral of depression that ultimately proved fatal, pain which can be sadly reminiscent of the psychological struggles faced by survivors.

Shortly after the baby's birth, Cheyenne entered a psychiatric facility for treatment; however, she attempted suicide at least two times afterward.

Cheyenne's depression became so grave that a judge ultimately declared her mentally disabled (Malnic, 1995). She later suffered a nervous breakdown and went missing from a clinic where she was undergoing treatment, before ultimately taking her own life in 1995. Cheyenne's agonizing story of abuse, debilitating depression, and suicide is not an anomaly. Research indicates that IPV survivors face a heightened risk of suicidal behaviors. In some ways, Cheyenne was uniquely privileged compared to most IPV survivors, as she had access to specialized treatment and resources by virtue of her familial connections and wealth. Her tragic death, despite these advantages, is a lesson in the enduring agony of domestic violence.

Not surprisingly, vulnerable women appear to be at a heightened risk for negative outcomes. In 2000, UNICEF conducted research in multiple countries including the United States, Fiji, India, Peru, Bangladesh, Sri Lanka, and Papua New Guinea and concluded that women and girls who had been abused committed suicide at 12 times the rate of those who had not been abused. Research has also uncovered a relationship between abused and low-income women in countries like Brazil and Egypt and heightened rates of suicidal ideation (WHO, 2001). Today, researchers conclude that ethnic minority, immigrant, and refugee female victims of IPV face a significantly heightened risk of suicide (Colucci and Montesinos, 2013). Victims and survivors who face the most serious institutional barriers to getting help are at the greatest risk of taking the ultimate step to escape their brutalization. This conclusion has important implications for treatment for victims and survivors of IPV. When these individuals attend psychiatric or psychological treatment, screening for suicidal ideations and behaviors should be a significant part of their evaluation. This is perhaps even more important when clinicians evaluate survivors who are historically marginalized and face additional institutional barriers to accessing treatment and assistance.

DOMESTIC VIOLENCE SURVIVORS AND SUBSTANCE USE

Domestic Violence Survivors and Smoking/Drinking

Some survivors of IPV turn to self-medication to try to numb the physical and emotional trauma that they have experienced. Both types of abuse can result in lifelong complications and pain, which may lead to a variety of self-destructive behaviors that are aimed at escapism and temporarily reducing the suffering from their trauma. Smoking is commonly viewed as anxiety-reducing despite its potential health hazards. Research indicates that survivors of IPV smoke at a higher rate than those who have not experienced domestic violence (Crane et al., 2013). In a similar fashion, research also suggests that IPV survivors have a heightened risk for excessive alcohol use (La Flair et al., 2012). Given the variety of negative outcomes that can result for people who suffer from alcohol addiction, ranging from serious legal issues to life-threatening physical problems, this finding is alarming and suggests that initial numbing and self-medicating behaviors on the part of IPV survivors can eventually morph into life-threatening addiction issues.

Studies have repeatedly found a connection between IPV experiences, the development of PTSD symptoms, and the victim's gradual addiction to alcohol (Stewart, 1996). Heavy use of alcohol can initially help numb various trauma-related symptoms, but it becomes the catalyst for addiction. For example, alcohol may initially help soothe some of the most severe PTSD symptoms, like extreme tension and hyperarousal (Stewart et al, 2000). A person who is traumatized is likely to turn to things that make them feel less hurt, even if just in the moment. Over time, however, an addiction to alcohol or any other substance may delay the development of more positive and prosocial coping skills, which the survivor can use to move forward in life.

Domestic Violence Survivors and Illicit Drugs

Sadly, the body of scholarship reveals an unmistakable connection between both past and present IPV and ongoing substance abuse challenges. For example, research in the United Kingdom indicates that around 40% of female crack users reported current abuse by a partner and almost 75% reported abuse from a past partner and/or past abuse by a current partner (Bury et al., 1999). These findings are consistent with the wider body of literature that concludes that a large percentage of substance-addicted individuals have either an ongoing history of abuse or are currently experiencing it. These conclusions are certainly suggestive that survivors of intense traumas like IPV may turn to illicit substances to self-medicate and that the popular conception of drugs for "partying" purposes may be shortsighted.

It is also important to note that the societal stigma toward illicit drugs can play a part in abusive relationships in a way that keeps abused partners somewhat trapped. Sixty percent of people who call the National Domestic Violence hotline say that their partners had tried to prevent them from getting help and almost 40% of callers indicate that their partners had strategically used their substance addiction against them in the relationship by threatening to report their activities to the proper authorities if the abused individuals sought custody of the children and/or sought protective orders. Perhaps most jarringly, roughly 25% of respondents reported that their abusive partners had either forced them to use a substance against their will or to take more of the substance than they wished. Collectively, these findings suggest that illicit substances can play a sinister role in the lives of abused people, serving as a helpful tool for the abusive partner and a desperate source of self-medication for some traumatized survivors of IPV. These findings continue to underscore the importance of the mental health community properly addressing the trauma of IPV and focusing on helping survivors to increase their coping skills and resiliency.

DOMESTIC VIOLENCE SURVIVORS AND PHYSICAL HEALTH CHALLENGES

While much of this chapter has focused on the physical and emotional legacy of IPV, it is also important to address the physical challenges that victims face. One study on women ages 21–55 who suffered from IPV indicated that they manifested a constellation of alarming physical symptoms at an increased rate as compared to nonabused women of the same age, including: headaches, back pain, rates of sexually transmitted infections (STIs), vaginal bleeding and infections, pelvic pain, painful intercourse, urinary tract infections, appetite loss, abdominal pain, and chronic digestive issues (Campbell et al., 2002). This study concluded that abused women faced a *50–70% increase* in gynecological, central nervous system, and stress-related disorders as compared to nonabused women (Campbell et al., 2002). These findings also underscore the legacy of IPV, as well as the importance of open communication between survivors of IPV and their practitioners so that they can receive the appropriate physical and sexual health screenings and begin early treatment when necessary.

The sexual health of IPV survivors is also important, as there are multiple studies that suggest that IPV survivors face heightened risks of STIs (Hess et al., 2012). Researchers posit that potential explanations for this include infidelity on the part of the abusive partner and decreased condom use (Hess et al., 2012). Being in past abusive relationships is associated with a higher likelihood of not using condoms in future relationships, which may correlate with a learned helplessness theoretical approach to domestic violence. As we have discussed, the main tenet of *learned helplessness* is that a repeatedly traumatized/victimized individual may slowly come to believe over time that they lack the necessary skills to change abusive circumstances and, therefore, "gives up." The connection between learned helplessness and the sexual health and autonomy of survivors of IPV appear to relate to how survivors of repeated violence believe that they cannot prevent it from happening again, and thus struggling to protect themselves and their sexual and emotional agency from predation. Higher rates of STIs and even infertility in IPV survivors reflect this phenomenon.

Consistent with this discussion are research findings that indicate previously abused young women (physically and verbally) were less likely to use condoms in their relationships than their nonabused counterparts and, accordingly, faced a heightened risk of HIV (Teitelman et al., 2008). As a result, an actual "causal pathway" exists between past and current abuse and risk of HIV. It must be noted that partner abuse is correlated with additional HIV/STI risk factors in addition to the lower likelihood of using condoms, which include a higher likelihood of substance use before sex and having a higher number of sexual partners (Teitelman et al., 2008). That is, IPV survivors carry the trauma of their experiences through multiple facets of their lives, including their sex lives. They appear to engage (more often) in risky behaviors that may please a partner but hurt them in the long run. It is essential that domestic violence survivors receive appropriate gynecological healthcare and necessary screenings so that they can recognize and confront trauma-based behaviors that may place them at a higher risk for distressing and life-altering health outcomes such as STIs, HIV, and infertility.

There are additional areas of concern for survivors of IPV that are wholly separate from gynecological-related ones, though equally alarming. Society's understanding of the debilitating nature of repeated head trauma has substantively grown in recent years, which has promoted increased research into the relationship between domestic violence survivors and traumatic brain injuries (TBIs). Research aimed at uncovering the most common physical injuries sustained by victims concluded that the most targeted areas centered around the face, head, and neck (Sheridan and Nash, 2007). This finding emphasizes the serious and malicious nature of IPV and is suggestive that of the estimated 42% of victims who suffer physical injuries from this violence, many should be screened for TBIs (Statistics Canada, 2016).

These findings are also concerning in terms of assessing the long-term health prospects for survivors of IPV. TBIs are associated with a variety of life-altering symptoms for sufferers, including brain degeneration, fatigue, depression, emotional lability/volatility, confusion, aggression, and a higher than normal risk of developing dementia (Langlois et al., 2006). When these symptoms are combined with the emotional and psychological symptoms that survivors of IPV experience, many face sustained challenges on their paths to recovery and healing. While estimates in the literature vary on the percentage of head injuries that IPV survivors sustain, what is important to note is that the research is consistent that TBIs are a substantial threat in violent relationships. In fact, one study found that a staggering *100%* of victimized respondents had sustained at least one TBI during their abusive relationship (Valera and Kucyi, 2017).

The body of the evidence supports the fact that survivors of IPV are likely to face a constellation of physical and emotional symptoms in the aftermath of their abusive relationships. Unfortunately, they often face societal judgment and stigmatization, rather than support. Researchers have found that victim blaming attitudes are common among study participants who are exposed to domestic violence scenarios, as are the propagation of domestic violence myths (Yamawaki et al., 2012). For example, when assessing these scenarios, participants tend to be quite judgmental and negative toward hypothetical victims who return to their abusers, even though as we discuss in other sections of this book, this behavior is common among victims of IPV. Enhanced social support and understanding would undoubtedly benefit survivors of IPV, who already face a difficult road to recovery. Emotional support cannot undo physical injuries and make something like PTSD disappear, but additional measures of caring and empathy can certainly give someone the strength to continue to fight to heal physical and emotional injuries. "You are not alone" is a powerful statement, both in word and deed.

CONCLUSION

The disturbing saga of former World Wrestling Entertainment (WWE) personality Tamara "Sunny" Sytch represents the ultimate cautionary tale of the convergence of trauma from domestic violence, mental health struggles, and the development of severe substance abuse. It illustrates why it is so essential to treat survivors of IPV before disaster ensues. Sytch, a member of the WWE Hall of Fame, was sentenced to 17 years in a Florida prison in November 2023 for DUI manslaughter after crashing her car into a vehicle at a stoplight, fatally injuring an elderly man (Bucksbaum, 2023). This was Sytch's sixth DUI, as well as the last of a long series of arrests. While this case represents, on the surface, a celebrity thoughtlessly taking another's life before facing justice, the sentencing hearing revealed layers of complexity, which represented a true cautionary tale for survivors of IPV.

According to the defense's psychiatric experts, Sytch had been involved in a series of abusive relationships and self-medicated with heavy amounts of alcohol. Despite numerous legal problems and physical complications including pancreatitis, Sytch fell deeper into addiction. At the time of sentencing, the experts diagnosed Sytch with an alarming host of problems, including bipolar disorder, borderline personality disorder, substance use disorder, PTSD, impaired executive function, depression, and anxiety (Fernandez, 2023). One of the diagnosing experts indicated that Sytch's PTSD seemed to center around grief and trauma, and heavy flashbacks to numerous abusive romantic relationships in her life. They asserted that Sytch had been improperly treated for her numerous problems. This tragic tale of the lost life of an innocent man and the lengthy imprisonment of a woman who faced multiple abusive relationships stands as a marker for how crucial it is that IPV survivors get appropriate and ongoing treatment for their trauma. Domestic violence is always a deeply unfortunate chapter in a survivor's story, but it need not be a life-defining one. While research is clear that survivors face numerous obstacles on their journey to healing, proper and ongoing treatment can serve as protective factors that ensure survivors take a path of positivity and growth. In our final chapter, we will turn our attention to contemporary issues within IPV with the hope that a deeper understanding of it can help prevent the catastrophic consequences discussed in this chapter.

SAMPLE CRITICAL THINKING QUESTIONS

1. Why does domestic violence intensify the risk for both PTSD and CPTSD?
2. How do stigmas toward borderline-diagnosed individuals create an obstacle to treatment for some survivors of domestic violence?
3. Given the lifelong physical and emotional injuries that survivors of domestic violence often face, do you think criminal penalties for this crime should be enhanced? Why or why not?
4. Depending on the jurisdiction, justice system policies and practices dealing with substance-addicted individuals can be characterized as punitive. Does the connection between domestic violence, trauma, and substance use affect your view on how to treat substance users in the criminal justice system?

CONTEMPORARY APPLICATIONS

National Center on Domestic Violence, Trauma, and Mental Health: https://ncdvtmh.org/our-work/mhsu-field/.

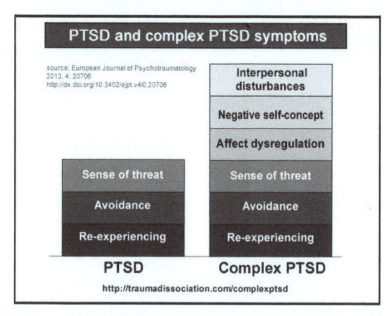

Figure 13.1. Post-Traumatic Stress Disorder (PTSD) and complex PTSD symptoms. From "Complex Posttraumatic Stress Disorder" by TraumaDissociation.com, http://traumadissociation.com/complexptsd. CC BY-SA 4.0.

C. Warshaw and G. Zapata-Alma, G. (n.d.). *In Honor of Domestic Violence Awareness Month: Responding to Substance Use Coercion in Treatment and Recovery Services.* Addiction Technology Transfer Center Network. https://attcnetwork.org/in-honor-of-domestic-violence-awareness-month-responding-to-substance-use-coercion-in-treatment-and-recovery-services/.

T. Harrison. 16 Borderline Personality Disorder Symptoms and Effective Treatment Approaches. *Mind Journal.* https://themindsjournal.com/borderline-personality-disorder/.

T. J. Peterson (February 1, 2022). PTSD From Domestic Violence, Emotional Abuse, Childhood Abuse. HealthyPlace. https://www.healthyplace.com/ptsd-and-stress-disorders/ptsd/ptsd-from-domestic-violence-emotional-abuse-childhood-abuse.

14

Domestic Violence in the Twenty-First Century

Lessons Going Forward

CASE STUDY

Kelly and her husband Johnny had been married for exactly one year when medical authorities issued the initial "stay at home" guidance for the COVID-19 pandemic in March 2020. Kelly is in her mid-20s and a Pilates instructor and Johnny is in his early 30s and a sales associate at Home Depot. Because both their jobs are put on hold during the "stay at home" period, they scramble for emergency benefits to make ends meet. Their finances are under severe daily strain. Within a week of each other, Kelly's grandmother and Johnny's aunt both die of the virus.

As they deal with isolation, financial stressors, emotional uncertainty, and grief, their marriage starts to implode. Their relationship has never been seamless but having to stay at home together brings immense tensions to the surface. Kelly has always been a fiercely career-focused introvert, and as things worsen between the couple, she feels that there is nowhere to turn. As a way to escape, Johnny is drinking the days away, and Kelly intensely dislikes the loud and arrogant person he becomes when he is drunk.

One evening right after Johnny summarily passes out, Kelly notices his phone on the bedside table. As Johnny slumbers, Kelly picks up the phone and sees it's unlocked. Curious, she proceeds to look through a series of shattering messages. Johnny is apparently talking to three different women on two social media platforms: a coworker, an ex, and a friend from high school. The messages are explicit, and all three women appear to be under the impression that Kelly and Johnny have formally separated and filed for divorce, which is untrue.

Kelly is a very private and controlled person. It takes all of her might to not immediately confront Johnny. She carefully places his phone in the same spot where she found it and tries to formulate a plan. She's not even sure that she wants to stay in the marriage anymore or if there is anything left to salvage, but she also doesn't want to lose to anyone else. She vacillates between pride and competitiveness all night, and when she wakes up, her decision is clear. Calmly, but authoritatively, she confronts Johnny and tells him she knows everything. Rather than offer any apology, he blames her for his affairs and their argument escalates. Kelly wants to leave their apartment to defuse an increasingly volatile situation, but as an asthma sufferer, she only leaves the apartment for emergencies, fearful of contracting COVID-19.

As their world grows smaller, Kelly's despair grows. Despite her introverted nature, she has connected with, and intrinsically trusts, her longtime therapist whom she has been seeing since her late teens. With the onset of the pandemic, her therapist can no longer safely practice in-person therapy, and so Kelly's sessions become virtual. While she is thrilled to be able to talk to someone, she can't truly talk openly because Johnny is always home and so much of what she yearns to discuss is all about him—how he cheated, how he is a full-fledged alcoholic, how he curses at her frequently and has even thrown things at her. Kelly entertains the thought of asking her therapist if they can text during the session as a private measure, but she ultimately demurs.

Fortunately for Kelly, by the summer of 2021 she is back to work full-time and has renewed access to multiple resources. With the support of her therapist and dearest friends, she leaves Johnny and officially files for divorce.

Kelly's harrowing and prolonged abuse illustrates one of the major recent trends within domestic violence—that the COVID-19 pandemic and its concomitant stresses and isolation exacerbated abuse within intimate partner relationships. Accordingly, this chapter examines where the nation finds itself in the fight against intimate partner violence (IPV) almost 25 years into the twenty-first century, as well as lessons and thoughts to carry forward. A thorough analysis of the concerning impact of the COVID-19 pandemic on IPV is conducted, and trends/evolutions in our collective understanding of this phenomenon are discussed and fully contextualized. Worrisome indicators that our society still does not take this phenomenon as seriously as needed is highlighted, including the impact of online misinformation and attacks on high-profile complainants. We close this book with a final note that understanding the complexities of IPV depends on exploring the scholarship rather than engaging in snap judgments. There are no easy answers to IPV, and combating it successfully requires a societal response to all the factors that play a role in its stubborn continuation.

COVID-19 AND DOMESTIC VIOLENCE TRENDS

COVID-19 and Domestic Violence Rates in the United States

One of the many social challenges that the COVID-19 pandemic fostered was a sudden and dramatic change in relationship dynamics worldwide. In the United States, the combination of stay-at-home orders, social isolation, pandemic stress and grief, possible health obstacles, and increased economic strain played a role in placing many intimate partner relationships under high levels of stress. An important note at the outset is that historically during crises periods, increased rates of IPV are reported (Curtis et al., 2000). Examples of this include heightened rates of domestic violence during the Great Recession in the United States (Schneider et al., 2016).

Researchers have identified additional areas of concern that likely played a role in the increased domestic rates of IPV, including lack of access to social services and other helpful resources (Kourti et al., 2023). Other factors include increased male unemployment, childcare stresses, and maladaptive coping strategies (Piquero et al., 2021). Forced isolation with their abusers impacted victims negatively. They were unwilling to contact authorities for help, which led to increased rates of IPV during the pandemic (note that this does not account for unreported violence) (Piquero et al., 2020).

An exhaustive meta-analysis of studies examining the impact of COVID-19 on rates of domestic violence indicate an average rise of approximately 8% for both the United States and the global community, though the increase in rates was slightly more pronounced in the United States (Piquero et al., 2020). Research indicates that there was an initial explosion in rates of IPV in some major cities in the United States following stay-at-home orders in March 2020, including a 10% rise in New York City throughout the month of March and an 18% increase in San Antonio, Texas (Boserup et al., 2020). From this data, it can be concluded that stressors from isolation and economic challenges emerged in relationships that were already fraught, likely intensifying already-abusive relationships.

Not surprisingly, certain vulnerable populations demonstrated the highest increases in IPV. Factors such as urban residency, being an essential worker, struggling to afford rent, experiencing unemployment or having an unemployed partner, pregnancy, and having tested positive for COVID-19 were all associated with higher rates of IPV (Peitzmeier et al., 2020). Additionally, races/ethnicities that have historically been disproportionately victimized by IPV demonstrated similarly high rates of pandemic related domestic violence. These disparities are most notable in Black women. Their rates of IPV were already disproportionately high even before the pandemic began and increased significantly during it (Kaukinen, 2020).

Researchers believe that there are multiple systemic reasons behind these racially based disparities in IPV during COVID-19. One manifestation of both structural racism and sexism in the United States is the disproportionate employment of Black women in both low-wage occupations and those that would be deemed essential (Holder et al., 2021). Unsurprisingly, these structural employment gaps placed Black women at a high risk for being infected with COVID-19, and both their infection rates and heightened mortality rates reflected the danger of essential work and the undue burdens placed upon them (Holder et al., 2021). Also notable is that Black women experienced the highest level of unemployment during the pandemic (Rushovich et al., 2021). They were also at a heightened risk for extreme financial stressors in their intimate relationships, with experts finding that diminished resources in a relationship often triggered higher levels of conflict (Kaukinen, 2020).

COVID-19 and Accessing Resources for Victims in the United States

Unfortunately, the pandemic caused a limitation of available resources and help for IPV-victimized individuals. Researchers found that one-third of victimized individuals had difficulties accessing the necessary help (Lindberg et al., 2020). Nonetheless, calls to domestic violence hotlines increased in the United States by around 10% during the pandemic, which indicates that the need for discussion and referral was significantly heightened during that time (Leslie and Wilson, 2020). Victims and perpetrators were isolated together when the medical community had recommended social distancing and isolation as a measure to avoid a collapse of the health-care system. The fact that calls to IPV hotlines were still up significantly during this period is telling, because, clearly, the ability of some victimized individuals to call for help was impeded by their close physical proximity to their abusers.

COVID-19 International Challenges

The worrisome relationship between the pandemic and significantly increased rates of IPV was not limited to the United States. Research indicates that IPV rates during the COVID-19 pandemic were alarmingly high worldwide. Studies conducted in the United Kingdom indicate that the rate of IPV there was even higher than in the United States, with over 11% of respondents indicating being victimized by either physical or psychological violence by their partners at some point after stay-at-home orders began (Kourti et al., 2023). Research conducted in Australia that focused on the 25- to 34-year-old age bracket also yielded concerning results, as both men and women in this age group expressed high levels of fear that they would be abused by their intimate partners during lockdowns (Biddle et al., 2020). This suggests that there was a significant proportion of relationships that were volatile and potentially already violent, and the fear of victimization by both men and women reflected that *their partners had already been exhibiting escalatory behaviors prior to the pandemic*. In other words, those findings indicate that high percentages of "young" relationships in Australia already were characterized by abusive tendencies before COVID-19, and partners' expressed fear for future victimization reflected this stealth abuse.

There were also deeply alarming metrics throughout mainland Asia. Domestic violence cases tripled in China after the lockdown started (Kunasagran et al., 2024). The statistics in South Korea were equally troubling. Data indicates that rates of IPV victimization for South Korean women increased significantly, but domestic violence arrest rates decreased by over 10% in 2020 as compared to 2019 (Yoon, 2023). The clear implication of these contradictory numbers indicate to IPV experts that the volume of IPV was clearly increasing in South Korea during the pandemic, but that because victims and perpetrators were often confined together under strict orders not to leave their residences, this severely hampered the ability of the abused partner to get help.

IPV has intensified in both scope and gravity in countries that were already experiencing high levels of gendered violence and discrimination against women. For example, over 35% of pregnant women in Iran indicated that they had experienced some form of IPV during the pandemic (Naghizadeh et al., 2021). Research in India reveals even more concerning jumps in IPV rates, as studies indicate that there was an almost 50% increase in domestic violence between March 2020 and July 2020 (Maji et al., 2022). Observers note that a central feature of some segments of Indian society is the freedom of movement that men enjoy compared to women, who are often only allowed to leave their homes to work or attend school (Maji et al., 2022). Gender norms, which had already isolated women before the start of the pandemic, made it even more difficult for them to get help once they were confined to their homes in an even more extensive and stricter manner.

When we assess the impact of COVID-19 on both domestic and global IPV rates, structural and gender bias issues were often responsible for staggeringly high rates in certain countries. One takeaway from these findings is that a worldwide health crisis contributed to precipitate a crisis of fear and violence in intimate partner relationships worldwide. Despite lockdowns and social distancing as measures to minimize the spread of COVID-19, there are numerous other metrics that suggest they took a disproportionate toll on victims of IPV. While it is neither reasonable nor realistic to expect governments to design future health interventions based solely on considerations of IPV, countries would be well-served to consider the impact of these policies on the most vulnerable segments of the citizenry, including victims of ongoing IPV.

TRENDS AND EVOLUTIONS IN COLLECTIVE UNDERSTANDING OF INTIMATE PARTNER VIOLENCE

The Impact of Social Media and Rising Hate Speech

Today, an inescapable facet of global life is the impact of various social media platforms on all aspects of daily existence. While social media platforms offer exciting opportunities for connectivity, learning, and even inspiration, they have a dark side—a high prevalence of misinformation (Allcott et al., 2019). Studies indicate that X (formerly Twitter) is alarmingly sensitive to the spread of false stories (Allcott et al., 2019), a concern that is exacerbated by Elon Musk's acquisition of the company in 2022. Musk asserts that he wanted to purchase the platform to promote increased free speech. Upon acquisition, he promptly unbanned multiple categories of accounts. Experts have found that these actions have resulted in a proliferation of COVID-19 and election deniers, White supremacists, White nationalists, QAnon believers, and other forms of extremists (Benton et al., 2022). Essentially, this has resulted in a situation, at least with X, where there is a considerable volume of hate speech and misinformation, but no real moderation of content.

Social Media and High-Profile Intimate Partner Violence

Widespread hate comments and misinformation have had considerable implications for the treatment of complainants of IPV within the social media sphere. The 2022 defamation trial between celebrated actor Johnny Depp and ex-wife Amber Heard is a clear example of targeted hatred and misinformation toward some complainants of domestic violence, particularly when they present as problematic in a way that challenges gender norms and expectations. Heard testified about incidents of abuse that she alleged the popular actor perpetrated against her, as well as her own substance use and bisexuality. Online outlets pounded and targeted Heard with a variety of scurrilous and demonstrably untrue allegations (Nelson, 2024), with sometimes misleading and doctored TikTok videos, stories, and tweets launching fantastic accusations against Heard, including that she snorted cocaine while on the witness stand in a globally broadcasted trial in which Depp was suing her for millions (Nelson, 2024).

Numerous social media users also commented on the trial in ways that completely excused clear evidence that Depp had behaved in an abusive manner on numerous occasions. For example, text messages introduced during the trial indicated that Depp insulted Heard in disturbing ways and even threatened to defile her corpse (Nelson, 2024). Yet trial watchers dismissed these instances as examples of Depp's offbeat charm, which observers assert is characteristic of a larger theme in which male abuses are minimized as misunderstood moments of humor (Manne, 2017). In short, the intense scrutiny on Heard's demeanor, makeup, hair, and courtroom interactions with her legal team while online trial observers ignored substantive evidence of Depp's abusive conduct in multiple aspects could indicate wider issues with societal misogyny (Nelson, 2024).

In addition to the concerns over possible manifestations of misogyny demonstrated by the social media activity during the trial, experts also expressed the concern that tweets from numerous social media users reflected a serious lack of understanding about domestic violence dynamics. For example, numerous social media accounts perpetrated the debunked notion that all victims of domestic violence have extreme physical wounds and injuries, and that "real" victims of IPV would be expected to behave in a certain fashion that was opposite to Heard's more assertive trial posture (Nelson, 2024). Again, these social media commentators seemed unaware of consistent intimate partner research that indicates there is no monolithic way in which survivors behave (Serisier, 2018).

A content analysis of social media commentary on the Heard-Depp trial indicated a proliferation of victim-blaming comments and disproportionate anger at Heard. In fact, 37% of the online comments reflected victim-blaming beliefs from users, ranging from attacks on Heard for not epitomizing the perfect victim to questions of her motivations (Whiting et al., 2019). Heard was variously called "a nutjob," "psychotic," "cold-hearted," and controlling (Whiting et al., 2019). One user's anger toward Heard was so visceral that they expressed the wish to witness her physical assault (Whiting et al., 2019). Only around 3% of the comments placed blame on Depp, with many of them attributing Depp's behavior to perceived issues with substance abuse (Whiting et al., 2019). In this way, online commentors somewhat mitigated the severity of Depp's alleged behavior by ascribing it wholly to substances.

As a result, researchers have urged therapists who work with victims of IPV to ensure that their treatment of abused partners is not unwittingly victim-blaming (Whiting et al., 2019). For example, there is a tendency on the part of some professionals to strongly encourage their clients to leave their abusive partners because the professionals themselves have great anxiety over their clients' safety. However, experts assert that aggressive attempts to cajole an abused partner into leaving their abuser can make survivors feel that their independence is being stripped from them (Whiting et al., 2019). Accordingly, researchers encourage professionals in IPV to ensure that their counseling and advice do not unintentionally blame victims for their decisions to stay or leave (Whiting et al., 2019).

As discussed earlier, the July 2020 shooting of Megan Thee Stallion gained worldwide attention and revealed deeper societal insensitivities to victims of IPV. Initially, Megan was untruthful with authorities about the source of her injuries, claiming that she hurt her feet on glass (Odusola, 2023). This lie reflected her concerns about reporting a Black man to the police less than two months after George Floyd's murder. When she eventually reported that the source of the incident was a shooting perpetrated by her intimate partner, rapper Tory Lanez, the social media vitriol was almost immediate. Oddly, rather than express any anger toward Lanez for shooting a naked and terrified woman in the feet, "antifan" accounts mobilized and targeted Megan on a variety of grounds (Odusola, 2023).

According to these social media accounts, Megan had "brought a Black man down" (Draggur, 2022), and her decision to seek justice for the IPV attack perpetrated against her meant that she was "trash," or even a traitor to Black people (Odusola, 2023). Recall our earlier discussion of guns and domestic violence and the significantly higher rate of fatal outcomes when the perpetrator had access to firearms. When Megan's decision to involve the authorities is contextualized with these research findings, one might think that her choice to cooperate with law enforcement would be celebrated and applauded as an inspiring choice to reclaim her power and hold her abuser accountable. However, the opposite happened.

Fellow celebrities participated in the spread of misinformation and hatred against Megan. Famed rapper 50 Cent posted a meme that compared Megan to actor Jussie Smollett, who had recently been convicted of perpetrating a hoax that centered around the idea that racist and homophobic Trump supporters staged a vicious attack against him (Pop Crave, 2022). Superstar rapper Drake heavily implied in one of his songs that Megan was lying (George, 2022). Equally concerning was the veneration of Lanez in some specters of social media. In fact, his follower count on Instagram grew by millions following the shooting (Odusola, 2023). Accordingly, some experts on IPV conclude that the online treatment of Megan reflects misogyny, racism, and a societal tendency to dismiss and minimize the pain of Black women hurt by IPV (Odusola, 2023).

CONCLUSION

In this book we have engaged in a full examination of as many salient aspects of domestic violence as possible. We have learned how prevalent this violence continues to be both domestically and globally, and have explored the topic considering laws, police, courts, interventions, batterers, victims, enduring impacts, social media, theories, COVID-19, economic strain, and other areas. We note that there is so much yet to discuss and explore because the scholarship on IPV continues to dynamically evolve.

The takeaway from this volume is individual, but all readers are encouraged to learn from the victim-blaming comments on social media, as outlined in this chapter, and contextualize them as part of a large theme in US society. Clearly, there is a continued knowledge gap on all aspects of domestic violence on the part of many members of the public, and it is our hope that this text explains and addresses some areas of confusion. We also encourage readers to immerse themselves in the available peer-reviewed domestic violence literature to best understand IPV. The social media comments we examined indicate that many individuals rely on anecdotes, stereotypes, outdated ideas, and hunches when they engage in discussions about IPV. Domestic violence is complex, and some experts do not fully understand every part of it, therefore, research continues.

Today, IPV continues and as discussed in this chapter, rates significantly increased during the COVID-19 pandemic. This issue is not going away, and there are numerous directions for future research. We hope that readers, and professionals in the field, continue to explore IPV through the lens of ongoing societal challenges, including the rise of extremism, wars, inflation, political polarization, the fentanyl epidemic, controversies over perceptions of diminished reproductive freedoms, and immigration tensions.

SAMPLE CRITICAL THINKING QUESTIONS

1. What impacts did the COVID-19 pandemic have on IPV worldwide?
2. What impact does hatred and misinformation on social media have on the public's understanding of IPV?
3. What do you think is the single most important factor behind continued high levels of IPV? What are your suggestions for addressing and overcoming this obstacle?
4. What is the most surprising thing you have learned about domestic violence, either from this book or elsewhere? Why?
5. Did you have any misconceptions about any aspect of domestic violence before reading this book? If so, what were they and what have you since learned that gives you a fuller picture?

CONTEMPORARY APPLICATION

The meme comparing Megan Thee Stallion to convicted hoaxer Jussie Smollett: @SaycheeseDGTL (December 17, 2022), "50 Cent compares Megan Thee Stallion to Jussie Smollett" [X post/meme], https://x.com/SaycheeseDGTL/status/1604270108020559873.

REFERENCES

Abhilash, B. S. (2015). Revenge, masculinity and glorification of violence in the godfather. *International Journal of Social Science and Humanities Research, 3*(2), 6–12.

Afifi, T. O., MacMillan, H., Cox, B. J., Asmundson, G. J., Stein, M. B., & Sareen, J. (2009). Mental health correlates of intimate partner violence in marital relationships in a nationally representative sample of males and females. *Journal of Interpersonal Violence, 24*(8), 1398–1417.

Aldana, A., Larralde, H., & Aldana, M. (2022). Modeling the role of police corruption in the reduction of organized crime: Mexico as a case study. *Scientific Reports, 12*, 19233. https://doi.org/10.1038/s41598-022-23630-x

Aldossari, M., & Calvard, T. S. (2021). The politics and ethics of resistance, feminism and gender equality in Saudi Arabian organizations. *Journal of Business Ethics.* Advance online publication. https://doi.org/10.1007/s10551-021-04949-3

Alejo, K. (2014). Long-term physical and mental health effects of domestic violence. *Themis: Research Journal of Justice Studies and Forensic Science, 2*(1), 5.

Alesina, A., Brioschi, B., & Ferrara, E. (2020). Violence against women: A cross-cultural analysis for Africa. *Economica, 88.* 10.1111/ecca.12343.

Ali, P. A., & Naylor, P. B. (2013). Intimate partner violence: A narrative review of the biological and psychological explanations for its causation. *Aggression and Violent Behavior, 18*(3), 373–382.

Allcott, H., Gentzkow, M., & Yu, C. (2019). Trends in the diffusion of misinformation on social media. *Research & Politics, 6*(2), 2053168019848554.

Al-Rawi, J. (2023). The case for relaxing Bruen's historical analogues test: Rahimi, 18 USC § 922 (g)(8), and domestic violence regulation in colonial and post-enactment America. *Berkeley Journal of Gender, Law & Justice.*

American Bar Association. (2008, July). Domestic violence civil protection orders (CPOs) by state. American Bar Association Commission on Domestic Violence. http://www.americanbar.org/content/dam/aba/migrated/domviol/docs/DV_CPO_ Chart_8_2008.authcheckdam.pdf

American Psychiatric Association. (2013). *DSM-5. Diagnostic and statistical manual of mental disorders* (5th ed.). Arlington, VA: Author.

Anderson, K. L. (2008). Is partner violence worse in the context of control? *Journal of Marriage and Family, 70*(5), 1157–1168.

Arnold, G., & Ake, J. (2013). Reframing the narrative of the battered women's movement. *Violence Against Women, 19*, 557–578.

Astin, M. C., Lawrence, K. J., & Foy, D. W. (1993). Posttraumatic stress disorder among battered women: Risk and resiliency factors. *Violence and victims, 8*(1), 17.

Avakame, E. F., & Fyfe, J. J. (2001). Differential police treatment of male-on-female spousal violence: Additional evidence on the leniency thesis. *Violence Against Women, 7*(1), 22–45.

Bacardi, F. (2019, March 20). *Emma Roberts and Evan Peters: From alleged domestic abuse to broken engagements.* Page Six. https://pagesix.com/2019/03/20/emma-roberts-and-evan-peters-from-alleged-domestic-abuse-to-broken-engagements/

Bachman, R., Zaykowski, H., Lanier, C., Poteyeva, M., & Kallmyer, R. (2010). Estimating the magnitude of rape and sexual assault against American Indian and Alaska Native (AIAN) women. *Australian & New Zealand Journal of Criminology, 43*(2), 199–222.

Baggett, A. (2014). *"Strike me if you dare": Intimate-partner violence, gender, and reform, 1865–1920.* Louisiana State University and Agricultural & Mechanical College.

Baggett, A. (2017). *Intimate partner violence in New Orleans: Gender, race, and reform, 1840–1900.* University Press of Mississippi.

Bagwell-Gray, M. E., Messing, J. T., & Baldwin-White, A. (2015). Intimate partner sexual violence: A review of terms, definitions, and prevalence. *Trauma, Violence, & Abuse, 16*(3), 316–335.

Bailey, B. A., & Daugherty, R. A. (2007). Intimate partner violence during pregnancy: Incidence and associated health behaviors in a rural population. *Maternal and child health journal, 11*, 495–503.

Barata, P. C. (2007). Abused women's perspectives on the criminal justice system's response to domestic violence. *Psychology of Women Quarterly, 31*, 202–215.

Bard, M., & Zacker, J. (1974). Assaultiveness and alcohol use in family disputes: Police perceptions. *Criminology, 12*(3), 281–292.

Barker, K. C. (2019). Police culture and perceived service value: Officer perspectives on psychological services utilization [Doctoral dissertation, Walden University].

Barker, L. C., Stewart, D. E., & Vigod, S. N. (2019). Intimate partner sexual violence: An often overlooked problem. *Journal of Women's Health, 28*(3), 363–374.

Barr, J. (2012). To love and to cherish: Marital violence and divorce in nineteenth-century America. *The Confluence (2009–2020), 4*(1), 5.

Barrett, B. J. (2015). Domestic violence in the LGBT community. In *Encyclopedia of Social Work.* https://doi.org/10.1093/acrefore/9780199975839.013.1133

Bauer, H. M., Rodriguez, M. A., Quiroga, S. S., & Flores-Ortiz, Y. G. (2000). Barriers to health care for abused Latina and Asian immigrant women. *Journal of Health Care for the Poor and Underserved, 11*(1), 33–44. https://doi.org/10.1353/hpu.2010.0590

Beck, E., & Mohamed, A. (2021, September 10). *A body speaks: State, media, and public responses to femicide in Guatemala.* MDPI. https://www.mdpi.com/2075-471X/10/3/73

Beeble, M., Bybee, D., & Sullivan, C. (2007). Abusive men's use of children to control their partners and ex-partners. *European Psychologist, 12*(1), 54–61. https://doi.org/10.1027/1016-9040.12.1.54

Bendlin, M., & Sheridan, L. (2021). Risk factors for severe violence in intimate partner stalking situations: An analysis of police records. *Journal of Interpersonal Violence, 36*(17–18), 7895–7916.

Bennett, L., Stoops, C., Call, C., & Flett, H. (2007). Program completion and re-arrest in a batterer intervention system. *Research on Social Work Practice, 17,* 42–54.

Ben-Porat, A., & Sror-Bondarevsky, N. (2021). Length of women's stays in domestic violence shelters: Examining the contribution of background variables, level of violence, reasons for entering shelters, and expectations. *Journal of Interpersonal Violence, 36*(11–12), NP5993-NP6012.

Benson, M. L., Fox, G. L., DeMaris, A., & Van Wyk, J. (2003). Neighborhood disadvantage, individual economic distress and violence against women in intimate relationships. *Journal of Quantitative Criminology, 19,* 207–235.

Bent-Goodley, T. B. (2007). Health disparities and violence against women: Why and how cultural and societal influences matter. *Trauma, Violence, and Abuse, 8,* 90–104.

Benton, B., Choi, J. A., Luo, Y., & Green, K. (2022). Hate speech spikes on twitter after Elon Musk acquires the platform. School of Communication and Media, Montclair State University.

Berkowitz, A. D. (2004). Working with men to prevent violence against women: An overview (part one). *National Resource Center on Domestic Violence, 9*(2), 1–7.

Bhambra, G. K., & Narayan, J. (2016). Introduction. In G. K. Bhambra & J. Narayan (Eds.), *European cosmopolitanism* (pp. 1–13). Routledge.

Bhaya, 2017. *New study highlights impact of domestic violence on workplace, productivity.* CGTN. https://news.cgtn.com/news/3051444f7a637a6333566d54/share_p.html

Biddle, N., Edwards, B., Gray, M., & Sollis, K. (2020). Mental health and relationships during the COVID-19 pandemic.

Black, M. C., Basile, K. C., Breiding, M. J., Smith, S. G., Walters, M. L., Merrick, M. T., . . . Stevens, M. R. (2011). *The National Intimate Partner and Sexual Violence Survey (NISVS): 2010 Summary Report.* Atlanta, GA: National Center for Injury Prevention and Control, Centers for Disease Control and Prevention.

Black, D. J. & Reiss Jr., A. J., (1967). Interrogation and the criminal process. *The Annals of the American Academy of Political and Social Science, 374*(1), 47–57.

Blumenstein, L. (2009). Domestic violence within law enforcement families: The link between traditional police subculture and domestic violence among police [Master's dissertation, University of South Florida].

Bonomi, A. E., Trabert, B., Anderson, M. L., Kernic, M. A., & Holt, V. L. (2014). Intimate partner violence and neighborhood income: A longitudinal analysis. *Violence Against Women, 20*(1), 42–58. https://doi.org/10.1177/1077801213520580

Boserup, B., McKenney, M., & Elkbuli, A. (2020). Alarming trends in US domestic violence during the COVID-19 pandemic. *The American Journal of Emergency Medicine, 38*(12), 2753.

Boy, A., & Kulczycki, A. (2008). What we know about intimate partner violence in the Middle East and North Africa. *Violence Against Women, 14*(1), 53–70. https://doi.org/10.1177/1077801207311860

Bozzatello, P., Garbarini, C., Rocca, P., & Bellino, S. (2021). Borderline personality disorder: Risk factors and early detection. *Diagnostics, 11*(11), 2142. MDPI AG. Retrieved from http://dx.doi.org/10.3390/diagnostics11112142

Braaf, R., & Barrett-Meyering, I. (2010, July). Economic wellbeing: What does it really mean for women and their children affected by domestic violence? In *11th Australian Institute of Family Studies Conference—Sustaining Families in Challenging Times, Melbourne* (pp. 7–9).

Brady, P. Q., Reyns, B. W., & Dreke, R. (2020). A sign of the crimes: Examining officers' identification of, and arrest for, stalking in domestic violence complaints. *Police Quarterly*, 23(4), 500–526.

Breiding, M., Basile, K. C., Smith, S. G., Black, M. C., & Mahendra, R. R. (2015). Intimate partner violence surveillance: Uniform definitions and recommended data elements. Version 2.0. https://stacks.cdc.gov/view/cdc/31292

Bucksbaum, S. (2023, November 27). *WWE star Tammy "Sunny" Sytch sentenced to 17 years in prison for deadly DUI crash*. EW.com. https://ew.com/wwe-tammy-sytch-sentenced-17-years-in-prison-deadly-dui-crash-8407185

Burnette, C. (2015). Historical oppression and intimate partner violence experienced by indigenous women in the United States: Understanding connections. *Social Service Review*, 89(3), 531–563.

Bury, C., Powis, B., Ofori-Wilson, F., Downer, L., & Griffiths, P. (1999). *An examination of the needs of women crack users with attention to the role of domestic violence and housing* (Report for Lambeth, Southwark and Lewisham Health Authority in collaboration with the National Addiction Centre and the Brixton Drugs Project).

Cadsky, O., Hanson, R. K., Crawford, M., & Lalonde, C. (1996). Attrition from a male batterer treatment program: Client-treatment congruence and lifestyle instability. *Violence and Victims*, 11(1), 51–64.

Caetano, R., Field, C. A., Ramisetty-Mikler, S., & McGrath, C. (2005). The 5-year course of intimate partner violence among White, Black, and Hispanic couples in the United States. *Journal of Interpersonal Violence*, 20(9), 1039–1057.

Caetano, R., Schafer, J., & Cunradi, C. B. (2017). Alcohol-related intimate partner violence among White, Black, and Hispanic couples in the United States. In Mangai Natarajan (Ed.), *Domestic violence* (pp. 153–160). Routledge.

Caetano, R., Vaeth, P. A., & Ramisetty-Mikler, S. (2008). Intimate partner violence victim and perpetrator characteristics among couples in the United States. *Journal of Family Violence*, 23(6), 507–518.

Calvete, E. (2008). Mental health characteristics of men who abuse their intimate partner. *Revista Española de Sanidad Penitenciaria*, 10, 48–55.

Campbell, J. C. (2002). Health consequences of intimate partner violence. *The Lancet*, 359(9314), 1331–1336.

Campbell, J., Jones, A. S., Dienemann J., et al. (2002). Intimate partner violence and physical health consequences. *Archives of Internal Medicine*, 162(10), 1157–1163. doi:10.1001/archinte.162.10.1157

Carbajosa, P., Catalá-Miñana, A., Lila, M., & Gracia, E. (2017). Differences in treatment adherence, program completion, and recidivism among batterer subtypes. *The European Journal of Psychology Applied to Legal Context*, 9(2), 93–101.

Cardefia, E. (1994). The domain of dissociation. In S. J. Lynn & J. W. Rhue (Eds.), *Dissociation: Clinical and theoretical perspectives* (pp. 15–31). Guilford Press.

Çelik, A. (2013). An analysis of mandatory arrest policy on domestic violence. *International Journal of Human Sciences*, 10(1), 1503–1523.

Cerulli, C., Kothari, C. L., Dichter, M., Marcus, S., Wiley, J., & Rhodes, K. V. (2014). Victim participation in intimate partner violence prosecution: Implications for safety. *Violence Against Women*, 20(5), 539–560.

Chambliss, L. R. (2008). Intimate partner violence and its implication for pregnancy. *Clinical obstetrics and gynecology, 51*(2), 385–397.

Chandan, J. S., Thomas, T., Bradbury-Jones, C., Russell, R., Bandyopadhyay, S., Nirantharakumar, K., & Taylor, J. (2020). Female survivors of intimate partner violence and risk of depression, anxiety and serious mental illness. *The British Journal of Psychiatry: The Journal of Mental Science, 217*(4), 562–567. https://doi .org/10.1192/bjp.2019.124

Chapman, C., Mills, K., Slade, T., McFarlane, A. C., Bryant, R. A., Creamer, M., . . . Teesson, M. (2012). Remission from post-traumatic stress disorder in the general population. *Psychological Medicine, 42*(8), 1695–1703. doi: 10.1017/ S0033291711002856

Cheek, N. N., Bandt-Law, B., & Sinclair, S. (2023). People believe sexual harassment and domestic violence are less harmful for women in poverty. *Journal of Experimental Social Psychology, 107,* 104472.

Cheema, R. (2016). Black and blue bloods: Protecting police officer families from domestic violence. *Family Court Review, 54*(3), 487–500.

Chen, J., Walters, M. L., Gilbert, L. K., & Patel, N. (2020). Sexual violence, stalking, and intimate partner violence by sexual orientation, United States. *Psychology of Violence, 10*(1), 110.

Cheng, T. C., & Lo, C. C. (2015). Racial disparities in intimate partner violence and in seeking help with mental health. *Journal of Interpersonal Violence, 30*(18), 3283–3307.

Chester, D. S., & DeWall, C. N. (2018). The roots of intimate partner violence. *Current Opinion in Psychology, 19,* 55–59.

Chiffriller, S. H., Hennessy, J. J., & Zappone, M. (2006). Understanding a new typology of batterers: Implications for treatment. *Victims and Offenders, 1*(1), 79–97.

Cho, H. (2012). Racial differences in the prevalence of intimate partner violence against women and associated factors. *Journal of Interpersonal Violence, 27*(2), 344–363.

Christensen, M. C., Gill, E., & Pérez, A. (2016). The Ray Rice domestic violence case: Constructing Black masculinity through newspaper reports. *Journal of Sport and Social Issues, 40*(5), 363–386.

Clements, K. A. V., Sprecher, M., Modica, S. et al. (2022). The use of children as a tactic of intimate partner violence and its relationship to survivors' mental health. *Journal of Family Violence, 37,* 1049–1055. https://doi.org/10.1007/ s10896-021-00330-0

Coker, A. L., Davis, K. E., Arias, I., Desai, S., Sanderson, M., Brandt, H. M., & Smith, P. H. (2002). Physical and mental health effects of intimate partner violence for men and women. *American Journal of Preventive Medicine, 23*(4), 260–268.

Coker, A. L., Smith, P. H., McKeown, R. E., & King, M. J. (2000). Frequency and correlates of intimate partner violence by type: Physical, sexual, and psychological battering. *American Journal of Public Health, 90*(4), 553.

Coker, D. (2001). Crime control and feminist law reform in domestic violence law: A critical review. *Buffalo Criminal Law Review, 4*(2), 801–860.

Colucci, E., & Montesinos, A. H. (2013). Violence against women and suicide in the context of migration: A review of the literature and a call for action. *Suicidology Online, 4,* 81–91.

Condino, V., Tanzilli, A., Speranza, A. M., & Lingiardi, V. (2016). Therapeutic interventions in intimate partner violence: An overview. *Research in Psychotherapy: Psychopathology, Process and Outcome, 19*(2), 79–88.

Conner, D. H. (2013). Financial freedom: Women, money, and domestic abuse. *William & Mary Journal of Women and the Law, 20*, 339.

Constantino, R., Kim, Y., & Crane, P. A. (2005). Effects of a social support intervention on health outcomes in residents of a domestic violence shelter: A pilot study. *Issues in Mental Health Nursing, 26*(6), 575–590. doi:10.1080/01612 840590959416

Cook, P. W. (Ed.). (2009). *Abused men: The hidden side of domestic violence.* Praeger Publishers.

Cordier, R., Chung, D., Wilkes-Gillan, S., & Speyer, R. (2021). The effectiveness of protection orders in reducing recidivism in domestic violence: A systematic review and meta-analysis. *Trauma, Violence, & Abuse, 22*(4), 804–828.

Crane, A., Hawes, S., & Weinberger, A. (2013). Intimate partner violence victimization and cigarette smoking. *Trauma Violence, & Abuse, 14*, 305–315.

Crenshaw, K. W., Ritchie, A. J., Anspach, R., Gilmer, R., & Harris, L. (2015). Say her name: Resisting police brutality against Black women. African American Policy Forum. Columbia Law School.

Cunradi, C. B., Caetano, R., & Schafer, J. (2002). Socioeconomic predictors of intimate partner violence among White, Black, and Hispanic couples in the United States. *Journal of Family Violence, 17*, 377–389.

Curtis, T., Miller, B. C., & Berry, E. H. (2000). Changes in reports and incidence of child abuse following natural disasters. *Child Abuse & Neglect, 24*(9), 1151–1162.

Dario, L. M., Fradella, H. F., Verhagen, M., & Parry, M. M. (2019). Assessing LGBT people's perceptions of police legitimacy. *Journal of Homosexuality, 67*(7), 885–915.

Davila, Y. R., Bonilla E., Gonzalez-Ramirez D., & Villarruel A. M. (2007). HIV-IPV prevention: Perceptions of what Latinas want and need. *Hispanic Health Care International, 5*(3), 101–108.

DeGrave, S. (2018, February 16). *APD apologizes for meme misfire it said made light of domestic violence.* Citizen Times. https://www.citizen-times.com/story/news/local/2018/02/16/apd-apologizes-meme-misfire-said-made-light-domestic-violence/344834002/

DeJong, C., Burgess-Proctor, A., & Elis, L. (2008). Police officer perceptions of intimate partner violence: An analysis of observational data. *Violence & Victims, 23*(6), 683–696.

Desmarais, S. L., Reeves, K. A., Nicholls, T. L., Telford, R. P., & Fiebert, M. S. (2012). Prevalence of physical violence in intimate relationships, Part 1: Rates of male and female victimization. *Partner Abuse, 3*(2), 140–169.

Devries, K. M., Mak, J. Y., Garcia-Moreno, C., Petzold, M., Child, J. C., Falder, G., . . . & Watts, C. H. (2013). The global prevalence of intimate partner violence against women. *Science, 340*(6140), 1527–1528.

Díez, C., Kurland, R. P., Rothman, E. F., Bair-Merritt, M., Fleegler, E., Xuan, Z., . . . & Siegel, M. (2017). State intimate partner violence–related firearm laws and intimate partner homicide rates in the United States, 1991 to 2015. *Annals of Internal Medicine, 167*(8), 536–543.

Di Marco, M. H., & Evans, D. P. (2021). Society, her or me? An explanatory model of intimate femicide among male perpetrators in Buenos Aires, Argentina. *Feminist Criminology, 16*(5), 607–630. https://doi.org/10.1177/1557085120964572

Douglas, H. (1991). Assessing violent couples. *Families in Society, 72*(9), 525–535.

Downs, D. A. (1997). *More than victims-battered women, the syndrome society, and the law.* University of Chicago Press.

Draggur [@dragga_cj]. (2022, December 21). *idk why we still stressing on this fake incident, Megan is jus been used by her record label* [Tweet]. Twitter. https://twitter.com/dragga_cj/status/1605581738851328001

Dragiewicz, M. (2008). Patriarchy reasserted: Fathers' rights and anti-VAWA activism. *Feminist Criminology, 3*, 121–144. doi:10.1177/1557085108316731

Dunn, J. L. (2005). "Victims" and "survivors": Emerging vocabularies of motive for battered women who stay. *Sociological Inquiry, 75*(1), 1–30.

Durfee, A. (2009). Victim narratives, legal representation, and domestic violence civil protection orders. *Feminist Criminology, 4*(1), 7–31.

Dutton, D. G. (1995). Intimate abusiveness. *Clinical Psychology: Science and Practice, 2*(3), 207.

Dutton, D. G., & White, K. R. (2013). Male victims of domestic violence. *New Male Studies: An International Journal, 2*(1), 5–17.

Dwyer, D. (2024, June 21). *Supreme Court says domestic abusers can be temporarily disarmed.* ABC News. https://abcnews.go.com/Politics/supreme-court-upholds-federal-ban-firearms-domestic-violence/story?id=111272685

Easteal, P., Holland, K., & Judd, K. (2015, January). Enduring themes and silences in media portrayals of violence against women. In *Women's Studies International Forum* (Vol. 48, pp. 103–113). Pergamon.

Eby, K. K., Campbell, J. C., Sullivan, C. M., & Davidson, W. S. (1995). Health effects of experiences of sexual violence for women with abusive partners. *Health Care for Women International, 16*(6), 563–576.

Edelson, M. G., Hokoda, A., & Ramos-Lira, L. (2007). Differences in effects of domestic violence between Latina and non-Latina women. *Journal of Family Violence, 22*, 1–10.

Edleson, J. L., & Syers, M. (1991). The effects of group treatments for men who batter: An 18-month follow-up study. *Research on Social Work Practice, 1*, 227–243.

Edwards, K. M., Mattingly, M. J., Dixon, K. J., & Banyard, V. L. (2014). Community matters: Intimate partner violence among rural young adults. *American Journal of Community Psychology, 53*, 198–207.

Edwards, K. M., Sylaska, K. M., & Neal, A. M. (2015). Intimate partner violence among sexual minority populations: A critical review of the literature and agenda for future research. *Psychology of Violence, 5*(2), 112–121. https://doi.org/10.1037/a0038656

Edwards, L. (2023). "The peace," domestic violence, and firearms in the new republic. *Fordham Urban Law Journal, 51*, 1.

Ellsberg, M. C. (2006). Violence against women: A global public health crisis. *Scandinavian Journal of Public Health, 34*(1), 1–4.

Eriksson, M., & Ulmestig, R. (2021). "It's not all about money": Toward a more comprehensive understanding of financial abuse in the context of VAW. *Journal of Interpersonal Violence, 36*(3–4), NP1625–1651NP.

Ertürk, Y. (2006). *Integration of the human rights of women and the gender perspective: Violence against women.* United Nations Economic and Social Council (Vol. 70793). https://doi.org/10.1017/S0020818300006640

Fagan, J. A. (1996). *The criminalization of domestic violence: Promises and limits.* United States Department of Justice.

Fapohunda, T., Masiagwala, P., Stiegler, N., & Bouchard, J. P. (2021, September). Intimate partner and domestic violence in South Africa. In *Annales Médico-Psychologiques, Revue Psychiatrique* (Vol. 179, No. 7, pp. 653–661). Elsevier Masson.

Feder, L., & Henning, K. (2005). A comparison of male and female dually arrested domestic violence offenders. *Violence and Victims, 20*(2), 153–171.

Fernández-Fillol, C., Pitsiakou, C., Perez-Garcia, M., Teva, I., & Hidalgo-Ruzzante, N. (2021). Complex PTSD in survivors of intimate partner violence: Risk factors related to symptoms and diagnoses. *European Journal of Psychotraumatology, 12*(1), 2003616. https://doi.org/10.1080/20008198.2021.2003616

Ferraro, K. J. (2017). Current research on batterer intervention programs and implications for policy. Battered Women's Justice Project. chrome-extension://efaidnbmnnnibpcajpcglclefindmkaj/https://bwjp.org/wp-content/uploads/2022/08/batterer-intervention-paper-final-2018.pdf

Ford, D. A., & Regoli, M. J. (1993). The criminal prosecution of wife assaulters: Process, problems, and effects. *Legal responses to wife assault: Current trends and evaluation*, 127–164.

Galea, S., Branas, C. C., Flescher, A., Formica, M. K., Hennig, N., Liller, K. D., . . . & Ying, J. (2018). Priorities in recovering from a lost generation of firearms research. *American Journal of Public Health, 108*(7), 858–860.

García-Moreno, C., Jansen, H. A. F. M., Ellsberg, M., Heise, L., & Watts, C. (2005). WHO multi-country study on women's health and domestic violence against women. *Geneva: World health organization, 204*(1), 18.

Gelles, R. J. (1977). Power, sex, and violence: The case of marital rape. *Family Coordinator, 26,* 339–347.

Gelles, R. J., & Straus, M. A. (2017). The medical and psychological costs of family violence. In R. J. Gelles & M. A. Straus (Eds.), *Physical violence in American families* (pp. 425–430). Routledge.

George, R. (2022, December 22). Joe Budden, Vivica A. Fox, Claudia Jordan join list of celebrities that voiced their opinion on Megan Thee Stallion and Tory Lanez case [full timeline]. *Atlanta Black Star.* Retrieved April 10, 2023, from https://atlantablackstar.com/2022/12/22/celebrities-that-voiced-their-opinion-on-megan-thee-stallion-and-tory-lanez-case-issues-apology/

Glenn, C., & Goodman, L. (2015). Living with and within the rules of domestic violence shelters: A qualitative exploration of residents' experiences. *Violence Against Women, 21*(12), 1481–1506. https://doi.org/10.1177/1077801215596242

Gold, L. H. (2020). Domestic violence, firearms, and mass shootings. *The Journal of the American Academy of Psychiatry and the Law, 48*(1), 35–42.

Goldberg, W. G., & Tomlanovich, M. C. (1984). Domestic violence victims in the emergency department: New findings. *Jama, 251*(24), 3259–3264.

Golding, J. M. (1999). Intimate partner violence as a risk factor for mental disorders: A meta-analysis. *Journal of Family Violence, 14*(2), 99–132. doi: 10.1023/A:1022079418229

Goldscheid, J. (2013). Rethinking Civil Rights and Gender Violence. *Georgetown Journal of Gender & the Law, 14*, 43.

Gómez-Casillas, A., van Damme, M., & Permanyer, I. (2023). Women's and men's status: Revisiting the relationship between gender equality and intimate partner violence against women in Europe. *Journal of Interpersonal Violence, 38*(15–16), 8755–8784. https://doi.org/10.1177/08862605231158760

Gondolf, E. (2004). Evaluating batterer counseling programs: A difficult task showing some effects. *Aggression and Violent Behavior, 9*, 605–631.

Gondolf, E. W. (1999). MCMI-III results for batterer program participants in four cities: Less "pathological" than expected. *Journal of Family Violence, 14*, 1–17.

Goode, W. J. (1971). Force and violence in the family. *Journal of Marriage and the Family, 33*(4), 624–636.

Goodmark, L. (2012). *A troubled marriage: Domestic violence and the legal system.* New York University Press.

Goodmark, L. (2018). Innovative criminal justice responses to intimate partner violence. In Claire M. Renzatti, Jeffery L. Edleson, & Raquel Kennedy Burgen (Eds.), *Sourcebook on violence against women* (pp. 257–274). Sage.

Gordon, S. F. (2018). *Violence against women in the developing world: Mexico and the migrant crisis.* Psicología Iberoamericana. https://www.redalyc.org/journal/1339/133959553002/html/

Gostin, L. O., & Record, K. L. (2011). Dangerous people or dangerous weapons: Access to firearms for persons with mental illness. *JAMA, 305*(20), 2108–2109.

Grau, J., Fagan, J., & Wexler, S. (2018). Restraining orders for battered women: Issues of access and efficacy. In Claudine Schweber & Clarice Feinmen (Eds.), *Criminal justice politics and women* (pp. 13–28). Routledge.

Green, K., & Browne, K. (2020). Personality disorder traits, trauma, and risk in perpetrators of domestic violence. *International Journal of Offender Therapy and Comparative Criminology, 64*(2–3), 147–166.

Gregory, D. R. (2002). Intimate partner violence: Societal, medical, legal and individual responses. *Journal of Legal Medicine, 23*(4), 609–616.

Grigsby, N., & Hartman, B. R. (1997). The Barriers Model: An integrated strategy for intervention with battered women. *Psychotherapy: Theory, Research, Practice, Training, 34*(4), 485.

Grinshteyn, E., & Hemenway, D. (2016). Violent death rates: The US compared with other high-income OECD countries, 2010. *The American Journal of Medicine, 129*(3), 266–273.

Guadalupe-Diaz, X. (2016). Disclosure of same-sex intimate partner violence to police among lesbians, gays, and bisexuals. *Social Currents, 3*(2), 160–171.

Hafemeister, T. L. (2010). If all you have is a hammer: Society's ineffective response to intimate partner violence. *Catholic University Law Review, 60*, 919.

Hamberger, L. K., & Hastings, J. E. (1989). Counseling male spouse abusers: Characteristics of treatment completers and drop-outs. *Violence and Victims, 4*, 275–286.

Hamberger, L. K., Saunders, D. G., & Hovey, M. (1992). Prevalence of domestic violence in community practice and rate of physician inquiry. *Family Medicine, 24*(4), 283–287.

Hampton, R. L., LaTaillade, J. J., Dacey, A., & Marghi, J. R. (2008). Evaluating domestic violence interventions for Black women. *Journal of Aggression, Maltreatment & Trauma*, 16(3), 330–353.

Han, Y. R., & Choi, H. Y. (2021). Risk factors affecting intimate partner violence occurrence in South Korea: Findings from the 2016 Domestic Violence Survey. *PLOS One*, 16(3), e0247916. https://doi.org/10.1371/journal.pone.0247916

Hare, S. C. (2010). Intimate partner violence: Victims' opinions about going to trial. *Journal of Family Violence*, 25, 765–776.

Harrison, L. A., & Esqueda, C. W. (1999). Myths and stereotypes of actors involved in domestic violence: Implications for domestic violence culpability attributions. *Aggression and Violent Behavior*, 4(2), 129–138.

Hattery, A. J., & Smith, E. (2007). *African American Families*. Sage.

Henning, K., & Feder, L. (2005). Criminal prosecution of domestic violence offenses: An investigation of factors predictive of court outcomes. *Criminal Justice and Behavior*, 32, 612–642.

Herman, J. L. (1992). Complex PTSD: A syndrome in survivors of prolonged and repeated trauma. *Journal of Traumatic Stress*, 5(3), 377–391. doi: 10.1002/jts.2490050305

Heron, R. L., Eisma, M. C., & Browne, K. (2021, June 7). Barriers and facilitators of disclosing domestic violence to the UK Health Service. *Journal of Family Violence*. SpringerLink. https://link.springer.com/article/10.1007/s10896-020-00236-3

Herstik, L., & Coscarelli, J. (2023). *Tory Lanez is expected to be sentenced for shooting Megan Thee Stallion*. The New York Times (Digital Edition), NA-NA. https://www.nytimes.com/2023/08/07/arts/music/tory-lanez-megan-thee-stallion-sentence.html

Hess, K. L., Javanbakht, M., Brown, J. M., Weiss, R. E., Hsu, P., & Gorbach, P. M. (2012). Intimate partner violence and sexually transmitted infections among young adult women. *Sexually Transmitted Diseases*, 39(5), 366–371. https://doi.org/10.1097/OLQ.0b013e3182478fa5

Hillman, J. (2020). Intimate partner violence among older LGBT adults: Unique risk factors, issues in reporting and treatment, and recommendations for research, practice, and policy. In Brenda Russell (Ed.), *Intimate partner violence and the LGBT+ community: Understanding power dynamics* (pp. 237–254). Springer.

Hines, D. A., & Douglas, E. M. (2014). Women's use of intimate partner violence against men: Prevalence, implications, and consequences. In Lisa Conradi & Robert Geffner (Eds.), *Female offenders of intimate partner violence* (pp. 26–40). Routledge.

Hodge, J. P., & Sexton, L. (2020). Examining the blue line in the rainbow: The interactions and perceptions of law enforcement among lesbian, gay, bisexual, transgender and queer communities. *Police Practice and Research*, 21(3), 246–263.

Hogan, K. F., Clarke, V., & Ward, T. (2021). Men's experiences of help-seeking for female-perpetrated intimate partner violence: A qualitative exploration. *Counselling and Psychotherapy Research*, 1–12.

Holder, M., Jones, J., & Masterson, T. (2021). The early impact of COVID-19 on job losses among black women in the United States. *Feminist Economics*, 27(1–2), 103–116.

Holtzworth-Munroe, A., Meehan, J. C., Herron, K., Rehman, U., & Stuart, G. L. (2000). Testing the Holtzworth-Munroe and Stuart (1994) batterer typology. *Journal of Consulting and Clinical Psychology*, 68(6), 1000.

Holtzworth-Munroe, A., & Stuart, G. L. (1994). Typologies of male batterers: Three subtypes and the differences among them. *Psychological Bulletin, 116*(3), 476.

Hotaling, G. T., & Sugarman, D. B. (1986). An analysis of risk markers in husband to wife violence: The current state of knowledge. *Violence and Victims, 1,* 101–124.

Houston, C. (2014). How feminist theory became (criminal) law: Tracing the path to mandatory criminal intervention in domestic violence cases. *Michigan Journal of Gender & Law, 21,* 217.

Htun, M., & Jensenius, F. R. (2022). Expressive power of anti-violence legislation: Changes in social norms on violence against women in Mexico. *World Politics, 74*(1), 1–36. doi:10.1017/S0043887121000186

Huecker, M., King, K., Jordan, G., et al. Domestic Violence. [Updated 2023 Apr 9]. In: StatPearls [Internet]. Treasure Island (FL): StatPearls Publishing; 2024 Jan-. Available from: https://www.ncbi.nlm.nih.gov/books/NBK499891/

Humbert, A. L., Strid, S., Hearn, J., & Balkmar, D. (2021). Undoing the 'Nordic Paradox': Factors affecting rates of disclosed violence against women across the EU. *PLOS One, 16*(5), e0249693. https://doi.org/10.1371/journal.pone.0249693

Huntley, A. L., Potter, L., Williamson, E., Malpass, A., Szilassy, E., & Feder, G. (2019). Help-seeking by male victims of domestic violence and abuse (DVA): A systematic review and qualitative evidence synthesis. *BMJ Open, 9*(6), e021960.

Huss, M. T., & Langhinrichsen-Rohling, J. (2000). Identification of the psychopathic batterer: The clinical, legal, and policy implications. *Aggression and Violent Behavior, 5*(4), 403–422.

International Institute for Population Sciences. (2007). *National Family Health Survey (NFHS-3), 2005–06: India (2 v.+ suppl.)* (Vol. 1). International Institute for Population Sciences.

Johnson, C. E. (1997). Rocket Dockets: Reducing delay in federal civil litigation. *California Law Review, 85,* 225.

Johnson, L. B., Todd, M., & Subramanian, G. (2005). Violence in police families work family spillover. *Journal of Family Violence, 20*(1), 3.

Johnson, M. P. (2008). *A typology of domestic violence.* Upne.

Johnson, R., Gilchrist, E., Beech, A. R., Weston, S., Takriti, R., & Freeman, R. (2006). A psychometric typology of UK domestic violence offenders. *Journal of Interpersonal Violence, 21*(10), 1270–1285.

Jones, M. S., Worthen, M. G., Sharp, S. F., & McLeod, D. A. (2021). Native American and non-native American women prisoners, adverse childhood experiences, and the perpetration of physical violence in adult intimate relationships. *Journal of Interpersonal Violence, 36*(23–24), 11058–11087.

Jonker, I. E., Sijbrandij, M., van Luijtelaar, M. J., Cuijpers, P., & Wolf, J. R. (2015). The effectiveness of interventions during and after residence in women's shelters: A meta-analysis. *The European Journal of Public Health, 25*(1), 15–19.

Joseph, J. (2017). Victims of femicide in Latin America: Legal and criminal justice responses. *Temida, 20*(1), 3–21. https://doi.org/10.2298/TEM1701003J

Karakurt, G., Smith, D., & Whiting, J. (2014). Impact of intimate partner violence on women's mental health. *Journal of Family Violence, 29,* 693–702.

Kaslow, N. J., Leiner, A. S., Reviere, S., Jackson, E., Bethea, K., Bhaju, J., . . . & Thompson, M. P. (2010). Suicidal, abused African American women's response to a culturally informed intervention. *Journal of Consulting and Clinical Psychology, 78*(4), 449.

Katz, E. (2014). Judicial patriarchy and domestic violence: A challenge to the conventional family privacy narrative. *William & Mary Journal of Women and the Law, 21*, 379.

Kaufman, J., & Zigler, E. (1987). Do abused children become abusive parents? *American Journal of Orthopsychiatry, 57*(2), 186–192.

Kaukinen, C. (2020). When stay-at-home orders leave victims unsafe at home: Exploring the risk and consequences of intimate partner violence during the COVID-19 pandemic. *American Journal of Criminal Justice, 45*, 668–679.

Keegan, G., Hoofnagle, M., Chor, J., Hampton, D., Cone, J., Khan, A., . . . & Cirone, J. M. (2023). State-level analysis of intimate partner violence, abortion access, and peripartum homicide: Call for screening and violence interventions for pregnant patients. *Journal of the American College of Surgeons*, 10-1097.

Keilitz, S. L. (1994). Civil protection orders: A viable justice system tool for deterring domestic violence. *Violence and Victims, 9*(1), 79.

Kelly, J., & Payton, E. (2019). A content analysis of local media framing of intimate partner violence. *Violence and Gender, 6*(1), 47–52.

Kelly, U. A. (2010). Symptoms of PTSD and major depression in Latinas who have experienced intimate partner violence. *Issues in Mental Health Nursing, 31*(2), 119–127. doi 10.3109/01612840903312020

Kessler, R. C., Molnar, B. E., Feurer, I. D., & Appelbaum, M. (2001). Patterns and mental health predictors of domestic violence in the United States: Results from the National Comorbidity Survey. *International Journal of Law and Psychiatry, 24*(4–5), 487–508.

Kim, M. (2012). Challenging the pursuit of criminalization in an era of mass incarceration: The limitations of social work responses to domestic violence in the USA. *British Journal of Social Work, 43*, 1276–1293.

Kisa, S., Gungor, R., & Kisa, A. (2023). Domestic violence against women in North African and Middle Eastern countries: A scoping review. *Trauma, Violence, & Abuse, 24*(2), 549–575. https://doi.org/10.1177/15248380211036070

Ko, C. N. (2001). Civil restraining orders for domestic violence: The unresolved question of efficacy. *Southern California Interdisciplinary Law Journal, 11*, 361.

Koirala, P., & Chuemchit, M. (2020). Depression and domestic violence experiences among Asian women: A systematic review. *International Journal of Women's Health, 12*, 21–33. https://doi.org/10.2147/IJWH.S235864

Kourti, A., Stavridou, A., Panagouli, E., Psaltopoulou, T., Spiliopoulou, C., Tsolia, M., . . . & Tsitsika, A. (2023). Domestic violence during the COVID-19 pandemic: A systematic review. *Trauma, Violence, & Abuse, 24*(2), 719–745.

Kubany, E. S., Hill, E. E., & Owens, J. A. (2003). Cognitive trauma therapy for battered women with PTSD: Preliminary findings. *Journal of Traumatic Stress, 16*, 81–91. doi 10.1023/A:1022019629803

Kumar, N. (2023). The Second Amendment battle: Domestic abuse case poses threat to gun future legislation. *Juris Mentem Law Review.*

Kunasagran, P. D., Mokti, K., Ibrahim, M. Y., Rahim, S. S. S. A., Robinson, F., Muyou, A. J., . . . & Yusoff, J. (2024). The global landscape of domestic violence against women during the COVID-19 pandemic: A narrative review. *Korean Journal of Family Medicine, 45*(1), 3.

Kyriacou, D. N., Anglin, D., Taliaferro, E., Stone, S., Tubb, T., Linden, J. A., . . . & Kraus, J. F. (2017). Risk factors for injury to women from domestic violence. In *Domestic Violence* (pp. 145–151). Routledge.

La Flair, L., Bradshaw, C., Storr, C., Green, K., Alvanzo, A., & Crum, R. (2012). Intimate partner violence and patterns of alcohol abuse and dependence criteria among women: A latent class analysis. *Journal of Studies of Alcohol and Drugs, 73*, 351–360.

Langan, M. (2018). *Neo-colonialism and the poverty of development in Africa.* Palgrave Macmillan.

Langlois, J., Rutland-Brown, W., & Wald, M. (2006). The epidemiology and impact of traumatic brain injury: A brief overview. *The Journal of Head Trauma Rehabilitation, 21*, 375–378.

Launius, M. H., & Lindquist, C. U. (1988). Learned helplessness, external locus of control, and passivity in battered women. *Journal of Interpersonal Violence, 3(3)*, 307–318.

LeCount, R. J. (2017, December). More black than blue? Comparing the racial attitudes of police to citizens. *Sociological Forum, 32*, 1051–1072.

Leisenring, A. (2008). Controversies surrounding mandatory arrest policies and the police response to intimate partner violence. *Sociology Compass, 2(2)*, 451–466.

Lenton, R. L. (2017). Power versus feminist theories of wife abuse. In Mangai Natarajan (Ed.), *Domestic violence* (pp. 227–252). Routledge.

Leslie, E., & Wilson, R. (2020). Sheltering in place and domestic violence: Evidence from calls for service during COVID-19. *Journal of Public Economics, 189*, 104241.

Letellier, P., & Island, D. (2013*). Men who beat the men who love them: Battered gay men and domestic violence* (1st ed.). Routledge. https://doi.org/10.4324/9781315801421

Lindberg, L. D., VandeVusse, A., Mueller, J., & Kirstein, M. (2020). *Early impacts of the COVID-19 pandemic: Findings from the 2020 Guttmacher survey of reproductive health experiences.* https://www.guttmacher.org/report/early-impacts-covid-19-pandemic-findings-2020-guttmacher-survey-reproductive-health

Lindhorst, T., Oxford, M., & Gillmore, M. R. (2007). Longitudinal effects of domestic violence on employment and welfare outcomes. *Journal of Interpersonal Violence, 22(7)*, 812–828.

Lipsky, S., Caetano, R., & Roy-Byrne, P. (2009). Racial and ethnic disparities in police-reported intimate partner violence and risk of hospitalization among women. *Women's Health Issues, 19(2)*, 109–118.

Lockwood, D., & Prohaska, A. (2015). Police officer gender and attitudes toward intimate partner violence: How policy can eliminate stereotypes. *International Journal of Criminal Justice Sciences, 10(1)*, 77.

Logan, T. K., Shannon, L., Cole, J., & Swanberg, J. (2007). Partner stalking and implications for women's employment. *Journal of Interpersonal Violence, 22*, 268–291.

Logan, T. K., & Walker, R. T. (2010). Civil protective order effectiveness: Justice or just a piece of paper? *Violence and Victims, 25(3)*, 332–348.

Logan, T. K., Walker, R., Staton, M., & Leukefeld, C. (2001). Substance use and intimate violence among incarcerated males. *Journal of Family Violence, 16*, 93–114.

Lott, L. D. (1995). Deadly secrets: Violence in the police family. *FBI Law Enforcement Bulletin, 64*, 12.

Lown, E. A., & Vega, W. A. (2001). Prevalence and predictors of physical partner abuse among Mexican American women. *American Journal of Public Health, 91(3)*, 441.

Lu, Y., & Temple, J. R. (2019). Dangerous weapons or dangerous people? The temporal associations between gun violence and mental health. *Preventive Medicine, 121,* 1–6.

Lynch, K. R. (2020). Female firepower: Gun ownership for self-protection among female intimate partner violence victims. *Violence and Gender, 7*(1), 19–26.

Lynch, K. R., & Logan, T. K. (2018). "You better say your prayers and get ready": Guns within the context of partner abuse. *Journal of Interpersonal Violence, 33*(4), 686–711.

Lysova, A., Dim, E. E., & Dutton, D. (2019). Prevalence and consequences of intimate partner violence in Canada as measured by the national victimization survey. *Partner Abuse, 10*(2), 199–221.

Maaddi, R. (2014, September 9). *Longer Ray Rice video shows obscenities, spitting (w/ video).* The Press Democrat. https://www.pressdemocrat.com/article/sports/longer-ray-rice-video-shows-obscenities-spitting-w-video/

Mahalik, J. R., Locke, B. D., Ludlow, L. H., Diemer, M. A., Scott, R. P., Gottfried, M., & Freitas, G. (2003). Development of the conformity to masculine norms inventory. *Psychology of Men & Masculinity, 4*(1), 3.

Maji, S., Bansod, S., & Singh, T. (2022). Domestic violence during COVID-19 pandemic: The case for Indian women. *Journal of Community & Applied Social Psychology, 32*(3), 374–381.

Malley-Morrison, K., & Hines, D. (2004). *Family violence in a cultural perspective: Defining, understanding, and combating abuse.* Sage.

Mallory, C., Hasenbush, A., & Sears, B. (2013). Discrimination against law enforcement officers on the basis of sexual orientation and gender identity. Williams Institute.

Malnic, E. (2019, March 5). Daughter of Brando Kills Herself in Tahiti : Suicide: The actor's child Cheyenne was the linchpin of the 1990 case in which her half-brother Christian was charged with killing her lover. She had been troubled by mental problems since. - Los Angeles Times. *Los Angeles Times.* https://www.latimes.com/archives/la-xpm-1995-04-18-me-56086-story.html

Maloney, K. E. (1996). Gender-motivated violence and the commerce clause: The civil rights provision of the Violence against Women Act after "Lopez." *Columbia Law Review, 96*(7), 1876–1939.

Manne, K. (2017). *Down girl: The logic of misogyny.* Oxford University Press.

Martin, E. K., Taft, C. T., & Resick, P. A. (2007). A review of marital rape. *Aggression and Violent Behavior, 12*(3), 329–347.

Martin, S. L., Mackie, L., Kupper, L. L., Buescher, P. A., & Moracco, K. E. (2001). Physical abuse of women before, during, and after pregnancy. *JAMA, 285*(12), 1581–1584.

Matamonasa-Bennett, A. (2015). "A disease of the outside people": Native American men's perceptions of intimate partner violence. *Psychology of Women Quarterly, 39*(1), 20–36. https://doi.org/10.1177/0361684314543783

Matias, A., Goncalves, M., Soeiro, C., & Matos, M. (2020). Intimate partner homicide: A meta-analysis of risk factors. *Aggression and Violent Behavior, 50,* 101358.

McDonald, B. D. (1986). Domestic violence in colonial Massachusetts. *Historical Journal of Massachusetts, 14*(1), 53.

McFarlane, J. M., Campbell, J. C., Wilt, S., Sachs, C. J., Ulrich, Y., & Xu, X. (1999). Stalking and intimate partner femicide. *Homicide Studies, 3,* 300–316. doi:10.1177/1088767999003004003

McFarlane, J., Malecha, A., Gist, J., Watson, K., Batten, E., Hall, I., & Smith, S. (2004). Protection orders and intimate partner violence: An 18-month study of 150 Black, Hispanic, and White women. *American Journal of Public Health, 94*(4), 613–618.

McFarlane, J., Soeken, K., Campbell, J., Parker, B., Reel, S., & Silva, C. (1998). Severity of abuse to pregnant women and associated gun access of the perpetrator. *Public Health Nursing, 15*(3), 201–206.

McLaughlin, K. (2024, February 9). *Sugar heir arrested for beating woman has violent past, Court Docs Say.* Court TV. https://www.courttv.com/news/sugar-heir-arrested-for-beating-woman-has-violent-past-court-docs-say/

Mercy, J. A., Hillis, S. D., Butchart, A., Bellis, M. A., Ward, C. L., Fang, X., & Rosenberg, M. L. (2017). Interpersonal violence: Global impact and paths to prevention. In Charles N. Mock, Rachel Nugent, Olive Kobusingye, & Kirk R. Smith (Eds.), *Injury prevention and environmental health* (3rd ed., chapter 5).

Merrill, G. S., & Wolfe, V. A. (2000). Battered gay men: An exploration of abuse, help seeking, and why they stay. *Journal of Homosexuality, 39*(2), 1–30.

Mertin, P., & Mohr, P. B. (2001). A follow-up study of posttraumatic stress disorder, anxiety, and depression in Australian victims of domestic violence. *Violence and Victims, 16*(6), 645.

Messing, J. T., Ward-Lasher, A., Thaller, J., & Bagwell-Gray, M. E. (2015). The state of intimate partner violence intervention: Progress and continuing challenges. *Social Work, 60*(4), 305–313.

Messinger A. M. (2011). Invisible victims: Same-sex IPV in the national violence against women survey. *Journal of Interpersonal Violence, 26,* 2228–2243. 10.1177/0886260510383023

Messinger, A. M. (2020). *LGBTQ intimate partner violence: Lessons for policy, practice, and research.* University of California Press.

Mihalic, S. W., & Elliott, D. (1997). If violence is domestic, does it really count? *Journal of Family Violence, 12,* 293–311.

Miller, B. A., Wilsnack, S. C., & Cunradi, C. B. (2000). Family violence and victimization: Treatment issues for women with alcohol problems. *Alcoholism: Clinical and Experimental Research, 24*(8), 1287–1297.

Miller, H. (2021). Police occupational culture and bullying. In Premilla D'Cruz, Ernesto Noronha, Loraleigh Keashly, & Stacy Tye-Williams (Eds.), *Special topics and particular occupations, professions and sectors* (pp. 387–413). Springer.

Miller, L., & Grollman, E. (2015). *The social costs of gender nonconformity for transgender adults: Implications for discrimination and health.* Wiley Online Library. https://onlinelibrary.wiley.com/doi/full/10.1111/socf.12193

Miller, S. (2005). *Victims as offenders: The paradox of women's violence in relationships.* Rutgers University Press.

Miller, T. R. (2012). *The cost of firearm violence.* Children's Safety Network.

Mills, L. G., Barocas, B., & Ariel, B. (2013). The next generation of court-mandated domestic violence treatment: A comparison study of batterer intervention and restorative justice programs. *Journal of Experimental Criminology, 9,* 65–90.

Muehlenhard, C. L., Humphreys, T. P., Jozkowski, K. N., & Peterson, Z. D. (2016). The complexities of sexual consent among college students: A conceptual and empirical review. *The Journal of Sex Research, 53*(4–5), 457–487.

Muelleman, R. L., & Burgess, P. (1998). Male victims of domestic violence and their history of perpetrating violence. *Academic Emergency Medicine, 5*(9), 866–870.

Mullen, P. E., Pathe, M., Purcell, R., & Stuart, G. W. (1999). Study of stalkers. *The American Journal of Psychiatry, 156*, 1244–1249. doi:10.1176/ajp.156.8.1244

Murakami, K. (2024). *The US Supreme Court weighs several gun right cases.* Route 50. https://www.route-fifty.com/management/2024/01/us-supreme-court -weighs-several-gun-right-cases/393282/

Murphy, W. J. (2001). The victim advocacy and research group: Serving a growing need to provide rape victims with personal legal representation to protect privacy rights and fight gender bias in the criminal justice system. *Journal of Social Distress and the Homeless, 11*, 123–138.

Naghizadeh, S., Mirghafourvand, M., & Mohammadirad, R. (2021). Domestic violence and its relationship with quality of life in pregnant women during the outbreak of COVID-19 disease. *BMC Pregnancy and Childbirth, 21*, 1–10.

National Coalition of Anti-Violence Programs. (2010). Lesbian, gay, bisexual, transgender, queer, and HIV-affected intimate partner violence. Retrieved from http://www.avp.org/storage/documents/Reports/2009_NCAVP_IPV _Report.pdf

National Task Force to End Sexual and Domestic Violence Against Women. (2012). Reauthorization of the Violence Against Women Act: Building on our successes. Retrieved from http://4vawa.org/pages/about-the-nationaltask -force-to-end-sexual-a

Nelson, C. (2024). "A public orgy of misogyny": Gender, power, media, and legal spectacle in Depp v Heard. *Feminist Media Studies,* 1–17.

Nicholls, T. L. (Ed.). (2006). *Family interventions in domestic violence: A handbook of gender-inclusive theory and treatment.* Springer.

Nowinski, S. N., & Bowen, E. (2012). Partner violence against heterosexual and gay men: Prevalence and correlates. *Aggression and Violent Behavior, 17*(1), 36–52.

Odusola, O. (2023). The People vs Megan Thee Stallion: Anti-fandom, spreadable misogynoir, and faux fandom. *The Motley Undergraduate Journal, 1*(2).

Okun, L. (1986). *Woman abuse: Facts replacing myths.* Suny Press.

Olivera, M. (2006). Violencia femicida. *Latin American Perspectives, 33*(2), 104–114. https://doi.org/10.1177/0094582X05286092

O'Sullivan, C. S., Davis, R. C., Farole, D. J., Jr., & Rempel, M. (2007). A comparison of two prosecution policies in cases of intimate partner violence: Mandatory case filing vs. following the victim's lead. *Criminology and Public Policy, 7*, 633–662.

Outlaw, M. (2009). No one type of intimate partner abuse: Exploring physical and non-physical abuse among intimate partners. *Journal of Family Violence, 24*, 263–272.

Owen, S. S., Burke, T. W., Few-Demo, A. L., & Natwick, J. (2018). Perceptions of the police by LGBT communities. *American Journal of Criminal Justice, 43*, 668–693.

Owusu Adjah, E. S., & Agbemafle, I. (2016). Determinants of domestic violence against women in Ghana. *BMC Public Health, 16*, 368. https://doi.org/10.1186 /s12889-016-3041-x

Paavilainen, E., Lepistö, S., & Flinck, A. (2014). Ethical issues in family violence research in healthcare settings. *Nursing Ethics, 21*(1), 43–52.

Pagelow, M. D. (1988). Marital rape. In *Handbook of family violence* (pp. 207-232). Boston, MA: Springer US.

Parish, J. R. (2010). *The Hollywood Book of Breakups*. Turner.

Parks, S. E., Johnson, L. L., McDaniel, D. D., & Gladden, M. (2014). Surveillance for violent deaths—national violent death reporting system, 16 states, 2010. *Morbidity and Mortality Weekly Report: Surveillance Summaries, 63*(1), 1–33.

Paymar, M. (2000). *Violent no more: Helping men end domestic abuse*. Hunter House.

Peitzmeier, S. M., Fedina, L., Ashwell, L., Herrenkohl, T. I., & Tolman, R. (2021). Increases in intimate partner violence during COVID-19: Prevalence and correlates. *Journal of Interpersonal Violence,* 8862605211052586. Advance online publication. 10.1177/08862605211052586

Peitzmeier, S. M., Malik, M., Kattari, S. K., Marrow, E., Stephenson, R., Agénor, M., & Reisner, S. L. (2020). Intimate partner violence in transgender populations: Systematic review and meta-analysis of prevalence and correlates. *American Journal of Public Health, 110*(9), e1–e14.

Pence, E., & Paymar, M. (1993). *Education groups for men who batter: The Duluth model*. Springer.

Perales, F., & Todd, A. (2018). Structural stigma and the health and wellbeing of Australian LGB populations: Exploiting geographic variation in the results of the 2017 same-sex marriage plebiscite. *Social Science & Medicine, 208*, 190–199.

Perilla, J. L., Bakeman, R., & Norris, F. H. (1994). Culture and domestic violence: The ecology of abused Latinas. *Violence and Victims, 9*, 325–339.

Perras, N., Sternfeld, I., Fei, S., Fischer, B., Richards, G., & Chun, K. (2021). Analysis of domestic violence related homicides in Los Angeles County: Media portrayals, demographics, and precipitating circumstances. *Journal of Family Violence, 36*, 629–636.

Peterson, C., Kearns, M. C., McIntosh, W. L., Estefan, L. F., Nicolaidis, C., McCollister, K. E., . . . & Florence, C. (2018). Lifetime economic burden of intimate partner violence among US adults. *American Journal of Preventive Medicine, 55*(4), 433–444.

Peterson, R. R., & Dixon, J. (2005). Court oversight and conviction under mandatory and nonmandatory domestic violence case filing policies. *Criminology & Public Policy, 4*(3), 535–557.

Petrosky, E., Blair, J. M., Betz, C. J., Fowler, K. A., Jack, S. P., & Lyons, B. H. (2017). Racial and ethnic differences in homicides of adult women and the role of intimate partner violence—United States, 2003–2014. *Morbidity and Mortality Weekly Report, 66*(28), 741.

Petrucci, C. J. (2010). A descriptive study of a California domestic violence court: Program completion and recidivism. *Victims and Offenders, 5*(2), 130–160.

Pico-Alfonso, M. A. (2005). Psychological intimate partner violence: The major predictor of posttraumatic stress disorder in abused women. *Neuroscience & Biobehavioral Reviews, 29*(1), 181193.

Pico-Alfonso, M. A., Echeburúa, E., & Martinez, M. (2008). Personality disorder symptoms in women as a result of chronic intimate male partner violence. *Journal of Family Violence, 23*, 577–588.

Piquero, A., Riddell, J., Bishopp, S., Narvey, J., Reid, J., & Leeper Piquero, N. (2020). Staying home, staying safe? A short-term analysis of COVID-19 on Dallas domestic violence. *American Journal of Criminal Justice, 45*, 601–635.

Piquero, A. R., Jennings, W. G., Jemison, E., Kaukinen, C., & Knaul, F. M. (2021). Domestic violence during the COVID-19 pandemic—Evidence from a systematic review and meta-analysis. *Journal of Criminal Justice, 74*, 101806.

Pispira, J., Cevasco, J., & Silva, M. L. (2022). Gender-based violence in Latin America (Ecuador and Argentina): Current state and challenges in the development of psychoeducational materials. *Discover Psychology, 2*(1), 48. https://doi.org/10.1007/s44202-022-00060-4

Polan, R. B. (2017). The context of violence: The Lautenberg Amendment & interpretive issues in the Gun Control Act. *Brooklyn Law Review, 83*, 1441.

Pop Crave [@popcrave]. (2022, December 17). 50 Cent compares Megan Thee Stallion to Jussie Smollett in new tweet. [Tweet; Image]. Twitter. https://twitter.com/PopCrave/status/1604252952197496832

Postmus, J. L., Hoge, G. L., Breckenridge, J., Sharp-Jeffs, N., & Chung, D. (2020). Economic abuse as an invisible form of domestic violence: A multicountry review. *Trauma, Violence, & Abuse, 21*(2), 261–283.

Potocznick, M. J., Mourot, J. E., Crosbie-Burnett, M., & Potocznick, D. J. (2003). Legal and psychological perspectives on same-sex domestic violence: A multisystemic approach. *Journal of Family Psychology, 17*, 252–259.

Price, B. J., & Rosenbaum, A. (2009). Batterer intervention programs: A report from the field. *Violence and Victims, 24*(6), 757–770.

Ptacek, J. (1999). *Battered women in the courtroom: The power of judicial responses*. Upne.

Rajan, H. (2018). When wife-beating is not necessarily abuse: A feminist and cross-cultural analysis of the concept of abuse as expressed by Tibetan survivors of domestic violence. *Violence Against Women, 24*(1), 3–27.

Rand, M., & Rennison, C. (2004). How much violence against women is there. In Bonnie Fisher (Ed.), *Violence against women and family violence: Developments in research, practice, and policy* (p. 8). National Institute of Justice.

Randolph, R. (2014). Gender, sex, and intimate-partner violence in historical perspective. In Rosemary Gartner & Bill McCarthy (Eds.), *The Oxford Handbook of Gender, Sex, and Crime* (p. 175). Oxford University Press.

Reaves, B. A. (2017). *Police response to domestic violence, 2006–2015*. US Department of Justice, Office of Justice Programs, Bureau of Justice Statistics.

Rennison, C. M., & Welchans, S. (2000). *Intimate partner violence*. US Department of Justice, Office of Justice Programs, Bureau of Justice Statistics.

Renzetti, C. M. (2009). Economic stress and domestic violence. University of Kentucky. https://uknowledge.uky.edu/crvaw_reports/1

Ristock, J. L. (2003). Exploring dynamics of abusive lesbian relationships: Preliminary analysis of a multi-site, qualitative study. *American Journal of Community Psychology, 31*, 3–4. 10.1023/A:1023971006882

Ristock, J., & Timbang, N. (2005). Relationship violence in lesbian/gay/bisexual/transgender/queer [LGBTQ] communities. Violence Against Women Online Resources.

Roberts, T. A. (2021). Black woman ungendered: How society failed Megan Thee Stallion. *The Word: Tha Stanford Journal of Student Hiphop Research, 2*(1), 4–15.

RoDe, D., & RoDe, M. M. (2016). Domestic violence and the functioning of the family system. *Problems of Forensic Sciences, 108,* 651–667.

Rohrbaugh, J. B. (2006). Domestic violence in same-gender relationships. *Family Court Review, 44*(2), 287–299.

Rollè, L., Giardina, G., Caldarera, A. M., Gerino, E., & Brustia, P. (2018). When intimate partner violence meets same sex couples: A review of same sex intimate partner violence. *Frontiers in Psychology, 9,* 1506. https://doi.org/10.3389/fpsyg.2018.01506

Rollè, L., Santoniccolo, F., D'Amico, D., & Trombetta, T. (2020). News media representation of domestic violence victims and perpetrators: Focus on gender and sexual orientation in international literature. *Gendered Domestic Violence and Abuse in Popular Culture,* 149–169.

Rushovich, T., Boulicault, M., Chen, J. T., Danielsen, A. C., Tarrant, A., Richardson, S. S., & Shattuck-Heidorn, H. (2021). Sex disparities in COVID-19 mortality vary across US racial groups. *Journal of General Internal Medicine, 36,* 1696–1701.

Sansone, R. A., Chu, J., & Wiederman, M. W. (2006). Domestic violence and borderline personality symptomatology among women in an inpatient psychiatric setting. *Traumatology, 12*(4), 314–319. https://doi.org/10.1177/1534765606297822

Sanz-García, A., Gesteira, C., Sanz, J., & García-Vera, M. P. (2021). Prevalence of psychopathy in the general adult population: A systematic review and meta-analysis. *Frontiers in Psychology, 12,* 3278.

Sardinha, L., Maheu-Giroux, M., Stöckl, H., Meyer, S. R., & García-Moreno, C. (2022). Global, regional, and national prevalence estimates of physical or sexual, or both, intimate partner violence against women in 2018. *The Lancet, 399*(10327), 803–813.

Saunders, D. G. (1996). Feminist-cognitive-behavioral and process-psychodynamic treatments for men who batter: Interaction of abuser traits and treatment models. *Violence and Victims, 11*(4), 393–414.

Saunders, D. G. (2008). Group interventions for men who batter: A summary of program descriptions and research. *Violence and Victims, 23*(2), 156–172.

Schneider, D., Harknett, K., & McLanahan, S. (2016). Intimate partner violence in the great recession. *Demography, 53*(2), 471–505.

Schwabauer, B. A. (2010). The Emmett Till Unsolved Civil Rights Crime Act: The cold case of racism in the criminal justice system. *Ohio State Law Journal 71,* 653.

Seabrook, J. (2016). *The horrifying details of what allegedly happened the night Chris Brown assaulted Rihanna.* Business Insider. https://www.businessinsider.com/chris-brown-rihanna-fight-2016-3

Seamans, C. L., Rubin, L. J., & Stabb, S. D. (2007). Women domestic violence offenders: Lessons of violence and survival. *Journal of Trauma & Dissociation, 8*(2), 47–68.

Semahegn, A., & Mengistie, B. (2015). Domestic violence against women and associated factors in Ethiopia: Systematic review. *Reproductive Health, 12*(1), 1–12.

Serisier, T. (2018). *Speaking out: Feminism, rape and narrative politics.* Springer.

Sheridan, D. J., & Nash, K. R. (2007). Acute injury patterns of intimate partner violence victims. *Trauma, Violence, & Abuse, 8,* 281–289. doi:10.1177/1524838007303504

Sherman, L. W., & Berk, R. A. (1984). *The Minneapolis domestic violence experiment* (Vol. 1). Police Foundation.

Sherman, L. W., & Cohn, E. G. (1989). The impact of research on legal policy: The Minneapolis domestic violence experiment. *Law & Society Review, 23,* 117.

Shimizu, A. (2013). Domestic violence in the digital age: Towards the creation of a comprehensive cyberstalking statute. *Berkeley Journal of Gender, Law & Justice, 28,* 116.

Shoos, D. L., & Shoos, D. L. (2017). Sleeping with the enemy, victim empowerment, and the thrill of horror. In *Domestic violence in Hollywood film: Gaslighting* (pp. 63–86). Springer.

Siegel, R. B. (1995). The rule of love: Wife beating as prerogative and privacy. *Yale Law Journal, 105,* 2117.

Silverman, E. (2023). *Proud boys protest drag queen story hour in Montgomery County. Washington Post.* https://www.washingtonpost.com/dc-md-va/2023/02/21/maryland-drag-queen-story-hour-proud-boys/

Slabbert, I. (2017). Domestic violence and poverty: Some women's experiences. *Research on Social Work Practice, 27*(2), 223–230. https://doi.org/10.1177/1049731516662321

Smith, B. E., & Davis, R. C. (2004). An evaluation of efforts to implement no-drop policies: Two central values in conflict. U.S. Department of Justice.

Smith, E. (2008). African American men and intimate partner violence. *Journal of African American Studies, 12,* 156–179.

Smith, E., & Hattery, A. J. (2008). Incarceration: A tool for racial segregation and labor exploitation. *Race, Gender & Class,* 79–97.

Smith-Marek, E. N., Cafferky, B., Dharnidharka, P., Mallory, A. B., Dominguez, M., High, J., . . . & Mendez, M. (2015). Effects of childhood experiences of family violence on adult partner violence: A meta-analytic review. *Journal of Family Theory & Review, 7*(4), 498–519.

Sorenson, S. B. (2017). Guns in intimate partner violence: Comparing incidents by type of weapon. *Journal of Women's Health, 26*(3), 249–258.

Stalans, L. J. (2007). Police decision-making factors in domestic violence cases. In N. A. Jackson (Ed.), *Encyclopedia of domestic violence* (pp. 543–548). Routledge.

Stalans, L. J., & Finn, M. A. (2000). Gender differences in officers' perceptions and decisions about domestic violence cases. *Women & Criminal Justice, 11*(3), 1–24.

Statistics Canada. (2016). *Family violence in Canada: A statistical profile* [PDF file]. Retrieved from http://www.statcan.gc.ca/pub/85-224-x/85-224-x2010000-eng.pdf

Stewart, D. E., & Vigod, S. N. (2019). Update on mental health aspects of intimate partner violence. *The Medical Clinics of North America, 103*(4), 735–749. https://doi.org/10.1016/j.mcna.2019.02.010

Stewart, S. H. (1996). Alcohol abuse in individuals exposed to trauma: A critical review. *Psychological Bulletin, 120*(1), 83.

Stewart, S. H., Conrod, P. J., Samoluk, S. B., Pihl, R. O., & Dongier, M. (2000). Posttraumatic stress disorder symptoms and situation-specific drinking in women substance abusers. *Alcoholism Treatment Quarterly, 18*(3), 31–47.

Stockman, J. K., Hayashi, H., & Campbell, J. C. (2015). Intimate partner violence and its health impact on ethnic minority women. *Journal of Women's Health, 24*(1), 62–79.

Strand, S. (2012). Using a restraining order as a protective risk management strategy to prevent intimate partner violence. *Police Practice and Research, 13*(3), 254–266.

Straus, M. A. (1995). Trends in cultural norms and rates of partner violence: An update to 1992. In *National Council on Family Relations* (Series Ed.) & S. Stith & M. A. Straus (Vol. Eds.), *Families in focus*, Vol. 2. *Understanding partner violence: Prevalence, causes, consequences, and solutions* (pp. 30–33). National Council on Family Relations

Straus, M. A., Gelles, R. J., & Asplund, L. M. (1990). *Physical violence in American families: Risk factors and adaptations to violence in 8,145 families.* Transaction Publishers.

Stuart, G. L. (2005). Improving violence intervention outcomes by integrating alcohol treatment. *Journal of Interpersonal Violence, 20,* 388–393.

Stuart, G. L., Temple, J. R., & Moore, T. M. (2007). Improving batterer intervention programs through theory-based research. *JAMA, 298*(5), 560–562.

Sullivan, C. M., & Bybee, D. I. (1999). Reducing violence using community-based advocacy for women with abusive partners. *Journal of Consulting and Clinical Psychology, 67*(1), 43–53. doi:10.1037/0022-006X.67.1.43

Sullivan, T. P., Weiss, N. H., Price, C., Pugh, N., & Hansen, N. B. (2018). Strategies for coping with individual PTSD symptoms: Experiences of African American victims of intimate partner violence. *Psychological Trauma: Theory, Research, Practice, and Policy, 10*(3), 336. doi: 10.1037/tra0000283

Swan, S. C., Gambone, L. J., Caldwell, J. E., Sullivan, T. P., & Snow, D. L. (2008). A review of research on women's use of violence with male intimate partners. *Violence and Victims, 23*(3), 301–314. https://doi.org/10.1891/0886-6708.23.3.301

Swan, S. C., & Snow, D. L. (2002). A typology of women's use of violence in intimate relationships. *Violence Against Women, 8*(3), 286–319.

Taccini, F., & Mannarini, S. (2024). How are survivors of intimate partner violence and sexual violence portrayed on social media? *Journal of Media Psychology: Theories, Methods, and Applications.*

Tavares, P. (2018). (PDF) Ending violence against women and girls—global and . . . https://www.researchgate.net/publication/349194682_Ending_Violence _Against_Women_and_Girls_-_Global_and_Regional_Trends_in_Women's_ Legal_Protection_Against_Domestic_Violence_and_Sexual_Harassment/ download

Teitelman, A. M., Ratcliffe, S. J., Dichter, M. E., & Sullivan, C. M. (2008). Recent and past intimate partner abuse and HIV risk among young women. *Journal of Obstetric, Gynecologic, and Neonatal Nursing, 37*(2), 219–227. https://doi.org/10 .1111/j.1552-6909.2008.00231.x

Terrill, W., Paoline, E., & Manning, P. (2003). Police culture and coercion. *Criminology, 41*(4), 1003.

Tillery, B., Ray, A., Cruz, E., & Waters, E. (2018). *Lesbian, gay, bisexual, transgender, queer and HIV-affected hate and intimate partner violence in 2017.* National Coalition of Anti-Violence Programs. https://avp.org/wp-content/uploads/2019 /01/NCAVP-HV-IPV-2017-report.pdf

Tilley, D. S., & Brackley, M. (2005). Men who batter intimate partners: A grounded theory study of the development of male violence in intimate partner relationships. *Issues in Mental Health Nursing, 26*(3), 281–297.

Tiyyagura, G., Bloemen, E. M., Berger, R., Rosen, T., Harris, T., Jeter, G., & Lindberg, D. (2020). Seeing the forest in family violence research: Moving to a family-centered approach. *Academic Pediatrics, 20*(6), 746–752.

Tjaden, P., & Thoennes, N. (1998). Prevalence, incidence, and consequences of violence against women: Findings from the National Violence Against Women Survey. Research in Brief. U.S. Department of Justice.

Tjaden, P., & Thoennes, N. (2000). Extent, nature, and consequences of intimate partner violence: Findings from the National Violence Against Women Survey. U.S. Department of Justice.

Tolman, R. M., & Rosen, D. (2001). Domestic violence in the lives of women receiving welfare: Mental health, substance dependence, and economic well-being. *Violence Against Women, 7*(2), 141–158.

Truman, J. L., & Morgan, R. E. (2014). *Nonfatal domestic violence.* US Department of Justice, Bureau of Justice Statistics.

Tsai, B. (2000). The trend toward specialized domestic violence courts: Improvements on an effective innovation. *Fordham Law Review, 68,* 1285.

UNICEF (2000). Domestic violence against women and girls. *Innocent Digest, 6.* http://www.unicefirc.org/publications/pdf/digest6e.pdf

United States Department of Justice. Federal Bureau of Investigation. (2011). *Uniform Crime Reporting Program data: Supplementary homicide reports, 2009.*

Valera E. M., & Kucyi A. (2017). Brain injury in women experiencing intimate partner-violence: Neural mechanistic evidence of an "invisible" trauma. *Brain Imaging and Behavior, 11,* 1664–1677. doi:10.1007/s11682-016-9643-1

Visher, C. A., Harrell, A., Newmark, L., & Yahner, J. (2008). Reducing intimate partner violence: An evaluation of a comprehensive justice system-community collaboration. *Criminology & Public Policy, 7*(4), 495–523.

Vizzard, W. J. (1999). The gun control act of 1968. *Saint Louis University Public Law Review, 18,* 79.

Walker, A., Lyall, K., Silva, D., Craigie, G., Mayshak, R., Costa, B., . . . & Bentley, A. (2020). Male victims of female-perpetrated intimate partner violence, help-seeking, and reporting behaviors: A qualitative study. *Psychology of Men & Masculinities, 21*(2), 213–223.

Walker, L. E. (2006). Battered woman syndrome: Empirical findings. *Annals of the New York Academy of Sciences, 1087*(1), 142–157.

Walker, L. E. (2015). Looking back and looking forward: Psychological and legal interventions for domestic violence. *Ethics, Medicine and Public Health, 1*(1), 19–32.

Waltermaurer, E. (2012). Public justification of intimate partner violence: A review of the literature. *Trauma, Violence, & Abuse, 13*(3), 167–175.

Walters, M. L., Breiding, M. J., & Chen, J. (2013). *The national intimate partner and sexual violence survey: 2010 findings on victimization by sexual orientation.* National Center for Injury Prevention and Control.

Wang, K. (1996). Battered Asian American women: Community responses from the Battered Women's Movement and the Asian American community. *Asian Law Journal, 3,* 151.

Wang, P. S., Demler, O., & Kessler, R. C. (2002). Adequacy of treatment for serious mental illness in the United States. *American Journal of Public Health, 92*(1), 92–98.

Wermuth, L. (1982). Domestic violence reforms: Policing the private? *Berkeley Journal of Sociology, 27,* 27–49.

Westley, W. (1970). *Violence and the police.* MIT Press.

Whiting, J. B., Olufuwote, R. D., Cravens-Pickens, J. D., & Banford Witting, A. (2019). Online blaming and intimate partner violence: A content analysis of social media comments. *The Qualitative Report, 24*(1), 78–94.

Wintemute, G. J. (2015). The epidemiology of firearm violence in the twenty-first century United States. *Annual Review of Public Health, 36*, 5–19.

Wolf, M. E., Holt, V. L., Kernic, M. A., & Rivara, F. P. (2000). Who gets protection orders for intimate partner violence? *American Journal of Preventive Medicine, 19*(4), 286–291.

Yalom, I. D., & Leszcz, M. (2020). *The theory and practice of group psychotherapy.* Basic Books.

Yamane, D. (2017). The sociology of US gun culture. *Sociology Compass, 11*(7), e12497.

Yamawaki, N., Ochoa-Shipp, M., Pulsipher, C., Harlos, A., & Swindler, S. (2012). Perceptions of domestic violence: The effects of domestic violence myths, victim's relationship with her abuser, and the decision to return to her abuser. *Journal of Interpersonal Violence, 27*(16), 3195–3212. https://doi.org/10.1177/0886260512441253

Yick, A. G., & Berthold, S. M. (2005). Conducting research on violence in Asian American communities: Methodological issues. *Violence and Victims, 20*(6), 661–677.

Yoon, M. S. Pandemic, violence and women: What data doesn't tell. The Korea Herald [Internet]. 2023 Jul 3 [cited 2023 Jul 3]. https://news.koreaherald.com/common/newsprint.php?ud=20220424000232

Zajecka, J. M. (2003). Treating depression to remission. *Journal of Clinical Psychiatry, 64*(15), 7–12.

Zawitz, M. (1994). Violence between intimates: Selected findings. US Department of Justice, Bureau of Justice Statistics.

INDEX

About the Author

Laura Elizabeth, PhD, most recently served as assistant professor of criminal justice at Methodist University in Fayetteville, North Carolina. She completed her undergraduate work at Duke University, and her master's and PhD at Virginia Commonwealth University before embarking on her academic career. Her research focus is intimate partner violence (IPV), and this is her first textbook on the topic. She invites readers to contact her at connormom@alumni.duke.edu for further questions and discussion on the issue of IPV.